Dr Dennis Grube is a Senior Lecturer in Politics in the School of Government and International Relations at Griffith University. His research interests focus on political rhetoric and its impact on public policy in both historical and contemporary settings. He lives in Brisbane, Australia.

AT THE MARGINS OF VICTORIAN BRITAIN

Politics, Immorality and Britishness
in the Nineteenth Century

DENNIS GRUBE

BLOOMSBURY ACADEMIC
LONDON • NEW YORK • OXFORD • NEW DELHI • SYDNEY

BLOOMSBURY ACADEMIC
Bloomsbury Publishing Plc
50 Bedford Square, London, WC1B 3DP, UK
1385 Broadway, New York, NY 10018, USA

BLOOMSBURY, BLOOMSBURY ACADEMIC and the Diana
logo are trademarks of Bloomsbury Publishing Plc

First published in Great Britain 2013 by I.B.Tauris & Co.
Paperback edition first published 2020 by Bloomsbury Academic

Copyright © Dennis Grube, 2013

Marilyn Dunn has asserted her right under the Copyright,
Designs and Patents Act, 1988, to be identified as Author of this work.

For legal purposes the Acknowledgements on p. vi constitute
an extension of this copyright page.

All rights reserved. No part of this publication may be reproduced or
transmitted in any form or by any means, electronic or mechanical,
including photocopying, recording, or any information storage or retrieval
system, without prior permission in writing from the publishers.

Bloomsbury Publishing Plc does not have any control over, or responsibility for,
any third-party websites referred to or in this book. All internet addresses given
in this book were correct at the time of going to press. The author and publisher
regret any inconvenience caused if addresses have changed or sites have
ceased to exist, but can accept no responsibility for any such changes.

A catalogue record for this book is available from the British Library.

A catalog record for this book is available from the Library of Congress.

ISBN: HB: 978-1-7807-6344-6
PB: 978-1-3501-6021-7
ePDF: 978-0-8577-2257-7
eBook: 978-0-8577-3402-0

Series: Library of Victorian Studies, vol. 7

Typeset by Newgen Publishers, Chennai

To find out more about our authors and books visit
www.bloomsbury.com and sign up for our newsletters.

CONTENTS

Acknowledgements		vi
Abbreviations		viii
1.	Introduction: 'Britishness' and the 'Other'	1
2.	British Law and the Irish Other	9
3.	Ireland on Trial: The Parnell Experience	33
4.	British Jews: The Search for Equality	55
5.	The Politics of Atheism	69
6.	Roman Catholics: The Enduring 'Other'	79
7.	The New Jewish Threat	97
8.	'Un-British' Women: The 'Problem' of Prostitution	109
9.	Containing Deviance: The Legal Limits of Male Sexuality	127
10.	Conclusion	153
Notes		163
Bibliography		201
Index		219

ACKNOWLEDGEMENTS

Writing a work of political history is a long haul up a sometimes dark road. I have been fortunate to have many friends willing to light the path. I express my deep gratitude to Margaret Lindley, for her years of support, good humour and continued belief in this project's success. I must express my great appreciation to Tomasz Hoskins at I.B.Tauris for his diligent commitment to getting this book out into the world. I thank Haig Patapan, John Kane and Pat Weller for refusing to countenance my periodic apathy, and for their many insights and useful pieces of advice. The Centre for Governance and Public Policy at Griffith University has provided financial support at crucial stages, and my colleagues in the School of Government and International Relations at Griffith have been unceasingly kind in their observations.

Staff at the Bodleian Library, British National Archives, British Library, Chifley Library at ANU, University Library at the University of Melbourne, Griffith University Library, and Morris Miller Library at the University of Tasmania have made the task of researching so much easier with their friendly professionalism.

I owe personal debts of emotional support and encouragement that are too many to mention. Nevertheless, I cannot allow the moment to pass without offering my deep thanks to Martin Grimmer and David Blaazer, who were kind enough to read a much earlier draft of this work and whose views were most helpful. I express my gratitude to my family – especially my Mum, Dad and brother Mark – for their patience and good humour. My lifelong friend, Daniel Bottaro, has always made me see the funny side of life and this study was no exception. To my wonderful wife Kathy, I express a heartfelt thank you. Whatever merit may be contained in the pages that follow is thanks to you most of all. The faults remain my own.

Dennis Grube
Brisbane

ABBREVIATIONS

CAB *Cabinet Papers*, cited by catalogue and folio numbers from the National Archives, Kew.

CRIM *Criminal Records*, cited by catalogue and folio numbers from the National Archives, Kew.

DPP *Papers from the office of the Director of Public Prosecutions*, cited by catalogue and folio numbers from the National Archives, Kew.

FO *Foreign Office Papers*, cited by catalogue and folio numbers from the National Archives, Kew.

HO *Home Office Papers*, cited by catalogue and folio numbers from the National Archives, Kew.

MEPO *Metropolitan Police Papers*, cited by catalogue and folio numbers from the National Archives, Kew.

WO *War Office Papers*, cited by catalogue and folio numbers from the National Archives, Kew.

CHAPTER 1

INTRODUCTION: BRITISHNESS AND THE OTHER

'Britishness' is a political question. But it is also a legal, social, and emotional one. For centuries British governments have played a leading role in shaping, defining and guarding 'Britishness'. They have framed the characteristics that define who is and who is not 'British'. The question of what it means to be British continues to be a topic of intense contemporary debate as twenty-first-century Britain comes to terms with challenges such as devolution, European integration and mass immigration.[1] In his introductory essay to a 2009 collection on *Being British*, Prime Minister Gordon Brown suggested that British national identity is centred not on race, religion or difference, but on shared values.[2] In this, Brown's view is consistent with much of the recent literature, which supports the assertion that British national identity is essentially a collection of values and ideas – the invisible ties that bind.[3]

The idea that a uniquely 'British' character is based on shared values of some kind is not new. In fact the contemporary debate is framed by decisions made over a century ago, in the Victorian era. The parameters for the modern debate were set in the age of Gladstone and Disraeli, when the shift occurred from a British identity based on religious difference to one based on shared moral values. Between 1829 and 1895 – from Roman Catholic emancipation to the Oscar Wilde trials – successive British governments slowly moved from viewing religious groups as 'others' to viewing moral 'deviants' as the chief outsiders against whom Britons should unify in shared disdain. As Jews, Roman Catholics and atheists were brought into a genuine sense of partnership in the British constitution by being allowed to seek election to Parliament, homosexuals, prostitutes and the allegedly innately criminal Irish found themselves further and more vehemently displaced. 'Otherness' stopped being a religious question and became instead a moral one.[4] That fundamental shift marks the moment that 'Britishness' became a values-based question. And we've been arguing about what those values are ever since.

What has changed is the absence in the modern debate of that most vital ingredient of any national identity – an 'other'. National identity is defined by its boundaries – by who is included and who is excluded. Current conceptions of 'Britishness' based on notions of 'tolerance', 'liberty' or 'fair play' provide values, but no 'other' to measure them against. They are universal values and by definition universalism embraces everyone. So if 'everyone' is a part of modern Britishness, it becomes a national identity without boundaries – meaning it becomes no identity at all.

Politics is a battle of definition. Political leaders create rhetorical frames through which to define how the public sees policy issues, how they decide on who is a friend and who is an enemy, and how they assess who are outsiders and who are insiders. This book scrutinizes how the frame of 'Britishness' was positioned in Victorian Britain; it examines who sought to define British national identity and how they did so. Political and legal rhetoric, backed by the force of legislation, set the boundaries of 'Britishness' and enforced those boundaries through the 'majesty' of an 'unproblematised' British law.

In Victorian Britain – through legislation, political rhetoric and the courts – successive governments identified a series of religious or moral 'others' who displayed a set of characteristics or behaviours incompatible with 'Britishness'. In doing so they reinforced the identity of the majority of British people as morally upright and religiously acceptable citizens.

In Victorian Britain the law was used and promoted as an instrument of unity while paradoxically being used simultaneously by lawmakers to ostracise religious or moral deviants from British society. The 'law' of course is not an objective entity. It is a definitional tool which provided the dividing line in Victorian Britain between those who obeyed the law and those who, by thumbing their nose at the law, were seen as thumbing their nose at one of the core components of 'Britishness' itself. The law could limit the rights of people professing an 'un-British' faith to sit in Parliament – the ultimate lawmaking body. It could also render as moral outcasts those whose nationality or sexuality threatened to undermine British social norms.

The 'Other'

British government, so changed in its character over the course of the nineteenth century, remained consistent in its defence of British law from the interference of groups deemed to be 'un-British'. For much of the first half of the nineteenth century Jews, atheists and Roman Catholics were all prevented on religious grounds from entering Parliament to make British law. These were people whose religion rendered them unfit to participate in lawmaking in a nation which defined itself as defiantly Protestant. As the century progressed these religious bans were slowly lifted, leaving lawmakers to define a replacement class of scapegoats: 'moral criminals'. Prostitutes, homosexuals and a certain class of Irishman came to dominate the imagination of the late Victorians as threats to the moral integrity of Britain. These people were not truly 'British' and could thus safely be excluded by laws that they had little hand in making.

Linda Colley's seminal work on British nationalism in the eighteenth century has stressed that the idea of 'Britain' has always needed to have an 'other' against which to define itself.[5] Colley's work has unleashed a now two-decade-long conversation on what it means to be British. Colley of course is not without her critics;[6] Keith Robbins has suggested that the United Kingdom in the eighteenth and nineteenth centuries moved towards a greater degree of cultural homogeneity than is allowed by Colley's theory of a British identity superimposed on distinct and continuing national identities.[7]

Hugh Kearney too has been critical of Linda Colley's approach as producing too holistic a picture of a Britain that was more fragmented by its composite nationalities than Colley's overarching analysis would suggest.[8] The composite work *Uniting the Kingdom: The Making of British History*, edited by Alexander Grant and Keith Stringer, similarly emphasises that the many forces which pushed the disparate nations of Great Britain together were matched by an equal number of forces pulling it apart.[9]

Paul Ward's work suggests perhaps a more harmonious relationship. He argues that the separate nationalities within the United Kingdom were not mutually exclusive with the broader nationality of 'British', and that in some ways the two forces were actually mutually reinforcing.[10] That of course does not mean that the distinctions between nationalities were always a source of pride for the whole. For instance, Peter Jupp has examined government in Ireland between 1801 and 1841 within the context of national identity. He argues that the union in 1801 simultaneously worked to incorporate the Irish as part of the United Kingdom while emphasising that they were different from their fellow British subjects.[11]

This debate about how to define Britishness has in many ways been a debate about competing nationalisms. It has been about what it means to be English, or Scottish or Welsh, or Irish, and extrapolating from that what it means to have a 'British' identity superimposed on these existing identities. This book is less about competing nationalisms and more about the buttressing of a values-based 'Britishness' in the late Victorian period. It's about the 'outsiders' *within* British society against which all British nationalities could define themselves as religiously, racially or morally legitimate.[12]

By stereotyping and ostracising certain minority groups, British politicians were building internal cultural boundaries – delineating moral and sexual outsiders who could be frowned upon equally by the Scots, the Welsh and the English. In the absence of a natural cultural hegemony based on language or a unifying church, the Scottish, the English, and the Welsh could be unified in their disdain for those whose religious beliefs, moral standards or sexual practices rendered them 'outsiders'. British law was the instrument that could define who these outsiders were. British governments were the keepers of law. They made law in parliament, appointed the judges who upheld the law in the courts, and chose the top policemen who would administer and execute the law at a practical level. These were all people very much at the core of that peculiarly British institution – the 'Establishment'.[13]

Governments could make and influence pathways to justice. By choosing to act against Oscar Wilde but not against the Duke of Clarence after the Cleveland Street Scandal, the Salisbury Government could decide who should be held up to the judicial mirror for judgement.[14] By passing a series of Contagious Diseases Acts isolating prostitutes from their own communities, successive governments in the 1860s and '70s were able to confirm with the force of law that these people, and not their clients, were sexual deviants who should be ostracised. Their detention for medical examination could be tested in court but the government had already, through legislation, made the outcome a formality. It was this subtle ability to decide the legal rules by which society's games were played that gave British governments the power to create and maintain outsider groups.

Of course, what also emerges when examining any group defined as 'other' is that each has its champions in the wider society that can affect when and if a group is welcomed into the fold. Jews, atheists and Roman Catholics all had vocal and articulate champions within Parliament and outside it that were willing to advocate for their cause. In the case of Jewish emancipation, by 1858 Whig governments had been willing to support change for a decade, only to be consistently stymied by an intransigent House of Lords determined to defend Britain's Protestant national character until the end. In the late Victorian period, even such widely feared moral outsiders as prostitutes and homosexuals had people at both a local and a national level that would seek to protect them from the harsh judgements of the law.

There have been many theories put forward on the relationship between society, government and the law. From Marx to Foucault and beyond, theorists have grappled with how best to characterise the power of the State with regard to its citizens. In Britain, legal historians have added to our understanding of the ways in which criminality impacted on the popular consciousness in eighteenth- and nineteenth-century Britain.[15] Douglas Hay, for example, referring to the criminal law in the eighteenth century, has argued that '[the law] allowed the rulers of England to make the courts a selective instrument of class justice, yet simultaneously to proclaim the law's incorruptible impartiality and absolute determinacy.'[16] Hay sees this as 'the peculiar genius of the law'.[17] It is this conception of reverence for the law being misused, as Hay suggests, which is important in understanding the power of the law as a tool of exclusion used to support particular conceptions of national identity.

The law was used not only to target criminals, but to isolate certain religious and moral minorities as outsiders within British society by labelling them as insufficiently 'British'. Laws passed or upheld that excluded Jews or atheists from becoming lawmakers served a function in keeping a certain set of people in power. They helped to define who was 'British' enough to be trusted to make British law.[18] Popular reverence for the idea of British law as an objective force for justice acted to buttress these definitions of who was and who was not British.

Every nation state and every system of law contains within it flexibilities and nuances, and I do not suggest that British political leaders had unfettered power to rule simplistically and overtly who was 'in' and who was 'out'. British lawmakers were defeated at times by the discretion of judges, as in the trial of the Irish leader Daniel O'Connell, or worn down by the persistence of Jews and atheists in seeking their rights to sit as elected members of the House of Commons. Such outcomes should not, however, hide the actions of British governments in attempting to use the law to ostracise outsiders, even when their attempts were unsuccessful.

The time period covered by this book stretches from Roman Catholic Emancipation in 1829 to the Oscar Wilde trials in 1895. The period marks the crucial years in the shaping of an outwardly more inclusive British society. In these years, following the Great Reform Act in 1832, more and more Britons became active players in their emerging democracy. Also over the course of this period, the pervading power of liberal thought saw governments of all political persuasions slowly move from seeing religious groups as 'others' to seeing moral 'deviants' as the truly 'un-British' outsiders.[19] In 1829 'true Britons' were Protestants who bore allegiance to the 'ancient' religious traditions of Britain. By 1895, they were morally upright heterosexuals of whichever religious persuasion.[20] This was no random change, but a reflection of the subtle manipulation of the law by British governments in support of changing perceptions of national identity.

This is not a book about empire. Much interesting work has already been done on the importance of conceptions of empire to how Britain and the British saw and continue to see themselves.[21] The external 'other' – whether in colonies or enemy nations – has been central to the work of Colley, and others and I don't seek to add to it here. Rather, I focus on the *internal* other – the ways in which certain people living within Great Britain itself were portrayed as 'other' – thus helping to define what true 'British' characteristics actually were.

Equally, this is not a book about class. Apart from the 'outsiders' already identified – atheists, Irish, homosexuals, Jews, Roman Catholics, and prostitutes – there is a clear case to be made that socio-economic class groups as a whole could be considered outsiders. The working class had little access to the means of creating greater wealth, and no say in electing a government that might fight to move a greater proportion of the nation's wealth in their direction. Gareth Stedman Jones's seminal work on the threat of the 'outcast' labouring poor addresses some of these issues, providing much of the economic context within which such class threats can be analysed.[22] A discussion of these class distinctions and their significance is beyond the scope of this study, except in so far as they intersect with specific minority groups.[23] For instance, Catherine Hall has examined the role of the Irish in mid-Victorian England and how they were distrusted not simply for their lower-class status, but for their perceived moral degradation which contemporaries feared might be transmitted to their English fellow citizens.[24]

British society during the Victorian era can be examined on the basis of how the law was used, and against whom. Different groups in society can be examined in terms of their legal position rather than in terms of the class of which they were members. For instance, the atheist Charles Bradlaugh could hardly be characterised as a member of the working class, nor could Charles Stewart Parnell, Lord Rothschild or Oscar Wilde. Yet they were all 'outsiders' in the sense in which I use the term here. Through their political, religious or moral beliefs, they offended 'British norms'. Victorian society, including representatives of all classes, was encouraged to use the outsider groups (identified here as 'others') to define their own superior status as Britons against. Lawmakers provided the justification for this self-righteousness by labelling a succession of minority groups as deviants from the core values of 'Britishness' as they perceived them to be.

In developing this values-based Britishness, the Victorians created the debate that still rages today. If Britishness is to be based only on values, are there in fact any values sufficiently unique to the British Isles as to be useful as a binding agent of national identity? In the absence of a clearly defined 'other', national identity dissipates into local or regional rivalries as people search for some boundary they can use to define who they are. A 'Britishness' based only on universal values thus effectively undermines British national identity by stripping away its meaning. The challenge is to embrace universal values – such as tolerance and fair play – but frame them within a set of characteristics or boundaries that are uniquely British and can be recognised as such.

CHAPTER 2

BRITISH LAW AND THE IRISH OTHER

By 1829 Britain was the pre-eminent colonial power in the world, a position it was to hold and expand on into the early twentieth century. Yet its most challenging relationship within the empire was not with a far-flung colony but with the nation that had joined it in partnership in 1800.[1] A constituent country of the United Kingdom itself, yet treated in many ways like a colony, Ireland was a nineteenth-century conundrum for British governments.[2] The Irish were rhetorically ostracised both within Ireland and within the broader United Kingdom. Within Ireland itself the Roman Catholic segments of the population were consistently restricted by coercion legislation that targeted the many for the crimes of the few. Following the Famine, Irish immigrants flooded into England itself, and the dual burdens of their Roman Catholicism and their levels of poverty made them easy scapegoats for British authorities. The tensions created within the British State of having a nation that was part of Britain and yet seen as alien culminated in the extraordinary highs and lows of the career of Charles Stewart Parnell, to be examined in detail in Chapter 3.

The Irish in Ireland

In theory Ireland was the political equal of England and Scotland in the union of the United Kingdom. The Emerald Isle had no

Parliament after 1800, for it had voted itself out of existence under the Act of Union. Irish members directly represented their constituencies at Westminster. Yet all was not well in this outward union. Doubted for its Roman Catholic religion, Ireland was often cast as the poor relation of the United Kingdom by British lawmakers, who repeatedly sanctioned laws to bring 'law and order' to a nation that was seen to be naturally lacking in those qualities.

It is important to differentiate between the Catholic Irish and those that were considered to be part of what has become known as the 'Protestant Ascendancy'. Members of the latter group had little difficulty in joining the British establishment. The Duke of Wellington is one Irishman in point. Lord Palmerston is another. Educated either at the University of Dublin or the main English universities, and tied by religion and class to England, such people were gladly welcomed where the bulk of their countrymen were not. Yet the Roman Catholic Irish were condemned not only for their religion but for their nationality in a way that the Protestant Irish on the whole were not. That is not to say that the Protestant Irish were one homogenous group – no more so than Protestants on the British mainland. Jennifer Ridden, for instance, has provided a useful analysis of the different groups of Protestant and Catholic elites and their understanding of and relationship to a 'British' nationality.[3]

Resentment seethed not far below the surface of Irish life. Absentee landlords, famine and land grievances led to the rise of nationalist leaders like Daniel O'Connell and later Charles Stewart Parnell.[4] More violently, they also led to the rise of Ribbonism, Fenianism, and armed rebellions in 1798, 1848 and 1869.[5] British law brought with it a set of British values that undermined Irish custom and Irish confidence. This was the context for the rise of Ribbonism and Fenianism, movements dedicated to the furtherment of Irish nationalism at the expense of British colonialism. Armed rebellions were tried and defeated, furthering the perception on mainland Britain that Ireland was a nation peopled by a violent, unruly, untrustworthy and ungrateful race.

The clearest way British Governments used the law to emphasise Irish 'lawlessness', and thereby differentiate the Irish from 'British' behaviour, was through coercion legislation. From the 1830s onwards, scarcely a year would go past without new legislation aimed at quelling agrarian discontent in Ireland. These acts typically gave greater powers to the police in Ireland and to the courts to deal with offenders in ways that would not have been acceptable under English conditions. The repetitive string of coercion acts encouraged the British public to continue to view the Irish as troublesome and unruly. The suggestion was that the Irish did not have the dignity and 'natural' civilisation which enabled English people not only to exist in peace but to share that skill by maintaining colonial rule over a quarter of the globe.

In 1886 T.P. O'Connor and R.M. McWade wrote *Gladstone–Parnell and the Great Irish Struggle*, in which they listed all the Coercion Acts passed by the British Parliament since the Act of Union in 1800.[6] Their work, coming squarely from the Irish nationalist viewpoint, implied the question: at what point does a legitimate government response to civil unrest become a concerted and continuous campaign labelling the Irish as criminal? There can be no question that, during the years of the most violent Fenian agitation in the 1860s, the British Government had to be seen to act in some manner to quell acts of outright violent rebellion. Yet even in these years the choice of language of British lawmakers tarred the Irish nation with a broad brush of criminality. It was the Irish nation that was criminal in the 1840s and 1860s, not merely the individuals who resorted to violence for political ends.

The 1833 Dangerous Disturbances Act made it lawful for the Lord Lieutenant of Ireland or the Chief Governor of Ireland to suppress any meeting which 'he or they shall deem to be dangerous to the public Peace or Safety.'[7] In other words it gave the Protestant British official who ruled Ireland unlimited discretion to stop public meetings. The Act gave the Lord Lieutenant the power to declare a district to be sufficiently disturbed to invoke the repressive measures of the Act.[8] All households within such an area could be forced to provide a list of all the male persons living in that household, the implication clearly being that adult Irish males were not to be trusted. The punishment for refusing to provide such a list was a fine of one shilling per day for each day of refusal to provide the list, or imprisonment.⁹ Approved individuals could hold meetings at their pleasure. The Lord Lieutenant had legal and social control over his domain. The discretion vested in him was the legal expression of his status as a bastion of British authority. He could decide who was allowed to have meetings and who was not.

Perhaps the strongest attack on the legal rights of the Irish in this Act is the provision in Section 11 disallowing bodies of persons to congregate in order to petition the Parliament without the prior consent of the Lord Lieutenant. Petitioning the Parliament was the constitutional right of all British citizens. It was a right generally even allowed to the residents of British colonies. But the people of Ireland, a constituent part of the United Kingdom itself, could not claim as of right an entitlement to approach their Parliament. Such a ban reinforced the status of the Irish as citizens who were untrustworthy.

The Irish leader Daniel O'Connell thought a ban on petitioning to be illegal because he believed all had the right to petition the monarch. He wrote to Chancellor Sugden in 1843: 'How can the Chancellor be of opinion that meetings to petition are not within the spirit of the Constitution, when the Constitution itself recognises, sanctions, aye, and enforces the right so to petition?'[10] O'Connell threatened to impeach the Lord Chancellor before an Irish Parliament when one was re-established.[11] Prime Minister Peel saw O'Connell's letter to Sugden and himself wrote to Sugden suggesting he look more closely to see whether O'Connell could be in breach of the law himself:

> Reference was made to the admissions in your Letter that the assemblages in Ireland were legal. Is it quite clear that they were so? There was a letter issued by Lord Stanley on the advice I believe of Lord Plunkett and Blackburne, when Lord Stanley was Chief Secretary, which lays down the position that immense assemblages – though peacefully conducted – and meeting for a legal object – might be illegal on account of ultimate danger to the public Peace – even though no depositions were made that parties were under the apprehension of immediate Risk to Persons & Property.[12]

O'Connell was a man who raised strong emotions inside British governments. William Ewart Gladstone, then President of the Board of Trade, described him in 1841 as 'a man regardless of all laws divine & human'.[13] Opinions of course could change with political agendas. In a second memorandum, this time in 1889, Gladstone recalled O'Connell as 'a great man' and recognised belatedly the role of the British Government in having defined O'Connell as a negative force:

> A very small part of this aversion may have been due to faults of his own, but in the main I fear it represented, taking him as the symbol of his country, the hatred which nations or the governing and representative parts of nations, are apt to feel towards those whom they have injured.[14]

The difference in language reflects the intellectual and political journey undertaken by Gladstone between 1841 and 1889. Beginning as the staunchest of conservative critics of the Irish and their Catholic religion, he became the strongest of their supporters, ultimately sacrificing his political energy in a vain attempt to bring about Irish Home Rule in 1886 and 1892–93.[15]

O'Connell recognised that the Irish were treated differently by British justice and wished it were otherwise. He assured a correspondent, Joseph Sturge, in 1843 that he did not wish to split Ireland from England: 'We know full well that it would be a great advantage to both countries to continue the connexion [sic] if it were placed on a basis of reciprocal Justice and Fair Play.'[16]

The 1833 Act further sought to introduce Courts Martial as an option for swift justice in proclaimed districts.[17] Under Section 15 a panel of eight officers hearing a case under martial law required only a bare majority of five to convict.[18] In effect the Act provided that lesser standards of justice were necessary to convict an Irishman than an Englishman. The law was again shown to be a useful exclusionary tool.

A curfew was put in place by Section 22, and anyone found violating it could be arrested.[19] The onus of proof was also reversed, with the defendant being required to satisfy the court that he was out of his house on lawful business.[20] Police could knock at any door and require named male inhabitants to show themselves or be deemed to have been absent and thus guilty of an offence.[21] Freedom of movement was restricted, notably within public spaces. The law again reflected underlying assumptions about the criminal nature of Irishmen that made it necessary to isolate them from the rest of society.[22]

The parliament reinforced its measures in 1835 with 'An Act for the better Prevention and more speedy Punishment of Offences endangering the Public Peace in Ireland.'[23] This Act went further than the 1833 Act in requiring inhabitants of houses to show themselves. A warrant was required to be issued, but that was the only formal bar.[24] Persons not showing themselves within ten minutes were deemed to be absent and became liable to a £1 fine or imprisonment for up to one month, or both, unless they could justify their absence to the court.[25] It was a sign that if you were Irish you were assumed not to be going about 'lawful business'. There was no place, even at home, where a law-abiding Irishman could feel that the law was no concern of his. The law could seek out people in their homes, not because they had committed a crime, but because they were thought to be likely to commit one.

The Irish were readily portrayed as a lawless race, and British lawmakers strove to uphold the majesty of the law in the face of such apparent Irish hostility. In the debate over a renewed Arms Bill against Ireland in 1843, Lord Eliot quoted to the House of Commons the observations of Colonel Millar, the second in command of the Irish Constabulary:

> There is, I regret to say, an unhappy propensity among the Irish peasantry to effect their ends, whatever those ends may be, by intimidation and violence; and even in cases of real injury occurring among themselves, where a legal remedy might doubtless be obtained, our police reports show that they are often prone to redress such wrongs by some cruel acts of retaliation, rather than proceed by course of law.[26]

The rhetoric in this case served the double purpose of highlighting the unruly nature of Irishmen while maintaining the Government position that legal recourse was available to all. The Irish were damned not only for their alleged criminality but for their unwillingness to 'proceed by course of law' in a legal system in which the odds were stacked against them.

Irish coercion laws were not a mere formality designed to enter Parliament's disapproval upon the statute book. Irish Members of Parliament lived with the knowledge that they could find themselves in prison for speaking to their massed constituents in a way that their political masters at Westminster judged to be rebellious. The arrest of Daniel O'Connell in late 1843 provides a case in point. Like Parnell 40 years later, O'Connell was arrested for a political crime. He had spoken to mass meetings in October 1843 and was arrested for conspiring to commit seditious acts.[27] In the judgement of historian Oliver MacDonagh, '[a] legal charge was only window dressing for what was a political act by the Government. While pretending to uphold "the rule of law", they really abandoned it.'[28]

Early 1844 saw some comment upon the case in Parliament. Thomas Duncombe, radical MP and Chartist supporter, alleged that O'Connell had not had a fair trial, and ridiculed the Government's reasons for acting: 'They [the House of Commons] were told that the object of the State prosecutions in Ireland was to vindicate what had been called the *majesty of the law*...'[29] (my emphasis). He was backed up by Lord John Russell, soon to be Prime Minister, who stated that 'whatever obloquy it may expose me to, I will never shrink from declaring that which I think, when it is my opinion that that person has not had a fair trial'.[30] William Sharman Crawford, MP for Rochdale, was keen to point out that Ireland was treated differently from England: 'What would have been said in England if an Arms Bill had been proposed in consequence of the Manchester riots? Ministers would not have dared to introduce it: England would not have submitted to it.'[31]

The possibility that O'Connell was the victim of unfair treatment at the hands of the British justice system was also noticed by some local office holders in various parts of the country. The magistrates of

Edinburgh sent a letter of protest to Prime Minister Peel on O'Connell's trial in Dublin. The letter expressed 'alarm' at the outcome of the trials, seeing them as an invasion of the 'British' right 'openly to canvass important measures'.[32] The letter went on:

> ...your memorialists participate in the opinion widely entertained, that in various respects, but especially in consequence of the irregularities committed in the selection of the jury, these parties have not had a fair trial, that justice has not been done to them, and therefore, that not only are the proceedings calculated to weaken the confidence of the people in the impartial administration of the law, but that the execution of the sentence, pending the discussion of the Appeal in the House of Lords, and having in view the State of Ireland, is at once unjust and impolitic.[33]

The magistrates' choice of words is revealing. It is not simply an unjust decision, but a politically unwise one. Why? Because it would 'weaken the confidence of the people in the impartial administration of the law'. In other words it would threaten that respect for British law which was the cornerstone of the successful rule of the British authorities. If O'Connell was found guilty in a case obviously biased against him as an individual, as an Irishman and as a Roman Catholic, it could threaten the popular reverence on which the law relied. The hold of British lawmakers on the fabric of society through control of the rule of law could only continue to work as long as the law was respected. Such a blatantly partisan case put that respect in doubt. The law lords saw this clearly, and overturned the guilty verdict. Somewhat ironically, what had begun as a clear Government attempt to make an example of an 'outsider' finished as something that could be held up as a vindication of the popular belief in the 'majesty of the law'.

The law officers of the Crown were asked by the Government for their opinion as to whether O'Connell's addresses to various mass meetings in 1843 constituted an attempt to corrupt the British soldiery in Ireland.[34] In essence, O'Connell in his speeches praised the average British soldier as Ireland's friend. He reserved his criticisms for their leaders and political masters. The Irish press, including *The Pilot*, were thought to have provided an improper amount of backing to O'Connell, and the law officers were asked to consider this also. In their opinion dated 15 September 1843, Fred Pollock and W.W. Tillett advised that O'Connell should not be prosecuted because his choice of words as reported did 'not amount to a malicious and advised endeavour to seduce the army from their allegiance'.[35] Similarly, while an article from *The Pilot* was considered by them to be a 'seditious libel', they felt it would be unfair to prosecute because similar libels were printed in English papers every week without any action being taken. The same law officers agreed in principle that a pre-planned meeting of 300 people could constitute 'a violation of the Convention Act' and that anyone present could be prosecuted.[36] However, they were at pains to suggest again that O'Connell should not be prosecuted for seditious language. The fact that the government chose to proceed against O'Connell, when he had done nothing prosecutable other than attending a meeting, shows the determination of the Home Secretary, Sir James Graham, amongst others, to make an example of an Irishman who dared to question the legitimacy of British rule in Ireland. Only through a successful prosecution, a practical demonstration of the majesty of British law, could O'Connell be brought to heel.

Graham wrote to Prime Minister Peel saying that he wished 'to meet Parliament with O'Connell convicted and in prison'.[37] Graham certainly seems to have entertained little thought that O'Connell might be innocent until proven guilty. The all-protestant jury might well have agreed, and even the diarist Charles Greville noted that the 'Chief Justice's charge was more like an advocate's speech than a judicial charge, stronger by far than any of our judges would have thought of delivering'.[38]

The House of Lords, against the expectations of the Government, threw out the conviction, and O'Connell was cleared. The extent to which this disrupted Government plans is revealed in the Home Secretary's reaction. Sir James Graham wrote to the diarist and MP, John Wilson Croker, of the decision:

[Baron Parke] is responsible; if he had not raised doubts, of which he was evidently ashamed, even Denman would hardly have dared to pander, as he did, to popular passion... I fear that no Irish juries will ever again convict in a political case; and it will be hard to find judges bold enough to do their duty when the House of Lords betrays its trust...[39]

Graham's choice of words is revealing. When the highest court in Britain finds an Irishman not guilty, Graham accuses the court of pandering to 'popular passions'. If the Lords had done their 'duty', as Graham saw it, O'Connell's conviction would have been upheld. The House of Lords, in finding for an outsider the Government was seeking to legally ostracise, had 'betrayed its trust'. Its 'trust' presumably was to make decisions in such contentious cases that reflected the position of the British authorities. In contrast James Whiteside, a future judge of the Queen's Bench in Ireland, congratulated O'Connell on the result, praising the Lords that had come down upon his side: 'You had in your favour Baron Parke, equal to any gown of the English Bench; Lord Denman, the Head of the Bench, whose integrity nobody can question; and Lord Cottenham, the best Chancellor since Lord Eldon.'[40]

What is identified consistently, both by contemporary parliamentarians and by historians, is that the Irish did not respect British law because it was a law imposed by an external force.[41] The British were prepared to go to lengths to impose their rule in Ireland that they would not have taken in other parts of the United Kingdom. As Alan Heesom has pointed out, the British Government did not move to suspend *habeas corpus* during the Swing Riots in England in the early 1830s.[42] Nor did they 'proscribe Nottingham or Bristol as revolted districts'.[43] Suspensions of such British constitutional rights in Ireland were accompanied by the use of soldiers as law enforcers, 'which many of the English military themselves, such as Sir Redvers Buller, noted would be unacceptable at home'.[44] That is not to say that stern measures had never been implemented in England. British troops had been used to quell Luddite disturbances in 1812. But these were individual responses to national security emergencies rather than a consistent policy of legal repression.

Whig/Liberal administrations showed themselves aware at different times that the law had to be seen to be impartial in Ireland as well as in England. The creation of a reverence for the law in Ireland was vital, a fact recognised by the Whigs in Government during 1835–41. As Virginia Crossman has noted,

> Public confidence in the law became a measure of public confidence in British rule. Reference to English notions of law and order served to emphasise the apparent contrast between England and Ireland in terms of public peace, and at the same time to place constraints on government in responding to Irish disorder.[45]

Later governments were equally aware that, for law to be respected, it had to be delivered by a local face. Michael Hicks Beach, when he was Irish Secretary in Salisbury's second ministry, needed to fill the position of Prison Commissioner for Ireland. Godfrey Lushington, permanent Under-Secretary at the Home Office, noted that 'Sir M. Hicks Beach is exceedingly anxious to find for the post a person who is an Irish Catholic and experienced in the management of prisons, and a reliable man'.[46]

That there should be a perception in Ireland that the law was not an objective adjudicator but merely a tool of a British elite is to some extent backed up by the structure of the legal system in Ireland. To quote nineteenth-century Irish historian W.E. Lecky,

> In 1833 – four years after Catholic emancipation – there was not in Ireland a single Catholic judge or stipendiary magistrate. All the high sheriffs with one exception, the overwhelming majority of the unpaid magistrates and of the grand jurors, the five inspectors-general, and the thirty-two sub-inspectors of police, were Protestant.[47]

Penny Bonsall has pointed out that Resident Magistrates in Ireland were not mere adjudicators on questions of law. They were also to some extent key government informants on the state of Ireland.[48] The majority of Resident Magistrates were from the upper and upper-middle classes, with a strong Protestant link, at least in the early years from 1836.[49]

Nonetheless Bonsall stresses that Roman Catholics were not excluded entirely, and that a small number continued to be appointed throughout the existence of the special magistracy.[50] Elizabeth Malcolm has also documented an increasing willingness by the British Government in the late 1830s to appoint Roman Catholic constables and magistrates in Ireland.[51] The question must be posed whether this illustrates that Roman Catholicism was not a bar. The fact that throughout the life of the Residential Magistracy the majority of the holders of that office were non-Catholics in a country that was overwhelmingly Catholic suggests that some non-specified selection criteria were at work. It may have been an economic question, as Bonsall suggests, with perhaps insufficient numbers of highly socially placed Roman Catholics to choose from.[52] Alternatively the Government may have been intelligent enough to know that, while it could not outwardly and absolutely discriminate against Roman Catholics from the 1830s onwards, it could massage the selection process to reflect political wishes. So much was this the case that, in 1884, only one out of the 74 magistrates in Co. Fermanagh was a Roman Catholic.[53] That all magistrates were unbiased on questions of religion seems unlikely. Clifford Lloyd, Special Resident Magistrate during the 1880s, described the Irish who were not from the Protestant north of Ireland (by implication Roman Catholics) as follows:

> ...the Irish of the south and west are disloyal by tradition, impulsive, reckless, ignorant, emotional, priest-ridden, and willing to be the slaves of the firstcomer who knows how to master them...[54]

The year 1848, against the background of armed uprisings in Ireland, saw further repressive legislation enacted. This included an Act suspending *habeas corpus*, and a Crime and Outrage Act.[55] The latter piece of legislation introduced a statutory duty on all males between

16 and 60 to join in a 'Search and Pursuit' of anyone suspected of murder or attempted murder, if asked by police. Failure to assist police to the utmost in this way could result in up to two years' imprisonment.[56] Such a measure could make peaceful law-abiding people into criminals simply for not wanting to join actively in a man-hunt for an accused neighbour. Once more British lawmakers were using the law to make outsiders of male Irish Catholics under the guise of introducing law-and-order legislation. By propagating the notion that all Irish were criminals, the Government was creating a body upon which the rest of Britain could place its insecurities about law and order. The clear implication was that the Irish would not pursue a murderer unless forced to do so. What is more, the Act provided that it was not necessary to prove that a district was in an insurrectionary state in order to proclaim that district for the purposes of the Act.[57]

This reveals one aim of the Government's strategy in utilising the law against the Irish. The Irish were to be treated as outsiders but it was important that they remained within 'British' boundaries. The 'outlaw' was a much more dangerous creature because the majesty of British law could no longer have meaning for such a person. The Crime and Outrage Act was forcing the Irish to respect British law by taking part in it, being forced to aid police in pursuing suspects. It was inclusion by force, and inclusion only in the subordinate position that British lawmakers would allow.

The Peace Preservation (Ireland) Act of 1856 reduced the penalties for some offences under the 1848 Act from two years' to one year's imprisonment.[58] It otherwise continued the 1848 Act until 1858.[59] The Peace Preservation (Ireland) Act of 1870 gave Justices of the Peace in proclaimed districts the power to summon witnesses and question them on oath even before any person had been charged with an offence.[60] Such judicial fishing expeditions were clearly an invasion of the legal rights of any person who might eventually be accused of a crime.

Persons found out after dark 'under suspicious circumstances' could be arrested and held without charge until the next petty sessions.[61] At the sessions, the person could be sentenced to six months' imprisonment if the justices believed that the person was not out on lawful business.[62] The term 'lawful business' is an accepted part of legal terminology, yet its meaning is not necessarily clear-cut. What in fact constituted lawful business? If it meant simply business that was not breaking the law, that was an effective mask for the fact that it meant not breaking the rules that Britain had imposed upon the Irish people. Nighttime was far more dangerous for British authorities because it was more difficult to control. It was a space associated with danger and conspiracy. 'British' credentials did not shine in the dark. By barring outsiders from that space, parliament implied that the Irish could not be trusted within it.

For agrarian crimes that resulted in 'murder, maiming or injury', the Grand Jury of the county in which the offence occurred could award compensation to the aggrieved party.[63] The problem with this state of affairs was that the money to pay such compensation was to be levied from the county or district in which the crime took place.[64] All the inhabitants of a district were therefore somehow guilty by implication for having allowed a murder to occur. The British Government was tarring the many for the crimes of the few. The Act implied that all Irish were necessarily involved in such crimes in their area and must be forced to pay. This provision was amended by the Peace Preservation (Ireland) Act of 1875, which restricted such payments to situations where the Grand Jury was convinced that persons in the district were withholding material evidence.[65]

The Government approach in Ireland suggested that the Irish people were not as committed to enforcing British law as their English counterparts. There is some evidence that this may in fact have been true. Acquittal rates by juries in Ireland were on the whole significantly higher than in England and Wales.[66] David Johnson argues convincingly that the largely rural and close-knit Irish population were little prepared to convict their neighbours, for reasons either of loyalty or fear of retribution.[67] He goes further and argues that assaults were considered much more a part of life in Ireland than in England.[68]

The behaviour of Irish MPs was also an aspect referred to as a reason for the negative view taken by British Governments of the Irish. Joseph Chamberlain, for instance, noted in 1882:

...some Irish members have acted as if their object were to embitter and prejudice all English opinion. The result is that nothing wd [sic] be easier than at the present moment to get up in every large town an anti-Irish agitation almost as formidable as the anti-Jewish agitation in Russia.[69]

Chamberlain's comments reflect the status of the Irish as outsiders, finding it hard to gain acceptance in a British society run by 'the rule of law'. Suspicion of the Irish was the starting point of many British Government actions. For instance, when the Boundary Commission was undertaking its work in 1884 under the leadership of Sir Charles Dilke, Lord Salisbury expressed great concern at the arrangements for Ireland. A separate Commission was being appointed for Ireland, and Salisbury was concerned that, due to the 'unscrupulousness of Irish politicians', the Commission must in no way appear to be biased.[70] Salisbury stated that he would have preferred the English Commission to have undertaken the task in Ireland.[71] While this might have created the impression of a more impartial result, it reinforced again the view that the Irish were not to be trusted with their own affairs.

The British Government certainly moved to take advantage of perceptions of Irish criminality to manipulate the justice system under the guise of 'law and order' policy. The jury procedure could clearly be manipulated in an attempt to gain more convictions. Under rules set down by Attorney-General Warren in 1867, the Crown had the right of limitless challenge to jurors. As Johnson points out,

> It is clear that the majority of jurors challenged were Catholics. Usually the Crown maintained the fiction that they were unaware of the religion of those it ordered to stand by and refused to provide information. It is clear, however, from occasional lapses from this stance that they were more aware of the facts than they admitted.[72]

The jury in Daniel O'Connell's trial in 1844 had been '...wholly Protestant and largely Conservative...'.[73] Thomas Bellew questioned

Lord Eliot in Parliament in March 1844, over reports that jurors in Ireland, specifically in the case of *R v O'Halloran, McKenna, and others*, were excluded on the grounds of their Roman Catholicism alone. Lord Eliot stated that there was no principle in operation excluding Roman Catholics.[74]

The way the law was applied against significant Irish figures as representatives of their nation reinforced the negative messages contained in the coercion acts. The imprisonment of Charles Stewart Parnell in Kilmainham gaol in Dublin in 1881, for his activities within the Land League, was an act of executive frustration with an outsider who was causing more trouble than could reasonably be allowed. The same motivations had caused the Whig Government to imprison O'Connell decades before. It was the Coercion Bill of 1881 that gave Prime Minister Gladstone the power to deprive a parliamentary opponent of his liberty in this way.[75] Under the Act, the Lord Lieutenant could hold without charge or bail anyone 'reasonably suspected' of having committed or attempted treason, violence or intimidation.[76] This effectively gave the authorities the power to arrest and detain anyone about whom they had suspicions for as long as they wished.

Parnell's chief colleagues in the Land League were imprisoned with him, causing that movement to falter. John Dillon, William O'Brien and J.J. O'Kelly were all imprisoned without due process of law, as allowed under the terms of the Coercion Bill.[77] They were imprisoned under the authority of the Government's Irish Secretary, W.E. Forster. Forster resigned from the Government over its subsequent agreement with Parnell, known as the Kilmainham Treaty, which brought about Parnell's release.[78] The new Chief Secretary for Ireland was Lord Frederick Cavendish, a close family relative of another Liberal minister, Lord Hartington, and of Gladstone's wife.[79] Cavendish and the Under-Secretary, T.H. Burke, were assassinated in the Phoenix Park murders on 6 May 1882, only four days after Parnell and his colleagues had been released from gaol. The assassination had the predictable effect of tying the Government to a new 'get tough' policy with Ireland, which English public opinion understandably demanded after the brutal murders.

The 1882 Prevention of Crime Act was amongst the most comprehensive yet enacted.[80] It allowed for Special Commissions to be established by the Lord Lieutenant to try such crimes as treason, murder, attempted murder, arson and attacking a dwelling house. These Special Commissions would consist of three judges who would try cases without a jury. The Act again put in place provisions against 'illegal' public meetings and absence from home at night, and for the arrest of strangers at any hour of the day or night. Witnesses could again be questioned without anyone having been charged with an offence. Section 18(3) of the Act allowed for additional police to be employed in certain districts 'by reason of the existence or apprehension of crime and outrage in any district'.[81] Importantly, the charge for such extra police was to be borne directly by the rate-payers of the district in which they were deployed.

The early 1880s were clearly troubled times in Ireland for law and order. The British Government undoubtedly wished to be seen to respond to concerns on that front. Yet its willingness to impose laws not applied to Britons in general implied again that the Irish were a class apart, a group of outsiders to be feared. Sections 25(4) and 27(5), amongst others, limited the right to object to the jurisdiction of a court of Special Commission. Section 27(12) made it clear that courts of Special Commission were empowered to find and enforce death-penalty convictions. It was thus envisaged that people in Ireland in 1882 could be sentenced to death without the privilege of a jury trial. Section 30 then proceeded to give the Lord Lieutenant of Ireland extensive powers to manipulate procedures for Courts of Special Commission as he saw fit.

Through the workings of statute law, Ireland remained an inferior society in English eyes. Like other indigenous peoples in the empire, the Irish were to be pitied rhetorically, but a firm hand had to be exercised to keep them from their natural state of violence and criminality. They displayed an 'un-British' disregard for the rule of law. A constituent nation within the United Kingdom, the Irish remained 'other' in the eyes of the British state.

The Irish in England

The Irish 'problem', as it was to be increasingly known in the nineteenth century, was not restricted to the Irish in Ireland. Irish immigration into England boomed during and immediately after the tragedy of the Potato Famine of 1846.[82] The Irish settled in the largest numbers in Liverpool, Manchester, Glasgow, Dundee and London.[83] The number of Irish-born people in England, Scotland and Wales jumped from 415,000 in 1841 to 805,000 in 1861, by which time they made up 3.5 per cent of the total population.[84] This might have been a small percentage of the British population, but represented a disturbingly high percentage of the native-born Irish population. As Fergus D'Arcy has pointed out, in 1861 'one in every three Irish lived out of Ireland'.[85]

Nineteenth-century Britain was not predisposed to welcome this influx of their Irish cousins with much warmth. Historian Donald MacRaild has convincingly suggested that contemporary 'observations' laid 'the foundation stone of a history which looks like demonology'.[86] Such a view was promoted, argues MacRaild, by the use of public inquiries by committees of the House of Commons. He suggests that the onset of this kind of inquiry in earnest in nineteenth-century Britain simply provided a more widely exposed vehicle through which elite views could be spread to the public:[87]

> Indeed, it is to this tradition – the local inspection and the government report, and not to Carlyle or Engels – that historians must turn if they are to understand the origins of what might be called the popular anti-Irish stereotype.[88]

MacRaild's research indicates that governments were informed through processes that exhibited a subjective bias against Irish immigrants in Britain.

The intellectual climate of the time also seemed to favour a divide between the British and the Irish, as a historiographical debate was played out over whether the Celts had long ago fallen to Anglo-Saxon superiority, or whether the idea of Anglo-Saxon racial purity was in fact a myth.[89] Thomas Carlyle wrote in *Chartism* about the superiority of Anglo-Saxons over Celts.[90] Such views were countered by the likes of James Cowles Prichard, who argued strongly during the nineteenth century that the Irish had a proud intellectual history, especially in the period following their conversion to Christianity.[91] Historian Sheridan Gilley has argued that '[r]ace was only one element among many in anti-Irish prejudice', suggesting that the Irish were 'damned for disloyalty before they were damned as Celts', in response to L.P. Curtis' 1968 work *Anglo-Saxons and Celts: A Study of Anti-Irish Prejudice in Victorian England*.[92] Paul B. Rich has likewise found Curtis's analysis to be too restrictive, suggesting that it was not that the Irish were a different 'race' that troubled the British, but that they did not want to be a part of the United Kingdom to which they legally belonged.[93] Ryan Dye stresses the distinction to be drawn between English Roman Catholics and Irish Roman Catholics in England. Dye suggests that English Roman Catholics were very aware of their identity as Englishmen and did not want Roman Catholicism to be tarred with the same brush as Irish nationalism.[94] This suggests that it was identification with Irish nationality over and above identification with Roman Catholicism that rendered Irish immigrants as doubly damned outsiders.

Roger Swift, a leading historian of the links between the Irish and crime in Victorian Britain, has postulated four reasons why the Irish were seen as 'outcasts' from British society.[95] He cites class, nationality, race and religion as the most important factors differentiating the Irish from the rest of the British population.[96] His research indicates that the perception that the Irish were by nature on the wrong side of the law was widespread: 'During the Victorian period the link between Irish immigration, crime, and disorder in England was widely regarded by contemporary observers as axiomatic.'[97] Contemporaries could also be swayed by the press to view the link between the Irish and crime as stronger than it actually was. The findings of Kristina Jeffes in her study of the Irish in early Victorian Chester certainly suggest such a conclusion.[98]

Whether through over-policing of Irish districts, or by a more visible condemnation of the Roman Catholic Church which was seen to be so closely linked to the Irish, the police and the press were responsible in large part for the maintenance of Irish outsider status.[99]

Research by Swift on the Irish in Wolverhampton has confirmed that they could be targeted by a police force keen to establish its own validity by strongly policing those perceived to be the instigators of so much urban crime.[100]

The link between anti-Catholicism and anti-Irish prejudice has been examined at length by Sheridan Gilley, who has pointed out that they were not one and the same thing and that the former was far broader than the latter.[101] Both carried connotations of disloyalty to the Queen, the head of society. For instance, as Oliver MacDonagh points out, the Irish party in the 1880s would sing 'God Save Ireland' as opposed to 'God Save the Queen'.[102] In a sense, such actions merely reconfirmed the outsider status of the Irish as disloyal to the traditions bound up with the idea of 'Britishness'.

Low attendance rates at Mass hardly backed up the image of an all-dominant Roman Catholic religion, at least until the years after the Famine.[103] Contemporary observer Henry Mayhew, in his study of Irish women as street sellers in London, concluded that 'as to the great majority, religion is almost a nonentity'.[104] He contradicts himself later, contrasting the alleged religious indifference of some Jews with the 'religious intensity of the majority of the Roman Catholic Irish of the streets'.[105] Ultimately it was the image of Roman Catholicism as a foreign religion, regardless of the level of genuine religious intensity on the ground, which worked to the detriment of those Irish who had come to seek their fortune on the British mainland.

Swift has found that the Irish were three times as likely to be prosecuted as their English counterparts, and five times as likely to be imprisoned.[106] It is against this wider backdrop of anti-Irish feeling that British attitudes need to be examined. By finding the Irish to be overtly criminal, British law-enforcement agencies were creating an 'other' against which the rest of British society could define itself. Swift's research supports such a conclusion, finding that 'to many contemporaries such disorders were the reflection of an inherent Irish weakness for collective violence which, paradoxically, served to highlight the relative orderliness of the host society'.[107] The Irish could be condemned equally for their 'petty' criminality, as well as the spectacular Fenian outrages that periodically raised their heads in the latter half of the nineteenth century.

In July 1858 the *Wolverhampton Chronicle*, describing a recent disturbance, asserted that 'misguided and ignorant men were taught that the law of England will not tolerate the interruption by brute force of a public lecture'.[108] The law of England as a body suddenly had the human abilities of tolerance and intolerance attributed to it by the *Chronicle*. Rather than the citizens of Wolverhampton, or the Government of Britain, it was the law of England whose integrity was said to be attacked by such interruptions to public events.

That the British Government took the alleged hostility of the Irish towards British law seriously is clear. On 8 April 1851, an Englishman named George Graham wrote to the Secretary of State, George Grey, expressing his concern at the outbreak of 'secret clubs' in England, consisting for the most part of foreigners, who were preparing to attack the royal family.[109] Graham claimed there were 90,000 foreigners involved and that 'they reckon upon the aid of 150,000 Irishmen now in the Country, and 60,000 Irishwomen, ripe at the word of Command to exterminate as many English as they possibly can'.[110] The Home Office was sufficiently concerned to send a police inspector to interview Graham, only to find that he 'appeared very anxious that his Son should be employed in what he called the Secret Service'.[111]

Historian Fergus D'Arcy has argued that what was remarkable was not the amount of anti-Irish ill-feeling, but rather that there was not more of it: 'That this invasion generated an enduring prejudice is hardly remarkable. That it generated hostile perceptions of the Irish was perhaps inevitable.'[112] D'Arcy's point is well made. Few mass influxes of 'others' are welcomed by the inhabitants already there. As van Duin notes, 'during the decade 1876–1885 alone another 130,952 Irishmen entered Britain, more than the total number of Russian and Polish Jews (estimated at some 120,000) to arrive in Britain during the entire period 1875–1914'.[113] British lawmakers, through their political rhetoric, had the capacity to inhibit or to aid any hostility which developed. By ensuring that most Irish interactions with the law were negative ones, British authorities undoubtedly increased the popular distrust of the newcomers. The link between that distrust and the agency of the law was recognised by contemporary commentators such as Nassau Senior in the *Edinburgh Review*.[114]

An examination of the key moments of Irish discontent within Britain reveals much about the status of the Irish before the law, and how that mirrored the outsider status of the Irish amongst their neighbours in British cities. The Garibaldi riots, the Stockport riots and the Fenian agitations saw outbursts of anti-Irish aggression, as well as anti-English aggression on the part of the Irish. The riots, and the involvement in them of the Irish, provided ammunition for the British Government in its attempt to present the Irish as outsiders. The large number of Irish arrests gave credence to the views of social commentators like Mayhew that the Irish had a fundamental opposition to obeying British law.

The Birkenhead disturbances in Cheshire in 1850 certainly demonstrate that anti-Catholicism and anti-Irish sentiment could be closely linked.[115] The local magistrates called a meeting to protest at the 'encroachment of Rome' represented by the Pope's restoration of ecclesiastical titles to Britain. Court cases came out of the disturbance, and the *Catholic Standard* was, perhaps unsurprisingly, quite certain the Protestants were to blame:

> Our readers have not, doubtless, forgotten the scene which took place at Birkenhead on the 27th of November last, when certain anti-Catholic brawlers, including half a dozen magistrates...attempted to pack a meeting of the ratepayers of the town, for the purpose of carrying an anti-Papal petition and series of resolutions.[116]

The involvement of magistrates in the meeting, and the share of the blame they should have carried for the accompanying disturbances, is significant. Magistrates were 'British' officials in their localities. They carried with them, by virtue of their position, the majesty of British law.

That the magistrates were aware of the significance of their support is demonstrated by a public notice which they posted on 27 November 1850, adjourning the meeting they had originally called:

> The Magistrates having called a PUBLIC MEETING, in pursuance of a most respectable requisition, for the purpose of presenting a LOYAL ADDRESS to the QUEEN, against the ENCROACHMENTS OF ROME, have found a Mob assembled round the place of Meeting... We the undersigned, under the circumstances, have not deemed it our duty, as Magistrates, to endanger the Public Peace, and have therefore adjourned the Meeting until the Inhabitants can be assembled to express their opinions with THE FREEDOM OF ENGLISHMEN.[117]

The inclusion of the last phrase, 'with the freedom of Englishmen', is significant. It emphasises the gulf that existed between those seen as having a reverence for the law and those, like the Irish Roman Catholic protestors, that did not. Once more, Roman Catholicism and Irishness were at least by implication linked to disrespect for the legal rights of their fellow citizens. In this instance, the link was so obvious that the Home Secretary, Sir George Grey, questioned the wisdom of the magistrates in convening such a meeting. Presumably in response to such pleadings from the Home Office, the magistrates refused to call a further meeting. In a public notice dated 3 December 1850, they stated:

> that it is not deemed expedient that they, as Magistrates, should take an active part in summoning a meeting likely to lead to such an amount of violence, as might renew the disgraceful and unprovoked riot that prevented the holding of the meeting on Wednesday last.[118]

The Irish were kept on the outer edges of British society by geography, by legislation, by policing methods and by the trials of Irish leaders. As the tumultuous debates over Irish Home Rule were to show, the

Irish were an 'other' that had to remain within the United Kingdom while still being excluded from positions of legal power. The tumultuous impact of this tension between wanting to exclude the Irish and simultaneously needing to retain them led to the confrontations between Charles Stewart Parnell and 'British' law that were to dominate British politics in the latter half of the 1880s.

CHAPTER 3

IRELAND ON TRIAL: THE PARNELL EXPERIENCE

In February 1886, the Liberal Government of William Gladstone was ushered in following the Conservative defeat in the general election of late 1885. The Government was to survive for under six months, and its demise was to be brought about by the issue of Ireland.[1] The Home Rule for Ireland Bill was announced in April 1886 and was brought before the Commons in June. Despite the efforts of Gladstone, with some measure of half-hearted support from the remainder of his Cabinet, the Bill was defeated. Joseph Chamberlain had resigned from the Cabinet two months previously, and it was his willingness to lead a group of his supporters to cross the floor that defeated the Bill.[2]

If legislation is the ultimate expression of legal authority, then the Home Rule Bill was perhaps the greatest legal recognition that the Irish did not really enjoy full equality within the United Kingdom. As Gladstone stated in his speech to the Commons when presenting the bill,

> ...rightly or wrongly, yet in point of fact, law is discredited in Ireland, and discredited in Ireland upon this ground especially – that it comes to the people of that country with a foreign accent, and in a foreign garb.[3]

The word 'foreign' carried with it a range of negative connotations in a country that always championed the 'British' way of life against the upheavals associated with 'foreign' nations on the Continent and beyond. By using the term, Gladstone gave recognition that Britain and Ireland were in fact, if not in law, separate nations.

Many MPs, even within the Liberal Party, failed to share Gladstone's belief that the rest of Britain cared sufficiently about the Irish to grant them Home Rule. As late as 1893, Henry Labouchere was able to write: 'Nobody cares for the rights and wrongs of Ireland. So far as I could make it out when going about electioneering – the only bait that took was the idea of getting rid of that troublesome country with its Mps [sic].'[4] This assessment by Labouchere, an English radical, is all the more significant because he had been a vocal supporter of Parnell and his claims for Ireland.

In some ways the most spectacular attempts to define the Irish as outsiders were the legal manoeuvrings which twice brought the Irish leader, Charles Stewart Parnell, to the political and social brink after 1886. The Protestant, aristocratic Parnell may at first glance have seemed a strange fit as the spearhead for a mass political movement of poverty-stricken Catholic Irishmen. But through his leadership during the 1880s in particular, Parnell came to embody for his Irish supporters all that was distinctive about their nation.[5] Until his fall, Parnell in many ways *was* Ireland. This made the symbolism of his fall all the greater.

The seeds of the extraordinary confrontation between British law and an Irish leader were sown initially from Parnell's own choices in his private life. From 1880 onwards, Parnell was smitten with Mrs Katherine O'Shea.[6] This in itself was nothing unusual. Many Victorian men, and indeed many parliamentarians, defied the moralistic official stance of the British Establishment to take a mistress. Parnell was unmarried and certainly an eligible bachelor. Parnell's problem was that Katherine O'Shea was the wife of a parliamentary colleague, Captain William O'Shea. The threat of possible exposure of this illicit relationship was therefore constant. But more of that later.

In March 1887, against a background of increased tenant discontent in Ireland's economic downturn, *The Times* newspaper began a campaign charging Parnell and his associates with murder and terror.[7] *The Times* published on 18 April a letter supposedly implicating Parnell in the Phoenix Park murders, a letter which Parnell duly pronounced to be a forgery designed to bring about his own political ruin. It was a pivotal moment. The political leader who embodied the very idea of Ireland and what it stood for was being accused by the establishment newspaper of being – in effect – just another criminal Irishman.

Katherine O'Shea recorded in her memoirs Parnell's strangely apathetic response to the publication of the letter. She had brought him *The Times* that morning, and had warned him of its contents before handing it over. According to her account, he read 'the whole thing' without reaction and did not seem disposed to worry about it at all.[8] 'I have never taken any notice of any newspapers, nor of anyone. Why should I now?', Parnell is alleged to have said.[9] Parnell may have seemed unconcerned, but he must have been aware that *The Times* would be a formidable opponent. The publication of the letter marked the start of a concerted campaign, run by *The Times* and leading members of the Government, to bring down Parnell and his brand of un-British Irish nationalism with him. *The Times* followed up in 1888 by publishing a further letter implicating Parnell even more directly in the Phoenix Park tragedy, which had so struck at the very heart of British rule in Ireland. The Salisbury Government responded to the sea of allegations and conjecture by establishing a Special Commission to inquire into the whole matter.

That *The Times* was acting as a Government lackey in agitating for a Special Commission was a point of view strongly put in Parliament in debates prior to the establishment of the Commission. The Irish MP, T.P. O'Connor, suggested that there must be collusion on the basis that the Attorney-General, whom he believed to have been consulted in the drawing up of the bill allowing the Special Commission, had just appeared for *The Times* in the case of *O'Donnell v Walter*, in which most of the allegations against the Irish parliamentarians had been made.[10] The Liberal Earl of Kimberley felt that the O'Donnell case had been central to giving the Government the political opportunity to appoint a Commission on a model of their own choosing:

> Parnell in the judgement of many people made a false move in demanding inquiry after the Atty. General's speech in the O'Donnell case. His position was excellent: he had asked for & been refused inquiry by a Committee... By demanding again inquiry, he gave the Govt. the opportunity of making the clever move of the Commission.[11]

Kimberley's colleague Labouchere used a speech in Parliament to condemn the Government for what he alleged was its complicity with *The Times* in seeking to bring down Parnell: 'As it was, the Commission was framed by *The Times*' Counsel and the Government to provide *The Times* with cogged dice in order to play the game against the hon. Member for Cork {Parnell}.'[12]

The response of the Liberal Unionist Joseph Chamberlain reinforced the 'majestic' view that those who administered British justice were above shallow conspiracies. Of Labouchere, he said:

> I am sure he must have been very unfortunate in his experience of human nature, if he cannot admit to himself that Englishmen, even although they happen to be Ministers of the Crown, are really filled with a desire for fair play and justice.[13]

This is an example of the rhetorical raising of 'Englishmen' and English justice to the rarefied heights that would encourage popular reverence. The English understood the rule of law, and it was their gift to the cumulative identity of the British state. It was exactly this picture which British lawmakers were attempting to present to the British public, that of the majesty of the law at work, a majesty that could not 'lower' itself to bias.

Sir Edward Clarke, Solicitor-General, returned to the theme when defending the lack of judicial procedure to be followed at the Commission: 'If we have three Judges, we can trust their experience and authority, surely, to guide the inquiry...'[14] It was a subtle defence of the institutions of law. By implying that anyone who questioned the make-up of the Commission was really questioning the professionalism of British judges, Clarke was asserting that a Special Commission deserved the same reverence as a court of law – even though it was clearly a very different institution.

The Government proved to be evasive over whether proper judicial procedures would be followed in the Commission. The Home Secretary Henry Matthews rejected calls for strict legality of procedure:

> It appears to me that, in showing a desire for a strict observance of the technical rules in a criminal pleading, hon. Members lay themselves open to the suspicion that they wish to evade inquiry into what is really material and substantial.[15]

Matthews effectively implied in his statement that if one wanted to get to the 'material and substantial truth', a normal British court of law was not the place to do it. Yet his speech came after A.H. Smith had spoken on behalf of the Government questioning why the Irish members had not sued *The Times* themselves for criminal libel.[16] He criticised the Irish for failing to trust the British justice system sufficiently to initiate a libel action, elevating the British justice system as something so objective as to be above the anti-Irish feeling that the Irish members feared. T.M. Healy, an Irish member, made the point that '[a]n English jury is now cracked up to us as the height of everything that is admirable'.[17]

Matthews himself does not seem to have been entirely in agreement with Government policy towards Ireland. He could see that the power of the law was being applied in a discriminatory fashion, making an example of Ireland and singling it out for treatment that could only confirm the 'outsider' status of the Irish. Lord Salisbury wrote to Lord Halsbury in 1889 asking the latter to use his influence to prevent Matthews resigning over the Government's refusal to 'extend the Irish Criminal Law Amendment Bill to England'.[18]

Labouchere ridiculed the Government for criticising the Irish for not pursuing a libel action against *The Times*. In doing so he again attacked *The Times* as a Government ally:

There was a journal known to many hon. Gentlemen opposite – *United Ireland* – which had made accusations again and again against the right hon. Gentleman the Chief Secretary for Ireland (Mr. A.J. Balfour) and against other Members of Her Majesty's Government, far more strong than any which had been made by *The Times* against the hon. Member for Cork and his Friends. Did hon. Gentlemen opposite consider that the right hon. Gentleman the Chief Secretary for Ireland was guilty because he refused to bring an action against *United Ireland*, or did they consider that *The Times* was a sort of sacred institution; and that if it made an accusation that accusation must be true, but that if another newspaper made an accusation it need not be true, although those accused did not choose to bring any action?[19]

As a rival newspaper editor himself, Labouchere undoubtedly had an axe to grind with *The Times*. Yet his insight is important. It showed that there was a contemporary perception that there were institutions which British Governments regarded as sacred and would protect. *The Times* was perhaps one such institution. The judiciary was another. Such institutions were sacred because they symbolised British values and the superiority of British law and British justice. Governments could protect these institutions – and the values they represented – by providing them with rhetorical backing, and by denigrating those who questioned the right of such institutions to superior status. By making it 'un-British' to question such institutions, British lawmakers could work to enshrine the sacred nature of such institutions in the fabric of British society.

Government responsibility for setting up the Special Commission extended to having partly brought about the evidence that led to the Commission. The series of articles on 'Parnellism and Crime' which *The Times* published from March 1887 onwards had set up the damaging backdrop against which the saga of the Parnell letters was to emerge. At least some of the articles were written by Sir Robert Anderson, Assistant Police Commissioner and Head of CID, as he admitted in 1910 in his autobiography.[20] The Government claimed to have been unaware of Anderson's authorship, but Anderson, writing in 1910, said he was told that '[e]verybody in Fleet-street knew that I was the author of them'.[21] How the Government could have been unaware of what everybody in Fleet Street supposedly knew is at best something of a mystery, although Anderson may well have been exaggerating to shift the blame from himself for having written the articles at all.

A man charged with upholding the law, in one of the highest positions in the police arm of the State, was actively contributing to the climate of fear and terror associated with Irish Members of Parliament. While all policemen were clearly also private citizens with private rights, Anderson utilised his public position to pursue a private agenda against Parnell. Clearly, in any attempt to discuss links between Parnell and crime, Anderson would have been in a position to utilise evidence and contacts that came with his position. That is certainly how The *Daily News* saw it in its 7 April 1910 edition, when responding to Anderson's admissions in his serialised autobiography in *Blackwood's* magazine:

> The position therefore stands thus: As a Home Office official he [Anderson] wrote the 'exposure,' and as a Scotland Yard official he was able to throw his influence into the defence of 'The Times' for the publication of his own 'revelations.' We do not think that the deplorable story of English official relationships with the Irish movement could reveal a more amazing incident than that which this gentleman discusses with evident self-approval on a page quaintly headed 'Radical dishonesty'.[22]

If Anderson had been in possession of sufficient evidence to bring a criminal charge against Parnell or any member of his party, he could have advised the Director of Public Prosecutions to that effect. Parnell and Gladstone both argued during the parliamentary debate over the setting up of the Special Commission that if the Government felt it had evidence to prosecute Parnell, it should use it. They rejected A.H. Smith's criticism of the Irish for refusing to go before an English jury in a libel claim, on the basis that the Government had it well within its power to put Parnell before a jury in a criminal trial if they really felt there was a case to answer.[23]

Anderson's background as a special agent dealing with Fenianism in the early 1880s undoubtedly influenced the views that were later expressed through *The Times*. In a letter to Home Secretary Harcourt in 1882, Anderson had described how the new coercion bill was working in Ireland, saying there could be no rest '... till the lesson which the people are now being taught has been far more plainly enforced...'.[24] His suspicions of Parnell clearly dated from the same period:

> I have mentioned in former memos that Henry Campbell, Mr Parnell's Sect., is implicated in the crimes of these people – or at least in the conspiracy wh. caused these crimes. I now learn that Parnell is 'hedging' by dismissing Campbell, who will leave the country.[25]

Anderson's name was to come up directly in parliament over his role in 'helping' *The Times's* case before the Special Commission. An Exchange between Henry Matthews and Sir William Harcourt in the Commons drew attention to Anderson's subterranean role as a Government enforcer.

> Harcourt: I would ask the Home Secretary on whose authority Mr Robert Anderson handed confidential papers in his possession, in his official capacity, to a man calling himself Le Caron (a witness for the *Times* newspaper), to be taken away by him and examined and used by Le Caron and Mr Houston?
>
> Matthews: Mr Anderson's action in the matter referred to by the right hon. Gentleman was without my cognizance; but, so far as I am acquainted with the circumstances of the case, he acted in accordance with what was due to the Special Commission.[26]

Matthews, upon further questioning, was forced to admit that the Special Commission had not directed Anderson to hand over those papers.[27] The clear conclusion to be drawn was that Anderson handed them over of his own volition. It is another example of how Government men were able to manipulate a process which appeared judicial without being formally acknowledged as a prosecution.

Sir Charles Russell QC, MP, appeared before the Commission as counsel for Parnell. He recognised the role of the Commission in perpetuating the place of the Irish as a people to be feared.

> I want to point out to your Lordships that in truth the attempt is here being made, in which your Lordships are asked to assist, to do what Edmund Burke declared had never been successfully done, to draw an indictment against a whole nation.[28]

By putting on trial the elected representatives of the Irish people, the Commission was questioning the character of the people who had sent these men to Westminster. Margaret O'Callaghan has argued that is precisely what the British Government wanted to do by setting up the Commission. She sees the Special Commission as a success for the Conservative Government, which had never believed that Parnell had written the letters that became the Commission's centrepiece: 'Substantially it had succeeded in establishing precisely what it had been constituted to establish – that nationalism and crime were one and the same thing.'[29]

Sir Charles Russell, appearing before the Commission, went on to ask why the Government had not pressed criminal charges if it felt that crimes had been committed or supported by members of the Irish party. He suggested that the Irish members and Irish people believed that the Government was pursuing a private prosecution where insufficient evidence existed to sustain a full criminal trial.[30] Sir John Simon recognised as much even before the Commission had begun, saying in parliament that '[t]he Government stood in no other position than that of public prosecutors'.[31]

Many of the counsel that appeared were MPs, a fact not unusual in itself. However, they included the Attorney-General appearing as leading counsel for *The Times*. The Attorney-General had earlier represented *The Times* in the libel action brought against it by F.H. O'Donnell, after being mentioned in the 'Parnellism and Crime' articles.[32] The anomaly of this position had been seized upon by opposition Members of Parliament in the debates over the Commission.[33] Certain charges against Parnell and his party had first been aired in a court of law in the *O'Donnell v Walter* case that the Government now claimed necessitated some action on its part.[34] Once rumours had been given credence by being mentioned in court, they had to be investigated, or such was the Government position.[35] Yet, ironically, the very person who had mentioned those rumours in court, thus necessitating a Special Commission, was the Attorney-General himself, Sir Richard Webster. The Attorney-General went on to represent *The Times* before the Commission that his own statements had forced the Government to initiate. It is an example par excellence of how a British government could use its access to legal machinery to protect itself while using the law to isolate 'outsiders'. Historian J.L. Hammond attractively summarises the anomaly of the situation:

> In one capacity, that of counsel for the *Times*, it was his duty to try to persuade a court, and incidentally the world, that this political opponent was a scoundrel. In another capacity, that of Attorney General, it was his duty to keep his judgement in suspense on all these charges, and only to decide on the fullest investigation whether or not that political opponent ought to be prosecuted.[36]

The Government was using all the powers at its disposal to try the elected representatives of Ireland. Hammond characterises it as a 'State prosecution'.[37] Sir Charles Russell, in his opening speech for Parnell before the Commission, highlighted the same fact:

> I say, while in form it is not a Government prosecution, it has in fact been conducted in a way which has given to the prosecutors all the advantages of a Government prosecution, and given to the accused none of the advantages to which they would have been entitled had it been in form a Government prosecution.[38]

The Government certainly used its control over legal machinery to advantage. It provided access for representatives of *The Times* to members of the Irish police, funds to pay for the transport of witnesses, and the assistance of magistrates and spies capable of asking gaoled criminals for information.[39] Harcourt, Irish MPs Timothy Healy and J.C. Flynn, and English MP Henry Cobb used parliament to question William Smith, the Government's Leader in the Commons, suggesting that constables had been allowed to offer their services to *The Times* and its agents. Smith denied that constables who might have been obeying the orders of Mr Shannon of *The Times*'s did so with the knowledge and authority of the Government.[40] That the Government was doing everything it could to assist *The Times*' side of the Commission is suggested by Cobb's admittedly provocative question, which Smith did not deny: 'Is the right hon. Gentleman aware that the courtyard in front of Mr Soames's office in Lincoln's Inn Fields has been crowded for weeks with constables from Ireland, many of whom were lolling about and smoking cigars?'[41]

The Government, to aid the Special Commission, allowed and supported the bringing over of various prisoners from Irish gaols to give evidence. The question of who had access to such prisoners caused a good deal of parliamentary controversy in 1888–89. That the Government was keen to avoid such scrutiny is clear from the instance of a visit by Pigott to a prisoner, John Daly, in Chatham Prison. A Home Office memo of 20 March 1889 contained a briefing for Home Secretary Matthews for a question on notice by the Irish Member Healy, relating to Pigott's visit. Matthews's answer in Parliament stated that 'Daly was entitled to a visit under the rules, and after being informed of Pigott's application he expressed a wish to be allowed to see him, and permission was accordingly sent to Pigott.'[42] That answer did not reveal what is included in the briefing note, namely that Daly had in fact wanted to see someone else, a personal friend, and Daly only said he would see Pigott when Daly's friend was not able to come, and he was asked whether he wished to see Pigott instead.[43]

In a triumph that was to raise Parnell to new heights of popularity, Pigott confessed during the course of the Commission to having forged the letters.[44] The confession followed a harrowing cross-examination by Defence Counsel Sir Charles Russell, in which Pigott had been greatly discredited.[45] Thus, in February 1889, Parnell returned to Parliament a vindicated man, with the new stature that British fair play accorded to one who had been wrongly accused. British law commanded widespread respect, and even an outsider like Parnell could find his reputation rehabilitated almost overnight for having been found 'within' the law.

The figure of Sir Robert Anderson again enters the story as the person entrusted with tracing the funding which enabled Pigott to flee England once his forgery had been discovered. Anderson found that some of the bank notes discovered in Pigott's possession had been drawn from the account of Mr Soames, counsel for *The Times*, although they were unable to trace how they had got into Pigott's hands. Instead of expressing distress at the involvement this suggested of *The Times* in the escape of a perjurer, Anderson cast aspersions elsewhere in a letter to the civil servant, Evelyn Ruggles-Brise, dated 24 March 1890:

> That no notice has been taken of the well known fact that Labouchere gave Pigott money is quite in keeping with the utter feebleness which has marked every step taken by *The Times*, & the Govt, in this wretched business.[46]

Government involvement in that 'wretched business' of trying to bring down Parnell seems to have been considerable. In April 1910, Mrs A.U. Thomson made application to the Home Office for a pension based on the services that her late husband, a policeman, had rendered to the country. Her earlier letter of 23 February 1910, referring to the events of the late 1880s, stated: 'The following year, I joined my husband on the Times Commission Case, and spent five most exciting months in America, resulting in the crushing of Parnell.'[47] Whether the crushing she refers to is the outcome of the Commission, which was hardly 'crushing', or the subsequent O'Shea divorce case is a matter for speculation. Either way, if Mrs Thomson's allegations are to be believed there seems to have been active Government involvement in Parnell's downfall. The Home Office was certainly not convinced by Mrs Thomson's credentials, being unable to substantiate her further claim that her husband had once conducted a secret mission to Russia.[48]

The full extent of Sir Robert Anderson's own role in the 'crushing' of Parnell was only confirmed in 1910, when the publication of excerpts from his autobiography confirmed his authorship of the articles on 'Parnellism and Crime' in the 1880s. It was of course already a matter of public record during the Special Commission that Anderson had provided documents to an agent of *The Times*. He gave information to an agent, Le Caron, who passed it on to Houston, a solicitor acting for *The Times*.[49] Anderson claimed in letters to the Home Secretary that the papers were unofficial and that he therefore did nothing wrong.[50] Home Secretary Matthews, under considerable parliamentary pressure, disagreed and told Anderson he could not reveal the contents of the letters without Government consent.[51] However, he defended Anderson's action in having provided information to Le Caron: 'Although Mr Anderson acted without my knowledge I think he acted properly in handing documents to Le Caron which had come from him, to enable him to give full evidence on any matter on which the Commission required it.'[52]

The Times was also quick to back up Anderson's action, perhaps unsurprisingly given that they bore much of the responsibility for the Commission having been set up in the first place. In 1889, *The Times* justified Anderson's giving of the documents to Caron as being necessary to shed light on the work of Fenians in America. The same editorial attacked Sir William Harcourt for daring to question the motives of the Government and suggesting that they may have assisted *The Times*. Anderson himself wrote a letter published in *The Times* attempting to exonerate his actions in providing documents to Le Caron by suggesting he had done it in the interests of justice, ensuring all the necessary evidence would be available before the Special Commission. Anderson's letter is also interesting because he quotes Caron as having said to him: 'He could not forget, said he, that he was an Englishman; he had gone into the conspiracy solely to serve his country, and now he would see the matter through, and face the consequences.'[53]

There seemed to be a firm belief that 'Englishness' equated with a certain form of justice. When Sir Robert Anderson was attacked in Parliament in 1910 over his revelations, he claimed that he had not had an opportunity to be heard in his own defence, and asked, 'Is this in keeping with our national ideas of justice and fair play?'[54] England was a nation ruled by law, and the Britain of which England formed the core was known for fair play. The law was, rhetorically at least, the inheritance of all.

In pursuing Parnell, the Government utilised all available aspects of the law. They knew that the findings of the Special Commission would have a marked impact on public opinion. Sir William Harcourt showed a good grasp of the Government's power to sway public opinion by setting up a Special Commission to investigate crimes that the Government itself had 'created':

> My right hon. Friend the Member for West Birmingham has said, also, that the charge is a charge of crime as popularly understood by the public of this country. It does not mean those artificial crimes which you have created by your legislation; it does not mean Boycotting, or those things which you have made crimes and which were not crimes before. That is not what the country understands by Parnellism and Crime. It is a totally different charge, and yet the action, as it is described here, is an action full of imputations of that character... [55]

Governments clearly had advantages in utilising legal machinery which they both created and ran. They were able to use it to reinforce the outsider status of the Irish, while at the same time seeking to uphold the mystique attached to the concept of 'British justice'. If a proceeding could be imbued with the characteristics of British law, its findings would be placed beyond question. Again, it was Sir William Harcourt, speaking from the less restrictive position of the Opposition benches, who understood what the Government was setting out to do:

> If they come forward now and tell us that this is to be a judicial proceeding, conducted according to judicial principles, of course one of the gravest objections to the form of the inquiry will be removed; but if that is not done then the Government are seeking to hoodwink the mind of the public and to induce them to believe that this is a judicial inquiry because you put Judges

upon it, while at the same time they are depriving it of the essential qualities that belong to a judicial inquiry.[56]

The fact that Parnell was ultimately cleared by the Commission can only have added to that mystique by increasing the perception that British justice was impartial. The reality appears to have been that the Government utilised every manoeuvre available and failed only because the forger – Pigott – confessed rather than because the Special Commission was an inherently 'fair' proceeding.

That the proceedings were an attempt to add to the poor reputation of the Irish was a point repeatedly made by Sir Charles Russell in appearing before the Commission:

> ...I charge that this case has been conducted with the purpose (unavowed, but with the purpose), by a repetition of the incidents of crime, by calling witness after witness to prove facts of crime which were not in dispute, I will not say of prejudicing your Lordship's minds (although it would be a marvel if it had not to some extent done so), but for the unavowed purpose of deepening in the public mind the prejudice existing, already grievous and sad enough, and suggesting that the Irish people are a nation of criminals.[57]

Reputation and outsider status were inextricably linked. The Government knew that if it could destroy the reputation of an individual or a group, it would ensure the outsider status of that individual or group.

The historian Tom Corfe has suggested that Parnell did in fact bear moral responsibility at some level for the Phoenix Park murders. Corfe suggests that Parnell 'was eminently skilful at impressing others with the belief that he sympathised with their violent plans and activities despite the fact that he could not publicly commit himself'.[58] This point in itself is somewhat speculative, yet even if true, it provides little justification for the Special Commission that followed. Politicians deal in words. Rhetoric is their tool of office. The fact that someone may have heard Parnell's words and decided that they were an encouragement to perform a violent act hardly constitutes a criminal offence. The fact that Parnell was not properly prosecuted in a court of law suggests that the Government was well aware of this.

A direct incitement to violence is of course another matter. That is why the letters purporting to be from Parnell that were published in *The Times* caused such an uproar. They specifically encouraged someone to commit violent acts. These letters were proved to be forgeries. Without them the case against Parnell retained no sting. All that remained was the broad principle of moral responsibility.

The Government had failed in its attempt to break the reputation of Parnell as an individual, and thus weakened its attack on the Irish people and their representatives as a whole. A vague claim of moral responsibility was no substitute for specific legal fault. The law could be a double-edged sword, and in this case it acted to vindicate someone who the Government had been trying to paint as an outsider – although there is not universal agreement that the outcome can be interpreted in that way. Margaret O'Callaghan for example has argued against such a conclusion:

> The investigations of the Special Commission had effectively destroyed Parnellism. The crude tactic of equating Parnellism with crime worked... By seeking to prove that they were not 'criminals' the parliamentary party had already lost the game. The drama of the battering ram was diversionary.[59]

Alvin Jackson has similarly suggested that the Commission ultimately achieved Salisbury's goal of tainting Irish nationalism with the broad brush of criminality.[60]

All the indications suggest that what captured the public imagination about the Commission was Parnell's vindication, not the variety of more general accusations about crime in Ireland that were upheld by the Commission. While the findings of the Commission may have provided some evidential base to support the Government's coercion policy, the spectacular clearing of Parnell's name was the Commission's centrepiece.

Parnell certainly seemed to understand the full power of the law. It was a defining part of the British identity, rooted in a peculiarly 'English' notion of justice. In her memoirs, Katherine O'Shea records a conversation with Parnell after he had been cleared by the Special Commission. Parnell observed:

> These people do not appreciate *me*, they only howl with joy because I have been found within the law. The English make a law and bow down and worship it till they find it obsolete – long after this is obvious to other nations – then they bravely make another, and start afresh in the opposite direction. That's why I am glad Ireland has a religion; there is so little hope for a nation that worships laws.[61]

The mentality promoted through the Special Commission – that the Irish were a rough and ready race, worshipping a foreign religion – was reinforced, upheld and maintained through the workings of British law. So great was respect for the law among the British that Parnell became suddenly popular, not because his views had changed or because he was any less committed to Irish nationalism, but because, as he stated, he had 'been found within the law'. To be 'within' the law, was to be exhibiting the best of British characteristics.[62]

Parnell's popularity was sufficiently great following the clearance of his character at the Special Commission that Edward Byrne, editor of the *Freeman's Journal*, thought his political career could go still further. In an 1898 memoir, Byrne suggests:

> As a matter of fact, Mr Parnell never intended to join the Irish government, but rather aimed at being Home Secretary for England, whence he could guide it, and possibly Prime Minister, for after the exposure and suicide of Pigott, the collapse of the *Times* Commission, and his own complete vindication, Mr Parnell was unmistakably one of the most powerful, if not one of the most popular politicians in England.[63]

Byrne's recollection smacks of panegyric more than reality, but it does serve to reiterate the importance for Parnell's reputation of having been cleared by British law of involvement in the Phoenix Park murders.

That re-found popularity was to be short-lived, as the lit fuse in Parnell's private life finally began to burn short. Captain O'Shea had hitherto had good reason to keep any suspicions he may have had about his wife and Parnell to himself. Katherine O'Shea had an aunt who was wealthy, but who was likely to leave her wealth elsewhere were she to discover her niece's infidelity. In May 1889, the 96-year-old aunt finally expired, leaving her fortune to Katherine, with legal protections stopping William making use of the money. With nothing to lose, William now decided to contest the will, in partnership with other relatives.[64] What followed again showed the power of the law in making and breaking reputations. The law finally did what the Government had failed to do through the Special Commission – remove Parnell and fatally damage his cause.

In December 1889, William O'Shea and his son Gerard visited Katherine's home, where Gerard was to find clothes and medicines belonging to Parnell.[65] Within a week, William had seen his lawyers to start divorce proceedings, filing his petition on Christmas Eve.[66] Parnell claimed that *The Times* was again behind the whole process, seeking revenge for its earlier failure.[67] The Irish leader also claimed that Captain O'Shea had long been aware of Parnell's close relationship with Mrs O'Shea, although he persuaded her not to press that charge at the court hearing.[68] Parnell's case for libel against *The Times* over the whole Phoenix Park murders affair was pending at the same time, and the Irish seem to have clung to their leader's assurance that there was nothing to fear in the allegations.[69]

In February 1890, *The Times* conceded defeat to Parnell's libel action and paid him damages of £5,000. It seemed that Parnell could do no wrong after all, and this further exoneration could only strengthen the belief of the faithful. Parnell had again succeeded, as with the Special Commission, in using the weapon of the law against the British Establishment which sought to wield it against him. Robert Kee argues that Parnell was so confident of success because he believed William O'Shea would be prepared to settle the matter for cash and withdraw the petition for divorce. The fact that Parnell was so convincing in telling his colleagues that he would be vindicated only made harder the fall that was to come. William was not to be bought, and the divorce case was heard on Saturday 15 November and subsequently, with Parnell refusing to appear to defend his case. Judgement therefore went as by default following the presentation of the Plaintiff's case, with the press publishing in great detail the evidence that came out in court.[70]

The revelation of Parnell's affair not only embarrassed him personally, it also embarrassed the Liberal Party which had come to support him in a partnership to gain Home Rule for Ireland. The Earl of Kimberley was aware of the significance of what might have seemed only a personal moral and legal issue: 'How shamefully Parnell is behaving! He will wreck Home Rule, & the prospects (up to this time) very bright of the Liberal party are completely over clouded.'[71] The Liberals had performed their duty as an Opposition in challenging the Government's Irish policy. Yet, when it came to matters of morality, they had to put their duty as 'British' men first in order to protect society's foundations. There was considerable pressure brought to bear on Parnell from both Liberal and Irish members to encourage him to resign, for no Victorian party could protect a leader proven in a court of law to have been morally lax.[72] Timothy Healy allegedly accused Parnell of 'having suffocated the alliance with the Liberal party of England in the stench of the Divorce Court'.[73] It was the proof in a court of law which was the key point. A court could turn rumour into fact in the minds of the 'law-loving' people of Britain. A series of letters from Labouchere to Harcourt attest to the Liberal will that Parnell must resign.[74]

It was morality that Parnell had offended against, and morality had to be defended as a foundation stone of Victorian society. The celebrated journalist W.T. Stead published an article on the matter entitled 'The Discrowned King of Ireland', in which he called on Parnell to resign, but seemed to suggest that the whole matter was rather more the fault of Mrs O'Shea in her role as temptress. He refers to 'one man's weakness' and 'one woman's sin'.[75] Parnell was merely weak, a victim of his quite understandable male urges, whereas Mrs O'Shea was to be seen as a sinful figure, someone who had offended against morality and in the process had brought down Ireland just as 'it was one woman's faithlessness that led the Greeks to the Trojan war'.[76] But Parnell could not escape culpability either. In Stead's view, once one had offended against morality, one was no longer fit to be a British lawmaker.

The emphasis by Stead and others on the finding of the court is significant. To offend against morality was bad, but it only became terminal when one got found out in a court of law. The language of Stead reads as if Parnell had been found guilty of a criminal offence, such was the power of the link between morality and decisions of the court:

> If Pigott had proved his case, Mr Parnell, all his immense services to the Irish race notwithstanding, would have instantly been swept into oblivion. Yet to the majority of Christian folk, both in Ireland and out of it, the offence of which Mr Parnell was found guilty before Mr Justice Butt was infinitely more serious than the offence of which he was acquitted by Mr Justice Hannan.[77]

Such was the hold of morality, upon Stead's imagination at least, that potentially being found guilty of involvement in the Phoenix Park murders and terrorist outrages in Ireland paled into insignificance when compared to having been pronounced 'guilty', in absentia, of adultery before a British court. Morality was the guide post, and the law, as intended by the Government, was the final arbiter. Stead quotes the *Independent* as saying, 'We simply cannot accept as a national leader one whom the Law Courts of the nation have convicted of odious crimes.'[78] Again, an offence against morality was here seen as an 'odious crime' of which Parnell was now deemed to have been convicted, although of course the use of the language of the criminal law masked the fact that Parnell could be sentenced to no criminal punishment.

The law provided the dividing line. The Liberal leader, Gladstone, wrote a secret Memo on the O'Shea affair:

> No man ought to suffer prejudice in his public capacity for any conduct, except such as is known: and the first question that arises is, what ought in such a case to be held to constitute knowledge. A line has to be drawn for practical purposes; and in my opinion knowledge, in a subject of this mind, is cognisance of what has been judicially established...[79]

Knowledge could destroy people. Governments could manipulate public knowledge through legal exposure or quiet cover-ups. The truth of that is revealed by one of the mass of people who wrote to Gladstone encouraging him to take a stand on the matter:[80]

> It wd, I am sure, be a fatal error in tactics for the Irish to retort with the case of Lord Hartington. Assuming that the two cases are on the same footing, it does make a difference in the public mind that Parnell has been publicly convicted, practically on his own confession.[81]

The whole divorce issue also gave scope to those who wished to stress the 'outsider' status of the Irish in general, by attacking those they chose as their representatives. That was the tone of a letter to Gladstone from Mr Moss, a former Vice-President of the Harrow Liberal Club, who suggested that Irish MPs 'should remember that English Judges are not like Irish Magistrates, & that the decision of the Divorce Court Judge was based on trustworthy evidence'.[82]

Defenders of Parnell were difficult to find, but one, Margaret Sandhurst, did emerge, at least in so far as she was prepared to confide in William Gladstone. She showed a real insight into the possibility that what ailed Parnell was not a unique lack of morality, but rather that the Government was trying to reinforce his 'outsiderness':

> The case is not brought forward or supported by persons who command the confidence of the Public. We do not know where the necessary money has come from, nor how much may have been spent; and it is more than possible that the same hands which pulled the strings in the cases of the 'Piggott' Commission

may be at work now, by much the same means and to obtain the same ends.[83]

The ultimate fall of Parnell is another link in the strong chain that successive governments had forged, joining the Irish to criminality and immorality. From the Irish immigrants who had 'terrorised' mid-Victorian England with their petty crimes to the fall of Ireland's 'criminally' immoral leader in the 1890s, the Irish were the perpetual outcasts of Victorian Britain.

CHAPTER 4

BRITISH JEWS: THE SEARCH FOR EQUALITY

Writing in 1901, jurist A.T. Carter described the position of Jews at the start of the nineteenth century:

> The Jew could not hold any office, civil, military, or corporate, he could not follow the profession of the law, as barrister or attorney or attorney's clerk, he could not be a schoolmaster or usher in a school. He could not sit in either House of Parliament, nor vote at an election if called upon to take the elector's oath.[1]

The range of offices from which Jews were banned provided an effective barrier against Jews achieving positions of 'British' power.[2] The heads of the civil service, the military and the Bank of England needed to be 'sound' British men. Practitioners of law had the power to argue points of law with the government, and could even hope to rise to the judiciary. By banning Jews from these positions and professions, British lawmakers were defining the boundaries which regulated the part that Jews could play in the life of the British nation. It was not until the Religious Disabilities Act of 1846 that Jews achieved the same rights that Dissenters had long enjoyed under the Toleration Act.[3] Even then, as Baron Lionel de Rothschild was to discover repeatedly from 1847 to 1858, democratic election could not guarantee that a man professing the Jewish faith would be accepted into the British parliament.

Rothschild's case revealed the tensions that could emerge when a 'liberal' state confronted the question of what religious and moral views rendered someone unsuitable to contribute to the making of laws for the nation. Even though legitimately and democratically elected, Rothschild was prevented by British lawmakers from taking his place amongst them for over a decade. By analysing the words and actions of those who resisted his inclusion to the bitter end, much is revealed about how the conservative British Establishment viewed British national identity in the Victorian era. To be British, and thereby worthy of making British laws, one had to be religiously and morally upright. Jews were an internal 'other', displaying religious and moral characteristics that the truly British could forge their own identity against. Britain, like all nations, has often been defined by what it is not as much as by what it is. In the view of battle-hardened parliamentary conservatives in the nineteenth century, Britain was not Jewish.

Parliament in the first half of the nineteenth century required a member to swear not only to serve Great Britain, but also its established religion. In 1828, the Test and Corporation Acts, which stopped both Dissenters and Roman Catholics from holding office under the Crown, were repealed. However, the House of Lords worded the new declaration upon taking office so that it ended: 'on the true faith of a Christian', to ensure that people of other religions could be specifically excluded from lawmaking.[4]

Positions of authority outside of Parliament were less fiercely opposed. For example, the exclusion of Jews from town corporations was lifted in 1845, which had an immediate beneficial effect for David Salomons, who had been elected a Sheriff in that year.[5] He wrote to Lord John Russell, thanking him for his support of the measure, acknowledging that 'although I have to thank my fellow citizens for the confidence reposed in me, that testimony would have been of little avail, if your Government had not been inclined to assist me in qualifying for office'.[6] Salomons remained a consistent campaigner in favour of religious liberties for all, writing to Russell again in 1846, urging his support for the Religious Opinions Bill left in the House of Lords by the previous Government.[7] Salomons later sent Peel a letter of congratulation on his son's maiden speech in 1849, at the same time thanking Peel for having supported the Jews Declaration Bill during his time in Government.[8]

Salomons was not the sole campaigner for a greater political and legal stake for Jews in Britain.[9] By the 1840s the Rothschilds were an established British family. Lord Rothschild had himself been born in Britain in 1808 and was one of the richest men in England. He moved in aristocratic circles, and he was undoubtedly a member of what might loosely be termed the 'upper classes'. Yet he was not a member of the 'British ruling elite' in terms of his ability to contribute to the civil and political life of the nation. He was Jewish, and for that reason alone he was ineligible to be a voting Member of Parliament. He would also have been ineligible for certain positions within the civil service.[10] This might have seemed of little significance had Lord Rothschild's interests been limited to finance, but they were not.

Rothschild was a Liberal in politics, and his status within the City of London gave him a strong recognition factor when he decided to stand for the House of Commons. The very act of putting himself forward for election positioned him as an advocate for minority rights, a wider cause which he passionately took up during his campaigning.[11] In 1847, 1849, 1852, 1854 and again in 1857 Rothschild was elected to parliament as a member for the City of London. He was then barred by Parliament from taking up his seat on the grounds of his Judaism.

The Whig/Liberal Government of Lord John Russell was sympathetic to his cause, due to a pragmatic mixture of moral principle and support for a fellow Liberal, and tried unsuccessfully over a number of years to introduce legislation removing this remaining Jewish disability.[12] On each occasion it was blocked in the House of Lords, where the Conservative peers held fast to the concept of a 'Christian' assembly. The consistent pressure of Lord Rothschild's frequent re-election finally forced a compromise in 1858 whereby each house was given the discretion over whether or not to allow Jewish members to take their seats.

The Bill of 1858 allowed each House of Parliament to decide whether it would waive the 'faith of a Christian' requirement in specific cases.[13] The will of the people in electing their representatives could still be blunted by the discretion of parliament if it so chose. The restriction seems largely to have been aimed at excluding Jews from the House of Lords, a concession which effectively allowed British Peers to retain the final say in who should be allowed to sit amongst them.

Modern historians have differed widely in their interpretation of Lord Rothschild's battle for acceptance and its wider significance. David Itzkowitz plays down the importance of the restriction on Jews entering Parliament, suggesting it 'affected only a tiny minority of English Jews', because most did not want to stand for Parliament.[14] He goes on to argue that, 'by the first half of the nineteenth century... though Jews had their own particular religious rites and beliefs that had to be respected, they were, in other respects, fellow subjects with all other British people'.[15]

The laws affecting the ability of Jews to sit in parliament were not just a symbolic difficulty. They reflected a difference between the Jews and the dominant Christian religion that carried very practical consequences. As Colin Holmes has stated, 'It should also be realized that whatever reasoning lay behind the restriction it succeeded in creating and sustaining an image of Jews as a problem.'[16] David Cesarani has made the similar observation that 'exclusion appeared to confirm the deeply held prejudices within a large part of English society, that Judaism was an inferior creed, and that Jews were not fit to participate in the affairs of a Christian nation'.[17] Various bills seeking to remove Jewish disabilities had been passed by the House of Commons as early as the 1830s, only to be rejected by the Lords on each occasion.[18]

David Feldman has argued that discrimination against Jews was a contributing factor in the defining of British national identity. He suggests that 'attempts to deal with the Jews' legal and political integration revealed and, in part, shaped conceptions of the nation'.[19] Feldman persuasively indicates that the whole process was about deciding what it meant for someone to be British.[20]

Some Jews claimed to be quite satisfied with the status quo, and even argued that they in fact had no right to be making laws for a

Christian nation. In 1857, one contemporary Jewish observer, David John Anderson, published a pamphlet entitled *Jewish Emancipation: A Voice from Israel*, which suggested that Jews already enjoyed 'with few exceptions the same liberty as the Englishman'.[21] Anderson realised that if Jews became lawmakers, that would bring them further within the fabric of British society, a result he viewed with suspicion:

> So soon as Jews are willing to forget their mission, to amalgamate themselves with, and consent to make laws for the nations with whom they live, they cease to be 'children of Israel,' they become naturalized subjects of the particular Government, and are no longer Jews.[22]

Jews who converted were labelled by Anderson as a disgrace to the Jewish community.[23]

Other pamphlets challenged such a hardline doctrinal approach. A pamphlet of 1845 written by 'An Israelite' was in favour of the political emancipation of Jews. The writer suggests, [W]e have considered ourselves as Englishmen, and England as our home; and as such, we have connected with it all the rights, the hopes, and the associations that belong to that honoured name'.[24]

The contemporary social observer Henry Mayhew made the rather startling observation, given the number of Jews running for political office, that Jews generally were not very interested in politics:[25]

> I was told by a Hebrew gentleman (a professional man) that so little did the Jews themselves care for 'Jewish emancipation,' that he questioned if one man in ten, actuated solely by his own feelings, would trouble himself to walk the length of the street in which he lived to secure Baron Rothschild's admission into the House of Commons.[26]

This was despite the fact that the same informant felt it was Rothschild's 'right' to sit in the Commons.[27]

An examination of the language used by the members of the House of Lords during the final debate on the 1858 Bill reflects their understanding of their role as 'British' men in protecting the foundations upon which British society stood.[28] The established church and the religion it served were to be inviolate, for they constituted one of the binding tenets of the nation. If religion was to be a societal foundation, the Anglican Church had to remain strong. When an outsider threatened that tenet by daring to practise a different religion, he had to be prevented from entering the sanctum of lawmaking. It was legislative law which could provide Rothschild's entry point, and the Lords were doing their best to show that it was they who controlled that entry point. What is more, certain members of the Lords saw the admission of Jews as being an attack on morality in its broadest sense. They argued that the denial of Jesus in religion 'constitutes a moral unfitness to take part in the legislation of a professedly Christian community'.[29]

David Englander argues that, until the middle of the nineteenth century, 'Jews were excluded from parliament and the universities because they were not Anglicans and not because they were Jews.'[30] Up until 1828–29, this was certainly true. Jews were simply being denied their rights equally with Catholics and Nonconformists. However, after the repeal of the Test and Corporation Acts and the passage of Catholic Emancipation, it was the Jews who remained on the parliamentary outer specifically because they were Jews. Catholics and Nonconformists were Christians, and as such had finally been allowed into a 'Christian legislature'. The Jews, due to the 'foreign' nature of their religious beliefs, remained unacceptable.

In the crucial 1858 debate, the Earl of Clancarty expressed an understanding that it was 'British' men who made and controlled law through legislation, and that anyone admitted to parliament could therefore threaten the power of the British ruling elite. In the second reading of the 'Jews Bill', as it was termed, Clancarty stated:

> Interwoven as Christianity is with the whole system of our Government both in Church and State, I see no way by which, without offence to the cause of truth, you could commit the interests of the Church and the *framing of our laws* to any who deny Christ and reject the divine laws.[31] (my emphasis)

The Bishop of Oxford made much the same point. He stated in debate that 'it was impossible safely to entrust a man, either in the capacity of a magistrate or a Judge, with the due and honest administration of those Christian laws from which he differed on fundamental points of view'.[32] His emphasis on legal offices is significant. To allow a Jew into civil society was one thing; to allow him to create or administer British law was quite another.

The defenders of exclusion made much of the fact that the status quo was enforced by law, as if that fact itself placed the Jewish bar beyond question. Charles Newdegate in the House of Commons expressed the wish that the House should allow 'the Members of this House an opportunity of declaring whether they will support the law as it exists, or whether they will support the Hon. Member for Finsbury in violating it'.[33] The Member for Finsbury, Thomas Duncombe, had proposed a motion that Baron de Rothschild should be allowed to take the oath 'in such a form as shall be binding on his conscience'.[34] Newdegate went much further in his speech on the second reading of the Jews Bill in the House of Commons, declaring that 'the Christian character of the Legislature and the constitution of the country constitute the great guarantee for the freedom of the people'.[35] He went on to criticise Rothschild for 'sneering'

> at the Lord Chief Justice of the Court of Queen's Bench, because that noble and learned Lord had declared that if the House of Commons had been so misguided as to attempt to override the law for the sake of admitting a Jew to a seat in this House, he would not have shrunk, in the performance of his judicial duty, from vindicating the majesty of the law...[36]

Newdegate's reference to the 'majesty of the law' indicates again what an important symbolic step it would be to allow Jews into a position where they could actually influence the making of law in Parliament. Newdegate warned in his speech that the Bill, or another like it, might allow atheists to take a seat in the House.[37] He would no doubt have nodded a sage head when the atheist Charles Bradlaugh was finally admitted to Parliament in 1885.[38] Newdegate's stand against the Oaths Bill as it was originally passed by the Commons was noted by Sir John Trelawny, Liberal MP for Tavistock, in his parliamentary diary:

> Report of the Oaths Bill Committee – first specimen, perhaps, of Judaic Handiwork, as Rothschild was upon it. Resolutions read. The Tories never heard a lesson more likely to be disagreeable to them... They seemed very much disconcerted – listening in a morose silence. At last Newdegate could hear it no longer & rose to protest. In vain. Other resolutions followed till the whole case of the Jew was fairly exhausted & formally accepted by a full House.[39]

In the Rothschild case, a majority in the House of Commons were prepared to concede something to the Jews of Britain because they could perceive that it would cost them less to acquiesce than to refuse. The religious difference of Jews was not seen as a political danger by 1858, and thus the concession could be given safely. The government may have been alive to the fact that it was dangerous to exclude a whole group of people and maintain their outsider status when certain individuals in that group were enormously wealthy.[40] Members of the House of Lords were more tenacious in clinging to a perception of Britain as a Protestant nation.

In the committee stage of the 1858 bill in the Commons, the Conservative MP for Northamptonshire South, Rainald Knightley, attacked the House of Lords for having compromised sufficiently to allow Jews to take seats in the House of Commons if the Commons so resolved: 'When a foreign nobleman came to that table as a representative of the City of London, and took an un-Christian oath, the guilt and responsibility would rest upon the House of Lords.'[41] It is noteworthy that, despite Rothschild's British birth, Knightley still considered him to be a foreigner, presumably on the ground of his religion as well as his foreign noble title. It illustrates again that not everyone born in England could consider themselves a 'true Briton'.

This was, of course, a matter of perception. David Salomons had stood and been elected for Parliament in the early 1850s, and been barred from taking his seat by the same disabilities that now stood in the way of Baron Rothschild. Salomons had claimed his rights not only as a Jew, but as an Englishman. Writing in 1851 to Lord John Russell, then Prime Minister, he said: 'The subject is one of great importance & anxiety to me, & I wish to fail in no respect whether as a gentleman, or as an Englishman desirous to maintain all his just rights.'[42] Salomons considered himself an Englishman, and thereby concluded that he had the right to sit in parliament. The House of Lords could not bring itself to look at Salomons in the same light. Salomons was well aware that 'the question is really one of law, and suggested that it be left to the courts, or the Lord Chancellor and Chief Justices, to decide.[43] He realised that if a court of law vindicated his claims, and implicitly also his Englishness, few would further question his legitimacy. Salomons felt such a course 'could not fail to give satisfaction to the public at large'.[44]

Ultimately, it was the Parliament alone that needed to act if Jews were to be allowed the right to join in the government of Britain. The fierceness of the debate over Rothschild's admission in 1858 demonstrates just what a leap the British Establishment considered that to be. Richard Spooner, MP for North Warwickshire, rose in the final debate on the day of Rothschild's admission to deny that he was actuated by anti-Semitic feeling. Yet all he would say was, '[t]he Jews are a most interesting nation – interesting, if we look to their past history, and more so if we contemplate their future destiny'.[45] This can hardly be counted as an embrace of the Jews as his fellow countrymen. Interestingly, there was not any link made during the debates between Jews and crime or other factors that could legitimate their barring from the law councils of the nation. Parliament was forced to acknowledge by its silence that it could not reinforce the status of Jews as outsiders in Britain through linking them with consistent breaches of the criminal law. The Parliament, or at least the House of Lords, was forced to rely openly on a lack of religious tolerance for Jews in a so-called 'Christian legislature'. Its methods of exclusion were thus less subtle than those directed against the Irish, and against poorer Jewish immigrants in the 1880s. Those proposing Jewish inclusion made reference to their law-abiding reputation, knowing it to be a strong point in their favour:

> [I]t was a principle of the Jewish religion that, wherever they might be carried away captive, or in whatever country their lot was cast, they must respect the law as established, and pray for the peace and order of the country serving as their temporary home.[46]

Having finally established himself as a 'British' parliamentarian, Lord Rothschild was allowed by the compromise of 1858 to take up his seat. Yet even then his 'inclusion' was not complete, as a subsequent incident a decade later was to demonstrate. Somewhat ironically, Rothschild was to be proposed by the Gladstone Government in 1868 as the first Jewish peer eligible to sit in the House of Lords. Lord Granville's letter to the Queen outlining the Liberal Government's selections suggests a motivation of political expediency in raising a Jew to the upper house:

> The notion of a Jew peer is startling. 'Rothschild, le premier Baron Juif,' does not sound as well as 'Montmorency, le premier Baron Chretien,' but he represents a class whose influence is great by their wealth, their intelligence, their literary connections, and their numerous seats in the House of Commons. It may be wise to attach them to the aristocracy, rather than to drive them into the democratic camp.[47]

This passage is revealing about Granville's perceptions of his role in government. He saw as the enemy the 'democratic camp', presumably people who would not respect the ruling traditions British lawmakers lived by. Granville's words suggest that, for British lawmakers, the risk of alienating rich and influential Jews was greater than the need to keep Jews out of the House of Lords. It was better to allow the wealthiest from this group of 'outsiders' into the aristocracy than to drive them into using their wealth and influence against British Government interests.[48]

Granville was, however, quite prepared to back down rather than force a confrontation with the Queen over the issue. When writing to Gladstone, Granville relayed the Queen's opposition to allowing a Jewish peer to sit in the Lords: 'I construe her assent to be given to everything but the Jew... I presume that you will not insist upon the Jew this year...'[49] Gladstone recognised the weakness in the Queen's wish to exclude Rothschild: 'Her argument is null and void. If it be sound, she has been wrong in consenting to emancipate the Jews.'[50] The Queen, as the symbolic head of British law, had to be treated with respect, even though Gladstone was theoretically free to ignore her views if he chose. Another letter of Granville's a week later only reiterated the Queen's opposition: 'I did not press her about the Jew, in consequence of Biddulph's advice, who said she was very strong on the subject.'[51] Granville's reference is itself revealing about the 'alien' qualities of British Jews. Granville's reference to 'the Jew' implies that Jewishness was the overwhelming characteristic of someone like Lord Rothschild, rather than his Britishness or one of his many personal attributes. Queen Victoria clearly retained a strong objection to the admittance of Jews to the peerage over a decade after Jews had been allowed into the House of Commons.

The Queen's objections were expressed merely as personal opinions, rather than being based on any particular demand of public policy. This accords with historian Colin Holmes's analysis of anti-Semitism prior to 1919: 'None of this turned upon a highly sophisticated theory of anti-Semitism; it was an in group–out group conflict which found parallels in the tension between English and German clerks or between British sailors and their Chinese contemporaries.'[52] The Queen wrote to Lord Granville that 'to make a *Jew a Peer* is a step she *could not* consent to. It would be very ill taken & would do the Govt great harm.'[53] Gladstone tried to make clear to the Queen what the consequences of her refusal were: '[I]f his religion were to operate permanently as a bar, it appears that this would be to revive by prerogative the disability which formerly existed by statute, and which the Crown and Parliament thought proper to abolish'.[54]

The Queen admitted to a 'feeling, of which she cannot divest herself, against making a person of the Jewish religion, a Peer...'[55]

She went on to link her refusal to the way in which Rothschild gained his wealth through loans and stock market speculations.[56] The Queen displayed the classic signs of anti-Semitism – a strong revulsion to promoting a Jew to a position of political importance and a claim to having the moral high ground over a people who were linked with monetary transactions. It is somewhat ironic that the Queen's eldest son was later criticised for being dominated by the Jews and for the number of Jews he had around him at court as King Edward VII.[57]

Rothschild was unsuccessful in gaining the peerage in 1869, and was proposed again by Gladstone in 1873. Lord Granville was in favour, but again did not wish to upset the Queen: 'I am for Rothschild being made a Peer – and in one sense his Peerage would be a complement to that of the Catholic.'[58] In this short sentence, Granville encapsulated the 'outsider' status of both Jews and Roman Catholics. It was clearly novel to think that such men could find their way into the British peerage. There is no indication that Granville, Gladstone or the Queen spent any time counting the number of Anglicans promoted to the peerage. Their religion was simply not an issue. It entitled them to an easier path to lawmaking power and respectability than that available to a Roman Catholic or a Jew.

There appears to have been a wider suspicion of the Rothschild family in particular on account of their international financial interests.[59] Historian R.W. Davis has argued against this view, suggesting that the Rothschilds were in fact readily accepted into English society because they were prepared to 'act like Englishmen'.[60] He contrasts this to the treatment of Disraeli who, despite being baptised a Christian, was subject to greater anti-Semitic abuse.[61] While Davis's point is well made, the degree of acceptance of the Rothschilds can be overstated; the evidence produced may be read differently. For instance, Davis acknowledges that the Queen could not be convinced in the first instance to raise Rothschild to the peerage, but suggests that she was 'favourably impressed by the Rothschilds because she thought their children "handsome" '.[62] The refusal of the peerage was of great symbolic importance, and arguably provides a stronger measure of the level of acceptance of the Rothschilds in royal quarters than the Queen's opinions of the family on a more personal level.

Similarly, Davis emphasises the fact that Rothschild was elected again and again between 1847 and 1858 by the City of London to represent it in Parliament.[63] This is undoubtedly, as Davis suggests, an indication that Rothschild was respected by the City of London. However, it only highlights again how powerful was the club of British lawmakers in Parliament that it could for 11 years refuse to abide by the wishes of the financial hub of the most powerful city in Britain by not allowing Rothschild to take his seat. This was despite the fact that they had for years been willing to take the Rothschild family's money, which had for instance helped to save the British economy in 1825, bailing out the Bank of England.[64] It illustrates well that money was not the defining characteristic of 'Britishness'. One could not buy the status of 'Briton'; it was useful to be wealthy, but it could only get outsiders so far unless they were of the right religious and moral fabric.

In light of the experience of Lord Rothschild and the Queen's apparent tendency towards anti-Semitic views, it is relevant to consider the case of Benjamin Disraeli. Can a Jew who became Prime Minister of Great Britain, and in later life a recognised favourite of the Queen, be seen as a triumph of British equality, invalidating the argument that Jews were an 'other' in the Victorian era?

Benjamin Disraeli was twice Prime Minister of Great Britain and Ireland, gained a seat in the House of Lords after being elevated to the aristocracy as an earl, and moved in the highest circles – yet he was never to sit comfortably within the British ruling elite. Contemporary observer T. Wemyss Reid wrote in 1880 that Disraeli was 'an "outsider" in our social and public affairs... A stranger and a sojourner in this land of his birth and his adoption.'[65] Lord Bryce wrote of Disraeli as 'not... really an Englishman'.[66] Historian Paul Smith notes:

> It did not matter that he was a baptised Christian. He was perceived as a Jew, and Jewishness in a racial if not in a religious sense was readily ascribed to him by those who thought to rebuff his pretensions to a role in English public life by assimilating him to an unfavourable stereotype, and occasionally by those who wished to claim him as a champion of his race.[67]

Disraeli had to battle against anti-Semitism all his political life, and Anthony Wohl has argued that this became more sinister once he had actually ascended to the Prime Ministership: 'The emotive force of "alien," as hurled at Disraeli, was much more sinister, for it cast him in the role of traitor and damned him as *anti-* rather than simply *un-*English.'[68] When Disraeli was a young man standing for politics he was subjected to personal abuse rather than labelled as the epitome of Judaism overrunning Britain.[69] Once he became Prime Minister, the virulence of the anti-Semitic tone of sections of the press and his political enemies reflected the greater danger he now posed to them. An outsider had risen to the top of British politics, and it was then that it became most important to reinforce his 'outsiderness' by stressing his Judaism.[70] David Feldman notes that it was at the peak of his popularity that Disraeli was subjected to negative stereotyping as a Semite while being labelled as un-English by his political opponents.[71]

Disraeli's ascension to the highest political office in the land illustrates the essential flexibility of Victorian society, and that outsiders could overcome all barriers that might theoretically have been in their way. Yet the real reason Disraeli made it to the top of the 'greasy pole' was because he was prepared to play the game by 'British' rules. He, or more accurately his parents, had been prepared to embrace Christianity sufficiently to be baptised in the Church of England. There must be considerable doubt whether Disraeli would ever have reached his high position had that early decision not been made. Disraeli's successful rise to the Prime Ministership stands more as a testament to his own flexibility, rather than to the flexibility of the society he came to govern.

CHAPTER 5

THE POLITICS OF ATHEISM

The established Church in England was a cornerstone of the nation, firmly ensconced in the unwritten constitution. The monarch was also supreme head of the church, thereby tying the symbolic head of the British Government to one of the foundation stones of society. The Church of England was essential for the British ruling elite's continuing hold on power.

The British state of the later nineteenth century had, through a process of painful change over preceding years, acquiesced in the rights of Dissenters, Roman Catholics, and finally Jews to sit as lawmakers in the British Parliament. In 1880, however, it could still not accept that someone might decline to worship God at all and still be considered as fit to take part in the government of Britain. Sir Stafford Northcote, Conservative Party leader in the House of Commons, in his notes for an 1883 speech on the controversy surrounding the admission to Parliament of the atheist Charles Bradlaugh, made it clear that anyone sitting in the ultimate lawmaking body of Great Britain must have a belief in God:

> But to look on the Oath simply as a Test of Theism is inadequate. It is rather a Test of a man's belief in his responsibility to a Supreme Being. Undoubtedly it was not imposed as a religious test at all; but that makes its significance all the greater. For it was imposed under the full understanding that every one believed in a God, and in his Divine Govt.[1]

The distinction was of more than academic interest, for it affected the rights of atheists to participate in the institutions of their nation. As the contemporary jurist Frederic Maitland pointed out, legally it remained a misdemeanour in 1888 for those who had once been Christian to deny publicly that the Bible was the word of God.[2] Northcote reiterated in the notes alluded to above that there was nothing wrong, in his eyes, in using the force of law to define the boundaries of society: 'It is said we have never had recourse to religious tests save for political objects – What can be a more important political object than maintenance of religion itself?'[3]

Charles Bradlaugh was not the first atheist to suffer at the hands of the law in nineteenth-century Britain. George Jacob Holyoake was convicted and imprisoned on those grounds in the 1840s, an experience he later recalled in *The History of the Last Trial by Jury for Atheism in England: A Fragment of Autobiography*.[4] Holyoake's case highlighted the real dangers that withholding belief could still expose one to in Victorian Britain. It was a misdemeanour at Common Law for any man to 'treat with contempt the Christian religion', as Justice Erskine pointed out at the Holyoake trial.[5] Holyoake's 'crime' had been that in giving a public lecture on 'home colonisation' he had, when answering a question from the audience, expressed a strong revulsion for Christianity and the Bible.[6]

The attitude of the bench towards Holyoake at his various trials reflected their deep belief in the value of religion as a cornerstone of 'British' society in the Victorian age. When Holyoake was brought before the magistrates, one member of the bench, Mr Capper, responded to a question by saying: 'We refuse to hold an argument with a man professing the abominable principle of denying the existence of a Supreme Being.'[7] Holyoake dryly records that '[t]his was not a very legal way of getting rid of my observations, but it answered in Cheltenham'.[8] At Holyoake's trial, the judge, Mr Justice Erskine, responded to criticisms of what Erskine had earlier told the Grand Jury, by saying: 'Inasmuch as this offence directly tended to take away that foundation on which real morality can alone be safely based, I told them what I feel, that without religion there is no morality.'[9] Justice Erskine retreated into an instinctive defence of morality and religion.

No public case of atheism was more celebrated, however, than that of Charles Bradlaugh, who was elected as MP for Northampton in the election of 1880, and subsequently re-elected four times without being allowed to take his seat until after the 1885 election.[10] Bradlaugh had built his reputation outside Parliament through decades of consistent secularism and radicalism. Born in 1833, he was the son of a lawyer's clerk. An orator, pamphleteer and founder of the National Secular Society, Bradlaugh never pretended to be restrained by the niceties of a socially conservative Christian society. He attracted support from those of the working class who were frustrated by piecemeal reforms and 'middle-class' Christian values.

In 1880, Bradlaugh had written to the Speaker of the House, declaring his atheism and his desire to affirm his oath of office rather than take the oath, with its Christian basis. The course of the controversy is well charted in the diary of Lord Hampden as Speaker of the House.[11] Hampden's entry for 3 August 1881 reads: 'Rough work with Bradlaugh. But when men take law into their own hands they must be dealt with effectually'.[12] This was, in essence, Bradlaugh's sin. He was claiming a legal right to sit in Parliament that British lawmakers were not yet prepared to concede to him. It was a lesson in who controlled the law. Bradlaugh's reliance on his popular mandate as being sufficient to allow him to sit was shown to be misplaced. It was the parliamentary lawmakers and not the electorate who would decide whether or not an atheist was fit to sit and make the laws of Britain.

It is perhaps little to be wondered at that British lawmakers were so reluctant to allow Bradlaugh into Parliament when, in addition to his atheism, he avowedly stood for the dismantling of all that 'British' tradition held dear. His 'appeal to the electors of Northampton', of unspecified date, indicates that Bradlaugh saw himself as standing for:

- the abolition of primogeniture
- greater taxation of landholders
- a complete separation of Church and State, including removing Bishops from the House of Lords

- the introduction of some kind of preferential voting system that would allow minorities seats in the House of Commons
- 'The abolition of all disabilities and disqualifications consequent upon the holding or rejection of any particular speculative opinion', and
- 'Peers habitually absent from Parliament to be deprived of all legislative privileges, and the right of voting by proxy in any case to be abolished.'[13]

Bradlaugh was effectively vowing to strip the British aristocracy of much of its power. This can only have strengthened Parliament in its resolve to protect the institutions of lawmaking from such an 'ungodly' man. Bradlaugh's manifesto did not stop there, and it is worth quoting a key paragraph at length because it embodies the idea that British ruling elites did not have a God-given right to make laws for the rest of their countrymen:

> The abolition as a Governing Class of the old Whig party, which has long since ceased to play any useful part in our public policy. Toryism represents obstructiveness to Radical progress, but it represents open hostility. Whiggism is hypocritical; while professing to be liberal, it never initiates a good measure or hinders a bad one. I am in favour of the establishment of a National Party which shall destroy the system of Government by aristocratic families, and give the members of the community born poorest fair play in their endeavour to become statesmen and leaders if they have genius and honesty enough to entitle them to a foremost place.[14]

These were revolutionary ideas. Bradlaugh was seen to be challenging both religion and morality. Northcote, in his speech notes from 1883, had noted a quote from Voltaire, 'And what will be the character of legislation when it ceases to rest upon the noble principle of religion and morality – *Godless Parliament*'.[15] Northcote went on to indicate just how openly the British Parliament used religion as a tool with which to control the levels of inclusion in society: 'No doubt it may be true that the main reasons for imposing religious tests have been political. Sometimes they have been imposed to protect a dynasty, *sometimes to exclude the foes of an Establishment*.'[16] (My emphasis)

A parliamentary committee voted to block Bradlaugh's right to affirm the parliamentary oath.[17] When Bradlaugh subsequently said he would then swear to the oath, a further Committee again voted against him.[18] It was decided that a confirmed atheist could not swear an oath that would have no meaning for him. When Bradlaugh was finally allowed to affirm, the affirmation was challenged in court and he was again prevented from taking his seat. On 22 June 1882, he was prevented from tabling a petition because he had not taken the oath, which he was prevented from taking because of his avowed atheism.[19] He was finally allowed to swear to the oath by the Speaker following the 1885 election.[20]

The years of turmoil associated with Bradlaugh's admission to Parliament reflect a degree of political obstructionism by the Conservative Party, but the incident also signified how slowly British lawmakers as a group were moving towards the full religious liberty that was the logical endpoint of nineteenth-century liberalism. When it came to atheism, the likelihood of mass uprisings in support of atheists' rights was not high, so Parliament could afford to be slow in its movements. It was able to paint itself as the defender of principle, rather than a barrier in the way of religious liberty. As Sir Stafford Northcote wrote to Bradlaugh:

> In the first place it is necessary that I should point out to you that the action of the House of Commons with respect to yourself has not been arbitrary or capricious, but has been founded on principles deliberately adopted by a large majority of its members of various political opinions, to which principles they have steadily adhered, and which they have always been prepared to justify.[21]

The Cabinet in 1880 and 1881 was consistently dogged by the need to discuss the Bradlaugh affair and its various problems, as the lack of workable solutions continued to drag out the controversy.[22] On 1 July 1880 the Liberal Government was successful in carrying a resolution allowing MPs to affirm.[23] A subsequent motion by the Conservatives that Bradlaugh should be prevented from taking the oath was won against Prime Minister Gladstone's wishes.[24] That it was an important event, overshadowing the affairs of the Parliament, is captured in the Earl of Kimberley's frustrated diary entry for 9 July 1880: 'The detestable Bradlaugh affair spoiled our short session utterly.'[25] Kimberley's choice of words reflects a certain distaste at Parliament having been forced to deal with an issue it would rather have seen left alone. Gladstone, in a letter to J.G. Hubbard, indicated that he thought Bradlaugh had been wrong to try and take the oath when he did not believe it, but argued against Hubbard that atheists did in fact have consciences.[26] Gladstone recognised that the law must still be obeyed, and wrote to Sir William Harcourt that 'the Speaker is right in proposing to debar Bradlaugh from the precincts [of the House]'.[27] John Bright made the suggestion in Cabinet that the Speaker should ask Bradlaugh whether he felt 'morally bound by the oath'.[28] The Cabinet rejected the suggestion.

The issue with Bradlaugh was not so much whether or not he believed in God, but that he was so vocal in saying that he did not. Appearance was everything, and if parliamentarians at least appeared ready to uphold the Protestant religion, that would be sufficient. The cynicism of such a stance was seized upon by one correspondent, Father Ignatius of Llauthaery Abbey, who wrote to Bradlaugh in 1880: 'Again, how can "Liberals" by any appeal to common sense or logic, cry out against your admission to parliament; they know that there are other atheists (not so honest as yourself) in the House; they however, for their dishonesty pass muster.'[29]

The significance of atheists gaining the same legal rights as other Britons is highlighted by a 1903 appeal by a prisoner at Dartmoor to be excused from attending chapel. Amongst the reasons he put forward for being excused was

> That my body, Atheists, are recognised in Courts of Law – House of Commons &c and are excused from anything that is opposed

to their belief – and I most respectfully Submit, that though a Convict – in this matter I am fully entitled to have my petition favourably accorded...[30]

The British Government had let Bradlaugh, an atheist of high stature, into full lawmaking rights. That allowed other atheists, like this prisoner, to seize upon Bradlaugh's case as a precedent. In this case, the prisoner's appeal was unsuccessful.

Bradlaugh's case was perhaps the most high-profile example of the legal difficulties that confronted those who dared to choose religious dissidence. The history of legal exclusion of atheists was a long one. In the mid eighteenth century, atheists had been unable to testify as witnesses because they could not sincerely swear the oath.[31] This restriction was slow to be removed. An Act of 1833 allowed certain dissenting faiths to affirm rather than give evidence on oath in court.[32] Quakers, Moravians and Separatists were by this Act enabled to take seats in Parliament by affirmation.[33] This right was extended, for civil court proceedings, to any who had a conscientious objection to taking the oath, by the Common Law Procedure Act of 1854.[34] An Act of 1861 allowed the same right for criminal cases, and a further statute of 1869 made it compulsory for people who indicated that an oath had no effect on their conscience to affirm rather than take the oath.[35] It was under all these statutes that Bradlaugh claimed his legal right to affirm and take his seat. In a letter to the Speaker in 1880, Bradlaugh said he would affirm under Act 29 & 30 Vict., Clause 19, Section 14, and Act 31 & 32 Vict., Clause 72, Section 11.[36] He equally claimed to be allowed to affirm under the Evidence Further Amendment Act of 1869, Section 4.[37] He cited in support of his argument the fact that he had long been entitled to affirm in a court of law, and had done so on numerous occasions before some of the highest courts in the land.[38]

Bradlaugh based his claims squarely upon the law. In effect, he challenged British lawmakers at their own game, claiming to have won by their rules. In an 1881 letter to Sir Stafford Northcote, Bradlaugh attacked the Parliament for refusing to play by the rules it had itself created. He suggested that, because the House of Commons was above judicial scrutiny in its activities, it should 'be most careful not to exceed its rights nor to strain its privileges'.³⁹ He asserted:

> In resorting to mere illegal physical force against one man it gives a lamentable encouragement to Law Breakers and it strikes a vital blow at that respect for Law which has saved this Country from mischief in many of its political crises.⁴⁰

Reverence for the rule of law was at the heart of British national identity. Bradlaugh recognised that if the Parliament's actions in any way lessened that reverence it would be to its own disadvantage. Parliament appears to have felt secure in discriminating against an atheist, believing that the majority of the country would agree with its actions on religious grounds alone. In this battle, the tension between lawmakers and the law itself was real, but public opinion limited the damage.

Bradlaugh failed to see that no matter how often he was re-elected for his constituency, it was not within the power of his electors to make him an 'insider'. Bradlaugh believed sufficiently in the majesty of British law to think that it would deliver him his seat. As he protested to Northcote,

> I was not elected as an Atheist, I was elected as an Englishman. I do not seek admission to the House as a heretic – I claim it as a duly elected legally qualified Englishman. The Law does not keep me out and illegal force shall not.⁴¹

What Bradlaugh failed to realise was that being an Englishman did not automatically entitle him to all the benefits of British law, despite the rhetoric. His 'Englishness' was not genuine if it was accompanied by atheism. He had to be accepted by his peers before he could be welcomed as a lawmaker. 'I answer that I am a law-abiding Englishman; that whatever views I have are mine, and that it is to the law alone I have to answer for them.'⁴² That is exactly the picture of reverence for the law that Bradlaugh was in effect fighting against. Bradlaugh, however, did not have to answer to some objective standard called 'the law'; he had to answer to those Britons who made the law.

The Bradlaugh issue also served to highlight the fact that Parliament, the ultimate lawmaking body, was itself above the law. As Bradlaugh lamented, '[t]here is apparently no court of law which can exercise jurisdiction & enforce the law against the House'.[43] It shows starkly that British law, which was wielded so freely against outsider groups, did have limitations – it did not fully extend to the body which created law. Symbolically at least, it placed those who sat in Parliament, including the unelected House of Lords, above the law.

Among the reasons why atheism was seen as such a threat to British stability was the fact that it challenged the 'right' of the British ruling elite to define the limits of the proper fabric of society. As S.J. Celestine-Edwards argued in 1889, speaking of atheists,

> If the laws which they acknowledge exist – viz., physical and moral – were produced by no one, it follows that we are responsible to no one for our conduct, and therefore it is an usurpation of power for one man or a number of men to make a law or laws which others are to obey.[44]

Celestine-Edwards felt that atheists threatened the governing right of the British Government. He listed amongst the objectives of political atheism plans to 'rob Christians of their prerogative of governing' and 'divest society of the means of keeping itself together'.[45] Religion and its soul mate, morality, were the foundation stones that successive governments had chosen for British society, and atheism seemed to threaten them both. It was this perceived link between religion, morality and the law, and what would happen to all of them if atheism were allowed to succeed, which dominated much of the Bradlaugh debates.[46]

The lengthy arguments over Bradlaugh's admission to Parliament are indicative of the tenacity with which the conservative British Establishment was prepared to hold on to what it saw as its prerogative – to make laws for the nation. Politics and lawmaking were activities that helped to define a nation, because in making laws, Parliament was also adding ingredients to Britain's ever fluid national identity.

Atheists – like Jews and Roman Catholics before them – were internal 'others' that by their differences helped to define 'Britishness'.

The fact that first Jews and then atheists were eventually to win their battle to be allowed to play their full constitutional part can be attributed to a number of factors. Firstly, it was a tribute to their persistence. Both Rothschild and Bradlaugh had to put themselves forward for election on numerous occasions, and embrace the turmoil associated with their exclusion, before they were finally allowed to take their seats in the Commons. Secondly, both Rothschild and Bradlaugh enjoyed the political support of the Liberal Party. Neither were a lone voice in the wilderness, and it was their ability to harness that wider political support that ultimately guaranteed their success. Thirdly, their eventual inclusion demonstrates that the strength of religious difference as a defining national characteristic was waning as the nineteenth century progressed.

Abhorrence at religious unbelief gave way to national condemnation of moral 'outsiders' such as homosexuals, prostitutes and the allegedly inherently criminal Irish. Events such as the fight over the Contagious Diseases Acts, the Phoenix Park murders, the Cleveland Street Scandal, and the Oscar Wilde trials helped to define clearer moral boundaries. As the nineteenth century drew towards a close, the characteristics of 'Britishness' came to be represented less by religious uniformity, and more by a commitment to British moral values.

CHAPTER 6

ROMAN CATHOLICS: THE ENDURING 'OTHER'

Atheists were not the only ones to face problems of exclusion from positions of power. While Roman Catholics might have been allowed into Parliament after 1829, their continued association with a foreign power, the Pope, and a 'foreign' religion rendered them a thorn in the side of 'Protestant Britain'. This tension, and how it spilled over in the Ecclesiastical Titles affair, showed how seriously such a thorn could still be taken by British lawmakers.

Roman Catholicism continued to prove an enormous disadvantage for those seeking to gain power in nineteenth-century Britain. It could also carry quasi-legal punishments for some. A soldier in 1840 was imprisoned briefly for consistently attending Roman Catholic services against the express wish of his commanding officer. John Walker, a Roman Catholic priest, brought the case to the attention of headquarters in a letter of 21 April 1840:

> John Brian, a drummer in a detachment of the 81st Regiment stationed at Scarbro' under the command at present of Captain Orange, has lately been subjected to punishment, & is even now undergoing punishment, for persisting in a determination to attend the Catholic Chapel here, rather than the Parish Church.[1]

A pencilled note on the back of an accompanying letter indicates that the matter was to be referred to the Home Secretary.[2]

Roman Catholic British soldiers in Ireland were a problem for British Governments throughout the 1840s. On the one hand, Roman Catholicism was supposed no longer to be an issue in terms of civic inequality, yet the military was the final arm of law enforcement, and no chances could be taken with its allegiance. The government was perfectly prepared to try to utilise the law to protect that allegiance. The Law Officers of the Crown were asked for a legal opinion on what action could be taken against Catholic priests who used divine service as a medium for political messages.[3] Lord Fitzroy Somerset had reported to Home Secretary James Graham on 11 December 1843 that often 'it has been necessary for the Officers in charge to withdraw the Troops under their Command from the Roman Catholic Chapels before the conclusion of divine Service in consequence of the allusion by the officiating Priest to political subjects'.[4] Amongst the alleged 'political subjects' were prayers for Daniel O'Connell, and criticism of the military as being 'the first to breed discord, and scandal', which was blamed on the officers.[5]

The law officers gave their opinion to Graham on 20 December 1843 on seven cases that had been referred to them. They concluded that no action was possible:

> We consider it very improper that a place of religious worship should be made the Scene of political discussions – and that it was very right under the circumstances to march out the soldiers; – But however indecorous it may be, it is not illegal merely to allude to political matters in Churches or Chapels – The question must always be whether seditious or defamatory language has been read or spoken.[6]

Roman Catholics, in the years immediately following emancipation, remained in the position of having to fight hard for legal recognition of their religious rights. As Linda Colley has asserted, 'Roman Catholics were beyond the boundaries, always on the outside even if they were British-born: they did not and could not belong.'[7] In 1830

George R. Morgan wrote to the Home Office on behalf of two Roman Catholic tradesmen who had been called upon in court to 'swear by the Cross'.[8] The Commissioner of the Court of Requests at Woolwich had not used the normal form of oath.[9] The tradesmen complained that the Commissioner was deliberately making an 'offensive aspersion' against their religion.[10]

Police files indicate that there was an awareness in the early nineteenth century of anti-Catholicism within the Metropolitan Police. An index of Historical Documents numbers 1–23 of Scotland Yard makes reference to a report upon the subject. The index refers to an 1835 document: 'A double page with notes by Mayne, which is obviously part of longer memo on subject of Police and political feeling in the Establishment. Of interest as mentioning charges of anti-Catholic bias...'[11] Unfortunately the document to which the index refers no longer seems to be extant. Religion was a nineteenth-century battleground, and the attitude of law-enforcers towards Roman Catholics had much to do with the popular perception that godliness was next to criminality where Roman Catholics were concerned.

The ability of Catholic priests to attend Roman Catholic prisoners was also an ongoing issue. In 1840, the Roman Catholic Bishop Thomas Griffiths appealed to Lord Normanby to allow a Roman Catholic chaplain to minister regularly to the Roman Catholic Prisoners at Bath Fields because 'the power given them of sending for a Catholic Clergyman has proved inadequate for securing his attendance'.[12] In 1847 the Roman Catholic Clergyman Stuart McCorry complained to the General Board of Directors of Prisons at Edinburgh of the restrictions placed on Roman Catholic clergymen which were not placed on those of the Established Church.[13] In 1863 The Prison Ministers Act provided local justices with the discretion to appoint priests to prisons where the numbers demanded it, and stated that priests 'may' be permitted to visit individual Roman Catholic prisoners.[14] The 1865 Prisons Act changed the wording to 'shall' be allowed to visit.[15] As late as 1892, Roman Catholic vacancies at Wandsworth and Maidstone prisons were not being filled due to the poor salaries being offered, at least in the opinion of Roman Catholic bishops.[16]

Throughout the nineteenth century, Roman Catholicism remained a significant bar to membership of the British ruling elite. Only two Roman Catholic cabinet ministers can be found in the period 1829–95.[17] Anti-Catholicism remained a defining characteristic of a Protestant nation.[18] It was a test of someone's 'British' credentials, and could affect the ambitions of Catholics who – for example – aspired to join the peerage, as was evidenced in discussions on peerages in the first Gladstone administration in 1869. In an ambiguous passage, Lord Granville wrote to Gladstone over the creation of Roman Catholic Peers: 'I shall leave it to you to discuss in conversation whether it will be wise as a general principle for the future to treat R. Catholics with disfavor, in order to rescue the Protestant Religion.'[19] It is unclear here whether Granville was advocating such an exclusion of Roman Catholics, or whether he was questioning a policy that was already in place to exclude them. It is also far from clear exactly what the Protestant religion needed to be saved from.[20] Either way, it is an interesting indication that members of government were aware of Roman Catholicism as an issue 40 years after Roman Catholic emancipation had been passed.

The Queen was prepared to be far less ambiguous about Roman Catholic equality. In a letter to Granville of 24 August 1869, she exhibited the kind of fervent anti–Roman Catholicism that reflected their continuing place as outsiders. The letter is worth quoting at length, such was the strength of the Queen's language regarding some of her subjects:

> Lastly with respect to the R. Catholic Peers – while she repeats the 2 proposed are unexceptionable, and that she will therefore not oppose their creation – she *does* object to the principle of treating them on an equality with the Protestants. The Govt. & many people in this country seem to the Queen to be totally blind to the alarming encroachments & increase of the R. Catholics in England & indeed all over the world... Every favour granted to the R. Catholics does *not* conciliate them, but leads them to be more & more grasping & encroaching & the danger of this to Protestant England cannot be overrated.[21]

The Queen was instinctively protecting what she continued to see as one of the cornerstones of British society – Protestantism. Roman Catholics should not be 'treated as equals', in the Queen's view, because that would accord them a dangerous status as legitimate incumbents of positions of political and moral power.

The Queen seemed to regard the Irish and Roman Catholics as one and the same. Writing to Gladstone on the subject of Fenian prisoners, Queen Victoria slipped from the specific to the general:

> ...firmness is absolutely necessary in Ireland & Mr Gladstone will see that it will not do either to give way to the Catholics in the hope of conciliating them. They will take everything & not be grateful for it. To treat them with perfect equality is an impossibility.[22]

That the Queen should have such a view of her Irish subjects, whose nation constituted a part of the United Kingdom itself, is indicative of the true position of both the Irish and Roman Catholics in Victorian Britain. They were not to be trusted. Formal civil disabilities were on the decline, but the more subtle distinctions continued to be seen as essential. In the eyes of the Queen, allowing Roman Catholics to make laws for a Protestant nation in the House of Lords was undesirable. To quote historian Frank Wallis, '[t]he most important dividing line in Victorian society was not between rich and poor, but between respectable Christians and unrespectable infidels'.[23] Only one of these groups could be allowed to make British law – and the Queen's preference was clear.

A later royal letter confirms the depths of Victoria's fears: 'Protestant to the very *heart's core* as the Queen is – she is shocked & grieved to see England forgetting her position & the higher classes & so many of the young Clergy tainted with this leaning towards Rome!'[24] The heart of Britain was to be England, and at the heart of England was to be Protestantism. Victoria continued to express anti-Catholic sentiments when the Irish Universities Bill was introduced by the Liberal Government in 1873, writing, in response to a measured letter from Gladstone: 'She entirely approves Mr Gladstone's decided expression of opinion that nothing more can be done for the Roman Catholics who have *no* right whatever to complain.'[25]

Education was one of the great anti-Catholic battlegrounds of the Victorian period.[26] If young Britons were to be brought up in Roman Catholic schools, this would eventually undermine the position of the Roman Catholic as an 'other'. But the most extreme disquiet was saved for the education of future Roman Catholic priests. The fear and controversy stirred up in the 1840s by government endowment of the Roman Catholic seminary at Maynooth is a good reflection of where education and religion combined in an explosive mix.[27] In some senses, Maynooth can be seen as the exception which proves the rule. The public and parliamentary outcry over the measure was such as to illustrate clearly the latent anti-Catholicism of British society. Denis G. Paz has argued that it was the issue which really led to the split of the Conservative Party, rather than the Corn Laws debate of the following year.[28]

On the other hand, the passage of the measure fits in well with the general pattern of movement towards religious and civil liberties throughout the nineteenth century. All reforms along religious lines were hard won against the opposition of significant numbers of British lawmakers. A proposal against the Maynooth grant was brought forward in every session of parliament from 1851 to 1863.[29] As the struggles over further Roman Catholic relief legislation in 1847, 1859, 1865, 1866, 1867 and 1872 show, the battle was fought vigorously to the bitter end.[30]

Anti-Catholicism was also a latent force in the courts throughout the Victorian period, where the attitudes of 'British' men who had become judges and barristers were naturally reflective of broader prejudices, albeit with the restraints that legal training could provide. Legal cases served to keep Roman Catholicism in the spotlight as an issue. Paz mentions *Connelly v Connelly*, *Achilli v Newman* and *Metairie v Wiseman and Others* as cases which led to an ongoing negative depiction of Roman Catholicism.[31] Such cases gave grist to the anti-Catholic mill, subtly reinforcing their outsider position through the press reports that ensued. The advocate for the Tichborne claimant in his perjury trial, Dr Kenealy, tried to portray the Government as being motivated by a Roman Catholic conspiracy to protect the Tichborne family against an alleged impostor.[32]

Roman Catholicism could be seen as a threat upon any ground that those allegedly threatened chose to put forward. Historian Walter Arnstein has indicated that one smaller aspect involved in the Anti-Catholic Murphy riots in 1867 was a fear amongst 'British' men that under Roman Catholicism the priest would challenge the authority of men over the women in their household.[33] The priest might become a competing authority. Frank Wallis has also supported that assessment.[34] William Murphy was the central figure in the Murphy riots.[35] A convert to Protestantism, he toured England exposing what he saw as the shortcomings of the Roman Catholic Church.[36] His lucid prose did not inspire all of his listeners, in particular the large numbers of Roman Catholics that protested during his speaking tour. On a number of occasions, violence erupted between Protestant supporters of Murphy and Roman Catholics, resulting in rioting.[37] Murphy presented grave problems for Englishmen as well as for the Irish Roman Catholics against whom his comments were directed. To quote Arnstein:

> The activities of William Murphy created a troublesome dilemma for respectable Englishmen, many of whom at bottom shared his distrust of Catholicism, but who were repelled by his lack of gentility...[38]

This was Murphy's problem. He may have been reflecting established British values, but this did not of itself make him acceptable to British powerbrokers. The Establishment recognised its own and saw in Murphy an unappealing if useful intruder.

Split Loyalties

Catholicism's greatest threat to a 'British' identity was its 'Roman-ness'. At an intellectual level, Roman Catholics could be deemed to hold a split loyalty – a double allegiance that diminished their 'Britishness'. To whom did the Roman Catholic owe his or her first loyalty, to Rome or the Crown? The split loyalties question was of extreme importance because it allowed Catholics to be seen as unpatriotic. What was more, it challenged the right of the Queen to the first allegiance of her subjects. The first duty of a British Government was to protect its head. Any threat to the prestige of the Crown was a threat to the majesty of the law. This was a central point in the furore that followed the re-introduction of the Catholic episcopal hierarchy into Britain in 1850.[39] Prime Minister Lord John Russell, in his open letter to the Bishop of Durham and through the subsequent Ecclesiastical Titles Bill, was reflecting the need to protect both the integrity of the monarchy and the strength of the religious foundation upon which society stood:[40]

> There is an assumption of power in all the documents which have come from Rome; a pretension of supremacy over the realm of England, and a claim to sole and undivided sway, which is inconsistent with the Queen's supremacy, with the rights of our bishops and clergy, and with the spiritual independence of the nation...[41]

The Government had been careful to gather information on how the Roman Catholic Church stood in the other nations of Europe before introducing the 1850 Ecclesiastical Titles legislation.[42] The ultimate result, however, owed more to the strong British aversion to papal pretensions than to a balanced desire to treat the Roman Catholic Church in the same way as it was treated in other Protestant countries. One correspondent with Foreign Secretary Palmerston, Anthony Perriers, protested against 'the attempts of a Foreign Potentate to establish in Great Britain an ecclesiastical Hierarchy independent of the authority of HM, the only legitimate head of all establishments within Her Realms...'[43] Once again, Victoria's position as the head of British society is highlighted. She was the legitimate head, and from her flowed the fount of British Law, forming the legitimate secular and ecclesiastical boundaries of 'Britishness'.

John Wolffe has placed the agitation surrounding the re-introduction of the Catholic hierarchy squarely within the context of nationalism: the picture of the British nation fighting against a foreign religion. He argues that 'a religious issue was serving to emphasize the common ground of identity between the component nations of Britain.'[44]

A necessary component of that common ground of course was the recognition of the Queen as being the supreme secular and ecclesiastical head of Britain. Her supremacy became the rallying point for a nation.

However, the principles of religious toleration had advanced sufficiently that the Ecclesiastical Titles legislation almost brought Russell's Prime Ministership to an end. In a memo of 24 February 1851, Russell noted that:

> Lord Aberdeen & Sir James Graham object decidedly to <u>any</u> legislative measure on the subject of the Ecclesiastical Titles Bill. This puts an end to the negotiation, & Lord John Russell has returned his Commission into Her Majesty's hands.[45]

The reason for Aberdeen and Graham's disapproval was that, even if changed, 'the Bill will still be resented as penal and offensive by the great body of Her Majesty's Roman Catholic subjects'.[46] Aberdeen and Graham realised the symbolic importance of such a measure in suggesting that Roman Catholics needed to be legislated against, separating them as outsiders from the rest of Protestant, 'British' society.

The popular mood, reflected by both the Government and the monarchy, was certainly one that perceived the restoration of ecclesiastical titles by the Papacy as a threat. David Newsome has argued that the Ecclesiastical Titles Bill helped to bring a greater sense of shared identity to English Roman Catholics by creating a common enemy in the form of a repressive State.[47] Protestant anger was not directed solely at the Roman Catholic Church. In Scotland there was concern that the Bill gave greater support to the Scottish Episcopal Church, whose leaders had also recently begun styling themselves as 'Bishops'.[48] A petition on the subject was sent to Home Secretary Sir George Grey on 25 March 1851, indicating that the Presbyterians wanted words specifically included in the Ecclesiastical Titles Bill to stop the encroachments of the Episcopal Church.[49] Five days earlier, Alex Ewing, 'styled Bishop of Argyle', had written to Sir George Grey indicating why the Episcopal Church saw nothing illegal in taking on territorial titles.[50]

That the Government explored all avenues of response to the papal imposition of ecclesiastical titles is clear. The Home Office files contain a legal opinion from John Romilly and A.E. Cockburn – the Attorney-General and Solicitor-General – on whether the assumption of Roman Catholic titles was an offence either at Common Law or under Statute.[51] The legal officers concluded that, because the titles did not attempt to fully usurp the exact titles of Anglican archbishoprics and bishoprics, the new names could not constitute a common law offence. They claimed that, had the new Roman Catholic Archbishop of Westminster instead tried to assume a title like the Archbishop of Canterbury, he could potentially have been charged with high treason. An Elizabethan statute did however come into play: 'We think that the publishing of such a Bull in this Country, the assumption of titles or dignities under it, the acting under it in any way, the mere reading of it in public as a document of authority, would constitute the offence under the Statute...'[52] Such laws provided a clear reminder of how long Britain had been a Protestant nation and how tenaciously it wished to maintain its national sovereignty in ecclesiastical as well as secular matters.

On this occasion, the law officers concluded nonetheless that a 'State Prosecution' was fraught with 'practical difficulties' based on the long-standing de facto acceptance by British Governments of the appointment of Roman Catholic bishops in Ireland by Papal Bull.[53] In the final analysis, the law officers argued against interference on the grounds of the potential public reaction. They concluded that

> the moral effect of the prosecution might under the circumstances of the case be against the Public Prosecutor and in favour of the Defendant as being the revival of an Old Law which had been treated as obsolete and ineffectual.[54]

Nonetheless, a spirit of anti-Catholicism was clearly motivating elements of the British Government in 1850. Contemporary Roman Catholic convert John Newman noted in a letter to the Conservative politician Spencer Walpole:

...a Royal Proclomation [sic] has appeared in the London Gazette; in which all whom it may concern are solemnly warned against a violation of the Act of 10 George IV, by which Roman Catholic ecclesiastics... are forbidden to exercise any of the rites or ceremonies of the Roman Catholic religion, or wear the habits of their order, save within the usual places of worship...[55]

Any papal assertions were seen as a threat to the Protestant way of life, and Britain was being exhorted to fight all such assertions.

The divisiveness of the Roman Catholic issue was illustrated again by the suggestion in a letter from the future Chief Justice Coleridge to Gladstone, the member for Oxford University, that he would love to be of help on any electoral issues, but that his name should not be published as a supporter because his brother had become a Roman Catholic.[56] In the tense atmosphere of the day, even being related to a deserter of the Protestant cause was something to be ashamed of.

This was emphasised again by Gladstone in 1870, when the disestablishment of the Anglican Church in Ireland necessitated the repeal of the Ecclesiastical Titles Act. He assured the Queen that 'The Lord Chancellor has undertaken to consider of fitting language for the preamble of a repealing Bill, in which the Constitutional principle with regard to Titles should be maintained.'[57] The Queen's paramount place as the head of Britain and fount of British law was not to be challenged. Gladstone had already made that quite clear when first broaching the subject in 1869. Any preamble was to ensure 'that any Titles not growing out of the Law of the Country have no legal force or effect whatsoever'.[58] The matter was clearly not an easy one because it was considered again in Cabinet on 7 May 1870, by which time a draft was available 'with recitals adequate to assert and maintain the established principles of law with reference to Your Majesty's Supremacy'.[59]

The issue of the Queen's supremacy over the Pope again came to the fore when Gladstone made it the subject of one of his widely selling pamphlets in 1874, *The Vatican Decrees in Their Bearing on Civil Allegiance: A Political Expostulation*.[60] Between November and December 1874, the pamphlet sold 145,000 copies.[61] The decree in question was that relating to Papal infallibility. Gladstone's main argument was that this doctrine might create a conflict of loyalties for Catholics.[62]

Loyalty to Queen and country was essential from the perspective of British lawmakers. Gladstone made this clear in his pamphlet, suggesting that 'no one can now become her [Catholic Church's] convert without renouncing his moral and mental freedom, and placing his civil loyalty and duty at the mercy of another'.[63] Gladstone quoted from Bishop Doyle giving evidence before a House of Commons Committee in 1825, where he indicated that in civil matters the highest allegiance of a Roman Catholic was to the British monarch.[64] He also quoted from the third chapter of the Papal Decrees, stating 'that none may re-open the judgement of the Apostolic See, than whose there is no greater authority; and that it is not lawful for any one to sit in judgement on its judgement'.[65] While the quote refers to ecclesiastical jurisdiction, it is easy to see why such language would seem threatening to British authorities. The Pope was setting himself above the majesty of the British law and above the majesty of the British monarch. Gladstone seized upon this as rendering British Catholics unpatriotic: 'Too commonly, the spirit of the neophyte is expressed by the words which have become notorious: "a Catholic first, an Englishman afterwards".'[66]

The Roman Catholic Archbishop of Westminster, Henry Manning, was adamant in a letter to *The Times* that Roman Catholics had no split loyalty:

> My desire and my duty as an Englishman, as a Catholic, and as a pastor is to claim for my flock and for myself a civil allegiance as pure, as true, and as loyal as is rendered by the distinguished author of the pamphlet or by any subject of the British Empire.[67]

The Vatican Decrees controversy reveals what can increasingly be seen as a pattern. When British elites wished to define a particular group as outsiders, they would be labelled as 'un-English', setting them apart from the rest of society, which could rejoice in its 'Englishness' at the legal expense of the targeted groups. It allowed governments to discriminate, rhetorically and legally, against outsider groups by not allowing them to enter into the birthright of 'British law'. If one chose not to be British by being Roman Catholic, or Jewish, or an atheist, or to act in an 'un-English' way, like homosexuals and prostitutes, then one could not expect to be protected by the majesty of British law.

Historian Josef L. Altholz characterises the British public in the 1870s as 'generally hostile to Roman Catholicism', although there was no major public display of that emotion at the time of the Vatican Decrees in 1874, as there had been in 1850.[68] The level of public emotion over the 1870s Papal encroachments is a point open for debate, Altholz's contention notwithstanding. *The Times* in September 1874 stated that '[t]o become a Roman Catholic and remain a thorough Englishman are – it cannot be disguised – almost incompatible conditions'.[69] The West of Scotland Protestant Association held two large public meetings over the Papal supremacy issue in 1875 and 1876, publishing the speeches that were made.[70] The meetings touched on the continuing suspicion felt amongst Protestants about trusting Roman Catholics with the majesty of British law. Speaking of a hypothetical Catholic, Sir Thomas Chambers MP stated: 'Well, they put him on a jury in a case of life and death, liberty, character, or property. Are sinister influences absolutely excluded, nay, are they not probable, in consequence of the Confessional?'[71]

From the personal space of the confessional to the public acknowledgement of the Queen's superiority, Roman Catholics were given no room to move. Religious toleration was one thing; allowing disloyalty to the head of British government, in whose name laws were promulgated, another thing entirely. Gladstone, in *Vaticanism: An Answer to Replies and Reproofs*, writing of his earlier work on the Vatican decrees, stated:

> In my Expostulation, I laid stress upon the charge of an intention, on the part of Vaticanism, to promote the restoration of the temporal sovereignty of the Pope, on the first favourable opportunity, by foreign arms, and without reference to the wishes of those who were once his people.[72]

While Gladstone may have been deliberately controversial in his choice of language, the target of his concern was the idea that the Pope might challenge the position of the monarchy as the highest body to which Britons owed allegiance. While Victoria remained the head of British society, her position had to be protected, because it was in her name that governments promulgated laws and defined the limits of British society.

Religious tolerance came slowly but relentlessly. Roman Catholics may have seen legal barriers slowly removed, but this did not automatically transfer them to being accepted members of British society. Concessions could and had been made because the entrenched British lawmakers felt safe in their power. Jews and Roman Catholics might now be permitted to sit in the British Parliament, but they certainly did not dominate Cabinets or Governments, with the exception of Disraeli. Henry Matthews, Home Secretary in the Salisbury administration from 1886 to 1892, was, according to Friedland, 'the first Catholic to be a cabinet minister since the seventeenth century'.[73] Friedland's claim is not entirely correct, given that Lord Ripon, a Catholic convert, held cabinet office under Gladstone in the short-lived Liberal administration of 1886.[74] Nonetheless, the point is well made that Roman Catholics in Cabinet were a rarity indeed.

Roman Catholicism was to remain a thorny issue right up to the end of the nineteenth century at least. For instance, the 1892 case of a father whose will stated that his son was to be sent to a Roman Catholic school caused some anxiety for the Home Office. The child was 14 upon his father's death, and had been baptised a Protestant. He expressed the wish that he preferred not to go to a Roman Catholic School.[75] On that basis, in the interests of the child, the Home Office decided the boy's decision would stand and the will of his deceased father was ignored. As the inspector dealing with the case noted in his report, it was a case 'in which the S[ecretary] of S[tate]'s decision, whichever way it is given, may be challenged'.[76]

The continuing strength of certain sections of popular feeling against Roman Catholics being allowed to assume positions of official and legal importance is indicated by the sizeable petition sent to Queen Victoria urging her to disallow the 1892 selection of the

Roman Catholic Alderman Stuart Knill as Lord Mayor of London.⁷⁷ The petition, from the Anti-Popery Association, contained over 2,000 signatures. Of course, the very fact that a Roman Catholic had been appointed to the position shows the extent to which resistance as a whole to religious outsider groups was diminishing. In this particular instance, it perhaps also reflected the extent to which the financial tycoons of the City of London were not as concerned as other areas of the country with religious sensibilities. After all, it had been the City of London that first sent Rothschild as its representative to Parliament. The language of the petition highlighted the classic, if by now no longer widely current, traditional 'British' concerns. The petitioners asserted that

> he approval by Your Majesty of the selection of Mr Alderman Knill as Lord Mayor of London will be an admission to the whole world that Your Majesty and the people of this Country are willing to submit to the domination of the Pope of Rome...⁷⁸

The petitioners were concerned that the Queen's position as the ultimate head of British society would be challenged by allowing her dominance in the ecclesiastical sphere to be challenged. A second concern was that it was illegal that '...the Office of Chief Magistrate and Lord Mayor be entrusted to a zealous and determined Roman Catholic owing allegiance to a foreign power...'.⁷⁹ Positions of legal and political power, even if only symbolic, were traditionally reserved for Protestant Britons. Seeing a Roman Catholic occupying such a position was a shock to those who had been accustomed for most of the nineteenth century to seeing Roman Catholics as outsiders. To add a further point to their argument, the petitioners again demonstrated that Catholicism, and in this case the Irish holders of that faith, were linked with lawlessness. They drew attention to the fact that 'at the present time in one portion of Your Majesty's dominions the Roman Catholic Priesthood are the aiders, abettors and champions if not the instigators of disobedience and opposition to the laws of the Realm'.⁸⁰

In 1890, the Liberals made an attempt to lift the restrictions remaining on certain offices that Catholics were proscribed from, including the Lord Chancellorship of England and the Lord Lieutenancy of Ireland. To overcome concerns at Roman Catholics having authority over any aspect of the Church of England, the Lord Chancellor's ecclesiastical role in bestowing benefices would be taken over by the Archbishop of either Canterbury or York.[81] The continuing controversy over these positions highlighted again which roles the British ruling elite held closest to its heart. They were those positions that carried legal as well as political authority. A rhetoric of equality masked a reality in which Roman Catholics were still to be the subjects rather than the originators of law. The potential difficulties suddenly made Home Secretary Matthews a little concerned at the strict legality of his own position as a Roman Catholic with some input into ecclesiastical appointments.[82] He had allowed Lord Salisbury to carry out these roles on his behalf during his period as Home Secretary, but the Home Office files reflect a desire for clarification in the wake of questions posed while the Liberals' Bill was before the House in February 1891.[83]

Whoever controlled the making and enforcement of law had control over how to define 'British' society. This was fully recognised by the Scottish Reformation Society, which sent a petition against the 1890 Bill. They were against the measure

> ...because the opening of the Lord Lieutenancy of Ireland to Roman Catholics would be a flagrant violation of the principle and spirit, if not also of the letter, of our Protestant Constitution. The clear principle of that Constitution is, that the Supreme Magistracy of Great Britain shall not be exercised by members of the Church of Rome. If the Sovereign in her own person cannot be a Romanist, as by law she cannot, it would seem to follow that neither in her Representative can she be a Romanist.[84]

The concentration on the legal symbolism of the position is clear. The law of the land protected the Protestant nature of Britain, and stopped Roman Catholics from assuming positions of legal superiority. It was the law which prevented Roman Catholics from becoming Lord Chancellor; and yet when the Liberals proposed to use archbishops and judges to take over any duties that touched on the working of the Anglican Church, that was thought by the Protestant Alliance to show 'that a Roman Catholic is unfitted for the duties of the Office of Chancellor'.[85] The law forbade Roman Catholics a judicial role, and then the very existence of that law supposedly rendered them 'unfitted' for the job anyway.

The working committee of the Portsmouth Protestant Institute also sent a petition, presented to the Queen, protesting against the proposed legislation. They reminded Victoria that she had sworn at her coronation to protect the Anglican Church and to protest against the 'superstitious and idolatrous' Roman Catholic Church.[86] This again suggests why the Queen was so crucial to the fabric of Victorian society. She was its head in the sense that laws were enacted and enforced in her name, and she had a strong interest in protecting the religious foundations of society because she was head of the Church of England. The United Protestant Societies of Brighton sent a resolution against the Bill, claiming to have been passed unanimously by a meeting of 'upwards of 3,000'.[87]

Every year or two from 1898 to 1904 saw a Bill introduced into Parliament attempting to remove remaining restrictions on Jesuits in Britain, and on Roman Catholics being barred from the Lord Lieutenancy of Ireland and the Lord Chancellorship.[88] British lawmakers were also aware of the importance of the greatest restriction of all, that royalty should have no link to Roman Catholicism. If the head of society could be contaminated with Roman Catholicism, the religious foundation stone might crumble, and with it the authority of British ruling traditions. Lord Salisbury wrote a long letter on the subject to Lord Halsbury, questioning the extent to which marriage to a Catholic disqualified an heir to the throne, and how one could tell if someone had genuinely converted from Roman Catholicism to being a Protestant: 'It may, therefore, become important to know by what precise procedure the stain of Papistry, which you do not think in this case indelible, can be washed off.'[89] Roman Catholicism was a stain that needed to be removed if one had any pretensions to the highest Establishment position of all – royalty.

CHAPTER 7

THE NEW JEWISH THREAT

London in the later nineteenth century had emerged as perhaps the most cosmopolitan city in Europe. The East End of London had a history of providing a refuge for those fleeing persecution or poverty. The Huguenots had long ago made it their home, fleeing France after the revocation of the Edict of Nantes.[1] In the nineteenth century, large numbers of Irish sought to make the East End their haven. Irish soldiers de-listed following 1815, and refugees from the potato famine of 1846 came to the streets of London in search of work. As Chaim Bermant has pointed out, the East End was a point of arrival, being so close to the London docks. It was often the first port of call for immigrants, and the poorer ones got no further as the need to bond with others of their ethnic or religious background asserted itself in a new country.[2] To this picture can be added Chinese immigrants who continued to arrive in small numbers throughout the nineteenth century.[3] They were predominantly young single males, and were mostly employed as seamen, with some finding work as personal servants.[4]

Fleeing the pogroms in the east, particularly Russia and Poland, Jewish immigrants came to England in general and East London in particular, in their thousands, in the years between 1880 and the turn of the century.[5] The numbers were large by any measure. Colin Holmes estimates that between 1881 and 1905 around 1 million Jews fled from Eastern Europe and Russia.[6] America soaked up the vast majority of these, but around 100,000 are thought to have settled in Britain.[7] Despite this, and the anti-alien hostility which flowed from it, Jews only accounted for 0.17 per cent of the British population in 1880 and 0.38 per cent in 1900.[8]

For much of the Victorian period, the total Jewish population was very small. David Anderson suggested in 1857 that the Jewish community in Britain numbered only 12,000.[9] Contemporary chronicler Henry Mayhew records it as being 35,000 in 1851, including 'foreign Jews' who remained largely in London.[10] It was Jewish difference, more than the sheer Jewish population size, that caught Mayhew's eye when he noted that 'among some the dominant feeling against the Jews on account of their faith still flourishes...'[11]

Mayhew makes reference to a Jewish tribunal, presided over by Chief Rabbi Adler, which twice a week sat to hear disputes over religious matters 'which are decided according to the Jewish law'.[12] Mayhew goes on to assert that, 'if the Lord Mayor or any other magistrate is told that the matter has already been settled by the Jewish Rabbi he seldom interferes. This applies only to civil and not to criminal cases.'[13] Although Mayhew does not make a great deal of it, this may be another reason why Jews continued to be viewed as outsiders. Their ability to manage their own affairs was such that they did not always have need even of that allegedly greatest of British gifts, British justice.

Jewish immigrants often survived and thrived in conditions many Englishmen would have considered abhorrent. Overcrowding in homes was the norm, and sweated labour an unfortunate fact of economic life. The dress and Yiddish language of the newcomers set them apart, and led to claims by anti-immigration campaigners like Arnold White that they were not assimilating into English society.[14] The concept of assimilation in this context is interesting. Did being truly British mean that one looked outwardly like an Anglican, soberly dressed and displaying the manners of an Englishman? Sir John Simon, amongst others, urged the newer Jews to take a greater pride in their British citizenship.[15] Some historians have suggested that the Jewish newcomers were more prepared and more likely to assimilate than the mass of Irish immigrants that had preceded them into Britain. Pieter van

Duin is one who makes that claim: 'This was a notable contrast to the behaviour of East European Jewish immigrants who, while retaining their religion, were generally anxious to assimilate the way most immigrant groups (including the Irish) in the United States were.'[16] This is consistent with the Beatrice Potter view of Jews that 'as a mass they shift upwards'.[17]

Colin Holmes has argued that there was a policy of toleration towards Jews in 1876–1914 by what he terms the 'British power elite'. It is difficult to escape such a conclusion when one looks at the pattern of liberalisation throughout the nineteenth century on questions of religion. Yet movement could only occur when the British Government was prepared slowly to remove the disabilities to which Jews were subject. David Feldman has found that 'Jewish integration was attended by more friction than is often allowed'[18] The final disabilities were not lifted until 1871.

As the immigration tide grew in the 1880s, so did concerns about links between Judaism and socialism and anarchism.[19] Jews could be criticised for their links to international capitalism and allegedly heartless materialism, while simultaneously being feared for their links with socialism and anarchism.[20] Immigrant Jews could be attacked for their pauperism; yet if they established themselves and made their fortune they were seen as threatening materialists who were looking to take over British society.[21]

By the 1890s, it had become clear that governments could no longer legislate specifically against Jews. To quote historian Todd Endelman, 'overt anti-Semitism' had now become 'disreputable'.[22] This did not mean that Jews had now become accepted as truly British. The Aliens Act of 1905 is an illustration that laws could still be made which were directed against Jews, just more subtly than previously. Despite the denials of contemporary politicians that the law had anything to do with anti-Semitism, one can only agree with Endelman that '[i]n fact, of course, anti-alienism and anti-Semitism were implicitly linked'.[23]

William Rubinstein, in his 1996 work, *A History of the Jews in the English-Speaking World*, goes some way towards defending Britain from claims of rampant anti-Semitism. He argues that '[i]t is fair to say that, compared with European Jewish history, in the English-speaking world 'nothing happened' – no ghettoes, no crusades, no pogroms, no Holocaust...'[24] Michael Ragussis has challenged that defence, and argues that: 'the history of Nazi atrocities should not make us inattentive to the subtle but nonetheless widespread, powerful, and deeply ingrained forms of anti-Semitism that are an important part of English history and culture'.[25]

A.L. Shane has suggested that the reactions of the Jews of England to the Dreyfus Affair in France was one of a people aware of their vulnerability.[26] It was that sense of vulnerability that motivated members of the established Anglo-Jewry to promote and support repatriation of Jews from Eastern Europe as the immigration waves rolled towards England during the latter part of the nineteenth century.[27] Endelman has suggested that as many as 50,000 Jews were repatriated between 1880 and 1914.[28] In the early 1900s there seemed, according to Hochberg, to have been an understanding between London magistrates and Jewish leaders to repatriate those found guilty of presumably minor offences.[29]

Alien immigration began to emerge as a serious social issue in the 1880s.[30] The term 'alien' sounds all-inclusive, but was aimed squarely at the flood of Jewish immigrants into London.[31] Most of these came from Eastern Europe and Russia, where pogroms were widespread following the assassination of Tsar Alexander II in 1881.[32] Britain's uninhibited immigration policy was to survive until the Aliens Act of 1905, but the seeds for its downfall were already being sown.

Newly arrived eastern Jews aroused strong feelings of resentment amongst both the longer-established Anglo-Jewry and among Gentiles.[33] There was a sense in the public mind that these newly arrived Jews were linked to crime. There was an underlying fear of their 'foreign' practices and beliefs, which surfaced in particular during high-profile murder cases. For example, such fears formed an underlying theme in the Jack the Ripper murders, as will be discussed shortly. They were also greatly apparent in the murder case of Israel Lipski the year before.[34] Lipski was a Jewish small-businessman who was accused of murder by poisoning. He was found in the same room as his alleged victim, who had been poisoned. Lipski was found unconscious under the bed, with traces of the poison around his own mouth. He claimed that two men had administered poison to him and left him for dead, having murdered the woman earlier.[35]

That the case was a significant one is highlighted by the fact that it was repeatedly raised in questions in Parliament. Mr Cunninghame Graham questioned the Home Secretary over the difficulties that Mr Hayward, Lipski's lawyer, had encountered in obtaining some crucial evidence from police, namely the phial containing the poison allegedly used in the murder.[36] In the end, the prosecution was triumphant in the case, and Lipski was sentenced to death. There is no evidence here of any direct government action or inaction that may have helped to convict Lipski. At most, there was a suggestion put forward by Hayward, and repeated by Sir Richard Temple in Parliament, that the Home Office was aware, before its announcement, that Lipski would confess and that this was why the Home Secretary had decided not to interfere and recommend clemency.[37] The Home Secretary denied the allegation.[38]

The Lipski case was an instance in which a legal proceeding with many doubtful elements was able to reinforce the outsider status of Jewish immigrants.[39] The case suggested that it took 'foreigners' to commit such crimes. Martin Friedland, in his 1984 work *The Trials of Israel Lipski*, writes of anti-Semitism at the time in the popular press, including the *Pall Mall Gazette*, which was one of Lipski's strongest advocates prior to his confession shortly before his execution. Friedland quotes Stead, the editor of the *Pall Mall Gazette*, in a letter he wrote to Madame Novikoff after hearing that Lipski had confessed: 'Lipski!!!! Alas could any human being not a Pole and also a Jew have played the PMG so scandalous a trick.'[40] Friedland concludes that there remains 'a reasonable doubt about Lipski's confession and guilt' and notes that 'Justice may in theory be blind, but in practice she has altogether too human a perspective.'[41] Despite calls for clemency in Parliament, Lipski was duly executed on 22 August 1887. *The Times* published a report of the execution in its Tuesday, 23 August edition, stating that

> [a] large crowd had meanwhile assembled within the precincts of the gaol in the Old Bailey, and upon the black flag being hoisted

indicating that the last sentence of the law had been carried into effect it was received with cheers.[42]

This report was sufficiently accurate to cause the Tory MP for Henley, Francis Parker, to call in Parliament for the abolition of the practice of hoisting a flag following an execution.[43] Henry Matthews, showing an awareness of how important it was that the public maintained a belief that the law was an active agent on their behalf, replied, 'Some intimation that an execution has taken place is, I think, desirable.'[44]

There was an air surrounding the Lipski case which suggested that Jews were a race apart, allegedly capable of barbarities that offended 'British' sensibilities. It was a viewpoint oft repeated during the Jack the Ripper murders. L. Perry Curtis, in his comprehensive study of contemporary media coverage of the Ripper murders, suggests that hostility towards Jewish immigrants was a contributing factor to people's willingness to accept that Jack the Ripper was likely to be a Jew.[45] By the labelling of Jack the Ripper as Jewish, British anxiety could be displaced onto a group seen as un-British, in the process labelling a whole immigrant Jewish community as outsiders.

The linking of Jews to crime was not necessarily new. Frank Wallis has noted that 'Sir Robert Peel claimed the Jews were the chief instigators of crime in London; they had a virtual monopoly on the disposal of stolen goods.'[46] David Cesarani, commenting on the late 1860s, argues that '[i]t remained habitual for local and national newspapers to identify as Jews criminals who happened to be Jewish, and to associate Jews with mendicancy.'[47] David Englander has argued that '[t]he unruliness of the Jewish lower orders was as notorious as that of the Irish, and in the absence of restraint they were comparable to the English labouring classes with whom they lived.'[48]

The broad facts of the Jack the Ripper murders have been extensively discussed in detail elsewhere.[49] It suffices to say that someone called Jack the Ripper is thought guilty of the murder of at least five women in London's East End in the autumn of 1888. Mary Ann Nichols, Anne Chapman, Elizabeth Stride, Katherine Eddowes and Mary Jane Kelly were all struck down between 31 August and 9 November 1888. They have become part of history, while the legend of their murderer continues to excite the popular mind to this day. The historical impression of the Ripper's victims as somehow wretched and pitiful has coloured perceptions of prostitution in the period. As Charles Booth noted, there were many varieties and classes of prostitutes who were not simply helpless victims of the social and economic world around them.[50] The Jack the Ripper murders implied that prostitutes were powerless creatures.[51] Anti-Semitism was running high at the time of the murders due to a widespread belief that a Jew was responsible.[52] The Jack the Ripper case, and the way it was handled by the authorities, gave anti-Semitism another outlet.[53]

The *Jewish Chronicle*, surprisingly at first sight, gave little coverage to the murders. David Cesarani has suggested that it was part of an editorial policy to play down any negative publicity for Jews, even if it was only in the process of denying their involvement in crime. Editorial recognition of the accusations would have meant a tacit willingness to take part in a debate that the *Jewish Chronicle* did not wish to begin. Editor Asher Myers did make an exception, stepping in personally to deny the alleged link between the murders and ritual Jewish knives.[54]

Central to the link between Jews and the murders was the suspicion cast upon a mysterious figure known as 'Leather Apron' by the press, portrayed as a sinister Jew. Some prostitutes did indicate that they knew 'Leather Apron' and that he had 'ill-used' them in the past.[55] The police tracked down a Jew by the name of John Pizer, a shoemaker, who did indeed wear a leather apron and work with sharp knives.[56] He was able to provide them with an alibi they found sufficiently convincing to release him. Suspicion of Jews persisted, and Sir Charles Warren, the Police Commissioner, appears to have been well aware of it. Following the murder of Katherine Eddowes, a piece of graffiti was found on a wall in Goulston Street which read either 'The Juwes are the men that will not be blamed for nothing', or 'The Juwes are the men that will be blamed for nothing'.[57] Sir Charles Warren personally attended the scene and ordered that the graffiti be immediately erased lest it start a riot against the Jewish population.[58] Stephen Knight has argued that Warren was in fact trying to cover up the murders through erasing the writing.[59] Superintendent Arnold's report to the Home Office supports Warren's explanation for his actions and claims that 'a strong feeling existed against the Jews generally'.[60] The statistics indicate that there was an exceptionally large Jewish population in Whitechapel.[61] It would not have been difficult for the local East End population, with the help of the anti-Semitic attitudes of individual policemen, to have blamed the newest part of the population for the atrocities.

What is more, there is likely to have been an underlying suspicion of the Jews on the basis of a fear of 'ritual murder', an alleged Judaic practice which led to several criminal cases on the Continent between 1880 and the First World War. The British adventurer Sir Richard Burton wrote a book alleging that Jews were responsible for some ritual murders in the Middle East, although the book was not published until after his death.[62] The allegations related to alleged murders outside Britain in 1840 and had no direct bearing on the Ripper case. But it is an example of the sort of underlying prejudice and suspicion which may have been influencing those involved in the Ripper investigation. Burton had earlier written a pamphlet on Disraeli stressing his Jewishness.[63] As Colin Holmes has argued, 'Burton was engaged in building up an image of the Jews which would bring home the threat they posed to non-Jewish interests.'[64]

The depth of feeling against the Jewish population would surely not have been helped by the claims later made by several high-ranking police officers. Sir Robert Anderson's memoirs, *The Lighter Side of My Official Life*, were originally published in 1910 in serialised form, in *Blackwood's Magazine*. He discussed the Jack the Ripper case, stating that

> the conclusion we came to was that he and his people were low-class Jews, for it is a remarkable fact that people of that class in the East End will not give up one of their number to Gentile Justice. And the result proved that our diagnosis was right on every point. For I may say at once that 'undiscovered murders' are rare in London, and the 'Jack-the-Ripper' crimes are not in

that category. And if the police here had powers such as the French police possess, the murderer would have been brought to justice...[65]

In this case, 'Gentile justice' clearly equates with British justice, and Anderson thought it 'remarkable' that anyone might fail to trust it with the freedom of their fellow citizens. Clearly the 'low-class' Jews were not displaying the kind of respect and reverence for British law that those who were truly 'British' displayed. There must have been some kind of backlash in public opinion, criticising Anderson for his comments on Jews, because the text was altered in the book, which was published later in the same year.[66] There Anderson included a new statement:

> In saying that he was a Polish Jew I am merely stating a definitely ascertained fact. And my words are meant to specify race, not religion. For it would outrage all religious sentiment to talk of the religion of a loathsome creature whose utterly unmentionable vices reduced him to a lower level than that of the brute.[67]

The damage was surely already done. If Anderson really did have genuine evidence against a particular suspect, then the case could have been brought to trial in a court of law at the time. If the suspect was dead by then, at least the evidence the police had against him could have been published with any allegation. If Anderson did not have sufficient evidence to convince a jury beyond reasonable doubt, then he arguably should have said nothing. To cast direct aspersions on the Jewish population of the East End, without bringing any suspect to trial, was an abuse of his power. Without actually accusing or imprisoning anyone, he had succeeded in placing the blame for the murders on the shoulders of the Jews. The Jewish community had no means of defending itself against such a vague charge, and no suspect was given the chance to clear his name in court. The only clue that Anderson gave in support of his statement is that the suspect was identified by a witness in the case but that he had refused to give evidence against him because he was a fellow Jew.[68] Such vague eye-witness identification evidence, not tested in court, does not make Anderson's case legally satisfying.[69]

Chief Constable Sir Melville MacNaughten wrote a memorandum in 1894 when a man by the name of Thomas Cutbush was being accused in the press of being the Ripper.[70] In defence of Cutbush, MacNaughten named the three suspects he claimed were most likely to be the Ripper. These were Michael Ostrog, a mad Russian doctor, Montague Druitt, a barrister and schoolteacher who committed suicide soon after the murders, and Aaron Kosminski, a Jew placed in an asylum after the murders.[71]

The naming of Kosminski has led leading 'Ripperologists' to conclude that he was the 'lower-class Jew' suspected by Anderson, and that he is therefore the suspect most likely to be the Ripper.[72] This is supported by the discovery of a marginal note written by Detective Chief Inspector Donald Swanson in his copy of Anderson's memoirs. Swanson wrote that the Jew in question was Kosminski.[73] On the evidence of the speculation of three police officers, who were operating in a climate where anti-Semitic feelings were strong in the East End, a Polish Jew has become the leading suspect in one of the most notorious series of murders in British history. The behaviour of Anderson in particular has meant that Kosminski is in danger of being found guilty by the judgement of history. As he had with Parnell, Anderson accused an individual of crimes in the absence of evidence while simultaneously calling into question the characteristics of the particular 'outsider' group the individual came from. Hideous murder was clearly an 'un-British' activity that only 'others' were capable of.

The majesty of the British law may have stood intact, but the agencies charged with its implementation did not always seem to be equally blind. During the height of the Ripper scare, Anderson took a tough approach to the protection of the group of people who seem to have been the primary target of the Ripper. In his autobiography, he discusses a conversation he had with the Home Secretary upon Anderson's return from a holiday on the Continent in 1888.

> ... I went on to say that the measures I found in operation were, in my opinion, wholly indefensible and scandalous; for these wretched women were plying their trade under definite Police protection. Let the Police of that district, I urged, receive orders to arrest every known 'street woman' found on the prowl after midnight, or else let us warn them that the Police will not protect them.[74]

Rather than apologising for the police failure to prevent a series of horrific murders, Anderson laid the blame at the door of the victims for daring to practise their trade outside at night. He feigned ignorance of the economic realities of life for East End prostitutes. Anderson was able to blame firstly the Jews and secondly the prostitutes themselves for the murders. Both were 'outsider' groups, and public attention focused on them would protect from criticism the government and police for not having arrested the perpetrator of the crimes. Would such an approach have been taken had any other class of people been involved? Were British officials in Ireland told, in the wake of the Phoenix Park murders of 1882, that if they insisted on travelling at night the police would not protect them? The police failed in the Ripper case not so much in their inability to catch the killer as in their uninterest in protecting his particular class of victim. Prostitutes were not to be seen as objects of sympathy, for this would undermine their status as morally unacceptable citizens.

CHAPTER 8

'UN-BRITISH' WOMEN: THE PROBLEM OF PROSTITUTION

Women in early Victorian Britain were legally disadvantaged. They could not vote in national elections until the twentieth century. They could not stand for or sit in Parliament. Married women could not refuse the sexual advances of their husbands, own their own property or enter into contracts in their own name. They could not sue or be sued in court except through their husbands. They could not enter universities or the 'professions' like medicine and law. Nevertheless, women as a whole were not an outsider group in the sense of the others so far discussed. They were not a group targeted specifically by the law for being in some way 'un-British'.

There was at least one glaring exception – prostitutes. Prostitutes were targeted by the law for being morally 'un-British'. That prostitutes were kept on the periphery by the laws created by male British lawmakers was appreciated by Josephine Butler in her fight against the Contagious Diseases Acts. Butler, listening to the complaints of a prostitute that she had been manhandled by men, from police to medical examiners to biblical rescuers, noted that 'it was a Parliament of men only who made this law which treats you as an outlaw. Men alone met in committee over it. Men alone are the executives.'[1]

The Victorian establishment in the second half of the nineteenth century was determined to face down two sets of 'un-British' moral deviants. Firstly, prostitutes had to be ostracised and regulated at one and the same time. And secondly, British lawmakers were faced with the emergence of the other great moral nemesis of late Victorian society – homosexuality.

Prostitutes in Victorian Britain were subject to legal physical interference which other women were spared. Like homosexuals, prostitutes represented a threat to the moral order, a potentially corrupting force which could reach to the very centre of power. Unlike homosexuality, prostitution was tolerated as a necessary evil, providing an outlet for the animal passions of otherwise respectable Victorian men.[2] Prostitutes on the streets represented a special threat because they could not be controlled or even measured. The Contagious Diseases Acts highlighted this need for control, which might neutralise the threat of a previously unquantified peril. As Helen Self has argued, it was the perception that prostitutes were 'abnormal' that legitimised the impulse to control them.[3]

Prostitution in London was not restricted to 'sordid' meetings in alleyways. There were several brothels in the West End specifically aimed at gentlemen of means.[4] Discreet and fashionable, they represented the respectable face of prostitution in a society increasingly concerned about the apparent abundance of that vice. Indeed, it was in the ranks of the prostitutes of the 'upper classes' that governments faced their greatest dilemmas. Such women could be amongst the most sought-after associates in high society. For instance, Laura Bell, supposedly notorious for her loose morals, was in fact very friendly with William Gladstone and his wife.[5] The Gladstones of course had an established reputation as rescuers of prostitutes, but that does not seem to have been their motivation in visiting Bell. It was a social friendship such as one might have with any other scions of London society.

Catherine (Skittles) Walters's reputation was so great that people would come to admire her on her drives in Hyde Park.[6] The Prince of Wales was a keen attendee of her parties.[7] The loose morals of the Prince of Wales were hardly a secret, and the fact that he attended the parties of a woman of doubtful reputation would come as no surprise. Nevertheless, it remains an interesting fact relating to the social status of Catherine Walters. Donald MacAndrew maintains that Skittles reflected the contradictions of Victorian society. He writes, 'Everybody knows the quiet tints of the Victorian wife, pious, noble, pure, highly progenitive. Reverse all these and you have the Victorian mistress.'[8]

Trevor Fisher has identified three distinct periods in the history of prostitution through the long nineteenth century.[9] The period 1790–1849 saw increasing publicity about prostitution and a push for more police action, led by the likes of Patrick Colquhoun in his writings.[10] The period 1844–64 marked, in Fisher's eyes, a time of 'uneasy toleration', which was then followed by a Puritan reaction that increased in strength through the remainder of the century.[11] As Fisher has indicated, the toleration of the middle years was indeed 'uneasy', as Parliament wrestled with the problems of addressing the vice without being seen to legitimate it by even discussing it. A succession of unsuccessful Bills finally gave way to the Protection of Women Bill, passed in 1849, which addressed the issue of procurement rather than prostitution per se.[12]

A stream of social commentators kept the issue of prostitution at the forefront of community fears for much of the mid and later nineteenth century.[13] Chief among these in the 1850s were William Acton and Henry Mayhew. Acton wrote a work specifically on prostitution, obsessed far more with the moral laxity of his subjects than with developing an understanding of the wider economic causes that may have led them to their situation.[14] Acton was hardly unique in this. Most contemporary commentators saw personal failings as the root cause of prostitution. To admit that economic causes were at the root of the evil would be to blame forces beyond the individual.[15] By sheeting home the blame to the practitioners of prostitution, an 'outsider' group was created that could assume all the burdens of troubled Victorian sexuality and deflect attention from wider social problems.

Writers such as Acton, Mayhew and W.R. Greg provided the intellectual foundation for treating prostitutes as outsiders. Prostitutes were threats to society and to British sensibilities because it was their personal moral corruption that was seen to drive them forth. They were not victims; they were a societal disease in search of victims. As Fraser Harrison has written, '... it was essential that the class from whom prostitutes were recruited was credited by the class that kept them in business with a fundamentally sinful sexual nature'.[16] The law was targeted towards achieving that end. Both through the Contagious Diseases Acts and through the system of regulation they introduced, prostitutes were left on the fringes of a society that could not live with them nor live without them.

The law emphasised the degraded nature of prostitutes, and by so doing validated the morality of the majority of middle- and upper-class women. To be 'British' was to be pure of such stains. To put it in utilitarian terms, the respect and dignity of a few had to be sacrificed to buttress the self-belief of the many. Mayhew seems to go a little further in recognising the financial aspects of prostitution. He describes how some young widows of street-sellers became prostitutes ('try the streets') in order to avoid starvation.[17] Yet he shares the difficulties of his fellows in being able to separate that fact from the idea of inherent character flaws amongst prostitutes. For instance, he writes that Irish women who fall 'into licentious ways' are the most 'savagely wicked'.[18]

It was in the East End of London that prostitution took on perhaps its most dangerous forms, where some prostitutes would meet with their clients outside, in dark alleyways or staircases. It was this practice that saw most of the victims of Jack the Ripper meet their death alone and without witnesses. Charles Booth, perhaps the most famous late-Victorian social commentator, was well aware of the dangers:

> The only utterly exposed class are the low women, who, under cover of darkness, make use of back streets and open spaces, and whose unprotected state gave rise to the horrible tragedies of a few years back.[19]

Historians simply do not know how many prostitutes were operating in London at various times in the nineteenth century. Police records only reflect the number of prostitutes actually identified as such or charged with an offence.[20] Mayhew, using these figures, asserted that 42,954 women had been taken into custody for prostitution between 1850 and 1860.[21] This figure in itself may be inflated, given that many of the arrests may have been of the same women year after year. To confuse the issue further, there were many women who were only part-time prostitutes, turning to it in desperation during hard times.[22] This unquantifiability was itself a threat to societal order. Like the unruly mobs of protest, a picture of faceless thousands must have seemed threatening to those seeking to regulate morality utilising people's awe of the law. To quote David Jones, 'These people of the streets mocked and appeared to threaten the very existence of an industrious, settled, Christian and family way of life...'[23]

Judith Walkowitz's work has shown that concern over prostitution by the 1880s went beyond fears over decay in family life, to unease about sexual and geographical freedom, especially for women. She writes:

> ...concern over 'dangerous' sexual practices focused on much more than disorderly sexual conduct: dangerous sexualities had as much to do with work, life-style, reproductive strategies, fashion and self-display, and nonfamilial attachments of urban men and women as with nonprocreative sexual activity.[24]

The law itself was of course far from comfortable in dealing with prostitution. Police and magistrates often clashed over the extent to which a police officer's uncorroborated charge was to be believed. For instance, 1864 saw correspondence between the police and the Secretary of State Sir George Grey about the practice of the magistrate at Westminster, Mr Selfe, of keeping a 'black book' in which he placed marks of credibility next to the names of various constables that appeared before him.[25] The case that triggered the activity involved the arrest of a prostitute, Emma Belgrave, and the extent to which the story of the arresting constable was to be believed in court. This led to a meeting in October between Selfe and the Metropolitan Police Commissioner, Sir Richard Mayne, to try and smooth out the communication channels between these two branches of law enforcement. Another magistrate, T.J. Arnold, was critical of police evidence so often that police were reluctant to appear in his court.[26]

Mayhew was not wholly condemnatory of all prostitutes, but his disgust for those who were unfortunate enough to be arrested was absolute:

> In an unreflective mood I should be inclined to say that prostitutes, taken collectively, were most abandoned, reckless, and wicked; but it is apparent, after a minute's study, that they must not be taken collectively. This forty odd thousand should be understood to represent, for the most part, the very dregs, the lowest, most unthinking, and vilest of the class.[27]

Public opinion, and the legislation which was to some extent driven by it, was aimed at the vices associated with prostitution as much as the practice itself.[28] 'Respectable' society was concerned at bawdy behaviour in the streets, at men being solicited on street corners. Concerted efforts were made to inhibit child prostitution, and the allurement of women to foreign countries in a trade that was known as white slavery.[29] There was similar concern at the spread of sexually transmitted diseases, which were largely blamed on prostitutes. The concern was most fervently expressed in relation to its innocent victims. Children born of a mother with venereal disease could suffer greatly, and appear to have had a significantly higher infant mortality rate than other sections of the population.[30] In a religious age, it was this contamination, more than sympathy for the prostitutes or their male clients, that drove the agenda. It was factors such as these that enabled prostitutes and their profession to be targeted by lawmakers. Few people had sympathy for women seen as morally culpable, and rife with venereal disease to boot. The Contagious Diseases Acts simply reinforced and legitimised the position of prostitutes as 'outsiders' – as 'un-British' women who had to be regulated and controlled.

State action materialised most readily when venereal disease was seen to be a health threat to members of the armed forces. Rates of infection in the army and navy were high, and it was in towns containing army barracks that action was first taken. The Contagious Diseases Acts of 1864, 1866 and 1869 subordinated women's liberties to the need of the state to control disease.[31] The Acts were both limited and specific in their operation. They were targeted mainly at controlling the spread of venereal disease in the army and navy and therefore operated in garrison towns only, excluding the large cities like London. They were also targeted solely at women, a fact not lost on contemporary critics of the scheme. Prostitutes who refused to comply when selected for inspection could be brought before a magistrate, who had the power to order inspection and even to impose prison sentences upon the uncooperative.[32] Prostitutes were portrayed as people whose profession disqualified them from the right to bodily integrity accorded to other Britons. They could be examined for disease and then held against their will for treatment. This legal apparatus isolated prostitutes from the rest of society, placing them within a legally enforced outsider status.

Judith Walkowitz has argued persuasively that the Acts were instrumental in reiterating that prostitutes were outcasts from respectable society.[33] By insisting that prostitutes became registered and be regularly inspected, the State was making it harder for younger women to enter and leave prostitution as a stage in their lives. Prostitutes were in effect branded by the State. Walkowitz indicates that part of the agenda may indeed have been to create an outcast group:

> The Acts represented an attempt to clarify the relationship between the unrespectable and respectable poor. They were designed to force prostitutes to accept their status as public women by destroying their private identities and associations with the poor working-class community.[34]

British lawmakers, in creating such laws, could get away by hiding behind the rhetoric of the law. To quote social geographer Miles Ogborn, 'The questions of the liberty of the subject raised by the policing arrangements were to be diffused by setting the whole administrative machinery well within the language and institutional framework of the law.[35] The 'normal' Briton was encouraged to revere the rule of law, and once something was declared to be a legitimate target for legal intervention it equally became a legitimate target for social ostracism. British lawmakers were rallying the people around the image of a morally pure Britain.

These new powers were, however, anything but uncontroversial. Agitation against them on the grounds of women's rights and of utility was strong and constant throughout the 1870s, finally leading to their repeal in 1886.[36] Under the leadership of Josephine Butler, the Ladies National Association lobbied loudly for the repeal of the Acts.[37] Josephine Butler was also the voice of the Vigilance Association for the Defence of Personal Rights, which in 1886 became the Personal Rights Association.[38] There was strong support from several Liberal Members of Parliament on the grounds that the Acts offended against civil liberties and gave the police a degree of power with which they could not be trusted.

Not all towns were willing to allow local prostitutes to be isolated from their communities by the force of law. A case at Dover in 1881 brought the community together in condemnation of the Contagious Diseases Acts. On 1 August, William Hobson of Dover wrote to Home Secretary Harcourt:

> On the 25th of April last I wrote you a letter as chairman of a crowded and enthusiastic public meeting, held in this town on the 31st of March, at which a resolution was passed strongly condemning the action of the C.D. Acts police in chasing a girl named Elizabeth Burley through the public streets, both unjustifiably and illegally...[W]hether the girl was or was not immoral has nothing whatever to do with the illegal conduct of the police, a fact that I think you will readily admit.[39]

The *Dover Express* of 18 March, 1 April and 8 April 1881 was supportive of the town's stance against the police action in the case. Elizabeth Burley, in attempting to evade the police, had either fallen or, according to police, jumped from the pier. She was charged with attempting to commit suicide.[40] Prostitutes had to struggle hard indeed to avoid the strictures of the law, in a society which relied upon them to verify its own morality.

Ranged against opponents of the Contagious Diseases Acts were the conservative figures who felt that not nearly enough was being done to combat the menace of prostitution. William Acton, in a new preface to his 1857 work, was a key supporter of the introduction of legislation to control venereal disease. He was convinced that the Acts represented progress:

> The working of this Act, and the public attention called to the subject, has been attended with the happiest results, both as regards the health of our army and navy, and the sanitary and moral improvement wrought in the unhappy women who have come within the scope of its provisions.[41]

The Association for the Extension of the Contagious Diseases Act was formed in 1866 to agitate for the medical examination of prostitutes to be universal, rather than limited to garrison towns.[42] Such a move had Acton's full support.[43] At the same time, Acton acknowledged that a large number of women were only prostitutes for a short time.[44] This did not sit well, as Walkowitz has made clear, with the stigmatising effect that registration could bring. Acton was providing intellectual grist for the rhetorical mill of British lawmakers. Prostitution was a moral evil, marking out prostitutes as moral outsiders who needed to be targeted by the law to prevent the extension of their moral contagion, as well as physical disease. Acton seems to have been more concerned for the clients of prostitutes than for the women themselves:

> The reader who is a conscientious parent must perforce support me; for, were the sanitary measures I advocate once in operation, with what diminished anxiety would he not contemplate the progress of his boys from infancy to manhood.[45]

In Acton's world, it was a given that young men might use prostitutes on their path to manhood. Acton saved his moral condescension for the women who provided that service.

The War Office was, on the whole, pleased with the Acts as a necessary measure to protect the men of the services. The War Office records for 1875, for instance, contain the observations of the Director-General of the army medical department 'on the effects of the Contagious Diseases Acts', and responds to a pamphlet by Dr Birkbeck Nevins, a supporter of the Association for the repeal of the Contagious Diseases Acts. Dr Birkbeck's objections can be summarised as follows:

1) that the Acts provided legislative recognition of prostitution, which was undesirable;
2) that the Acts encouraged men's 'licentiousness'; and
3) '...whilst they legislate for man as if he was an object requiring extraordinary protection, they treat woman as if she was little more than an instrument for the satisfaction of male passions, and reduce the subjected women to a depth of moral degradation below that of ordinary prostitutes not subject to such enactments'.[46]

Captain Harris, an assistant C.D. Acts Commissioner, and Mr Sloggett, Inspector of Certified Hospitals, responded to Birkbeck's criticisms point by point in their War Office report. They claimed vindication by

> the testimony of the magistrates, clergy, and influential inhabitants of the towns of Plymouth, Devonport, Stonehouse, and Dartmouth, of the town council, the clergy, and most influential inhabitants of Winchester, of the magistrates and clergy of Dover, of the board of guardians of Farnham Union, at all of which places the Acts are in force, expressed in memorials or petitions to the Board of Admiralty or the Secretary of State for War, praying for their continuance.[47]

In other words, the authorities in the various towns supported the Acts. Magistrates and 'influential inhabitants' saw the necessity for using the force of law to isolate moral deviants. Given the later town meetings at Dover over the Elizabeth Burley affair, one must take the assertions of Harris and Sloggett with a grain of salt. The War

Office records of 1883 contain 'statistics relative to the suspension of the Contagious Diseases Acts'.[48] It was asserted by the compiler of the information that, 'If the Contagious Diseases Acts had been universally applied, they would, by the same reasoning, have prevented at least 186 men being permanently in hospital.'[49] Again, the emphasis on the wellbeing of men, as against the disregard for the wellbeing of sexually impure women, is striking. There could be no chivalry for those who had shown themselves unworthy of 'British womanhood'.

The Association for the Extension of the Contagious Diseases Acts argued that prostitutes as a whole in fact supported the Acts and realised that they were in place for their own good.[50] Not all contemporaries agreed with that analysis, Annie Clark saying she 'would rather spend fourteen years in prison than submit to it'.[51] Historian Jane Lewis indicates that 'women on the whole were in favour of protective legislation', while suggesting that there was working-class resentment at the inspections.[52] The Association defended the lack of similar checks for the men who used prostitutes by insinuating that the prostitutes, as temptresses, bore greater moral guilt than the men who had been unable to fight such temptations of the flesh.[53] It is noteworthy that arguments ran essentially along lines of civil liberties rather than any defence of prostitutes as a morally wronged class of persons. Both camps were united in their disgust with prostitution, and disagreed only on whether to suppress, regulate or ignore the vice.

The agitationists for abolition eventually won the debate, and the Acts were repealed in 1886, having been suspended in 1883. In some ways the Contagious Diseases Acts can be seen as an example of where the British elite made an incorrect judgement. They underestimated the extent of the opposition to such a measure. They had used the law in a way that even 'respectable' women found offensive. The mobilisation of high-profile women in the campaign for repeal again may well have taken British lawmakers by surprise. It undermined the ability of the British Government to utilise the measures as a method of defining female conformity, because a significant section of women refused to accept that prostitutes should be made legal outcasts in this way. No-one was arguing that prostitution was a moral good, but there was significant and effective opposition to the idea that the law had a role to play in physically invading women's bodies.

The Criminal Law Amendment Act of 1885 attempted to address crime that revolved around prostitution, as well as the less savoury parts of the profession itself.[54] W.T. Stead, the editor of the *Pall Mall Gazette*, had revealed facts about levels of child prostitution in the metropolis, and these were to be addressed by the legislation.[55] The series of articles printed under the collective title of 'The Maiden Tribute of Modern Babylon' excited public debate in unprecedented fashion.[56] The National Vigilance Association, with William Coote as its secretary, was formed in 1885 to ensure that Stead's revelations were addressed and that the social purity of Britons was encouraged.[57] The so-called revelations provided by Stead were hardly unknown.[58] Henry Mayhew had documented 25 years earlier that English women could be sent overseas as prostitutes and that foreign women were imported into England for the same reason.[59]

The Metropolitan Police took Stead's revelations seriously enough to initiate an extensive investigation of his claims. The reports of various superintendents, forwarded to the Commissioner on 26 July 1885, did their best to dismiss the allegations. Superintendent 'B' stated that 'the superintendent is of opinion that the violation of young girls to the extent described in the *Pall Mall Gazette* does not exist'.[60] The police were however well aware of the hypocrisy entailed in attempts by the Government to crack down on prostitutes, when some of their best clients came from within the ranks of society's privileged:

> That vice is largely supported and encouraged by what is called the upper class is patent at the West End, but this is a very different matter from the eyes of the police being deliberately closed to the wholesale debauching of young children.[61]

The starkest outcome of Stead's revelations was his own arrest on a charge of abduction in relation to his 'trapping' of a young woman in order to test how easy it was to lure someone into prostitution. The police then used Stead's status as an 'accused person' to justify not seeking his help to throw light on the allegations on child prostitution printed in the *Pall Mall Gazette*.[62] As one policeman assigned to investigate the claims in the *Pall Mall Gazette* wrote to Police Commissioner Munro, 'I had no wish to have dealings with a person, who broke the law under pretence of being actuated by benevolent motives'.[63] The 1885 Act signified the growing strength of morality as the foundation stone of late-nineteenth-century Britain, replacing the religious hatred of earlier years as a binding force for national unity. As Trevor Fisher has put it, 'From this point onwards, repressive attitudes towards prostitution became set in stone. Victorian Values at their most puritanical became the norm both legally and socially.'[64]

The police inevitably failed to please either side of the prostitution debate. They were reluctant to persecute prostitutes outright, because it could lead to falsely accusing innocent young women of being prostitutes simply because they were out alone at night. This in fact did happen on a number of conspicuous occasions, and the subsequent outcry against police invasion of private lives was hardly an incentive for police action.[65] In one particular case, Miss Cass, a milliner, was arrested for soliciting in Regent Street. The uproar that followed brought forward a picture of Miss Cass as an unblemished character, the epitome of wronged innocence.[66] This willingness by 'respectable' society to stand up for the accused should not be mistaken as providing a broader support for all women to be free to walk the streets without fear. Walkowitz argues that 'real' prostitutes were still to be considered outsiders whose lifestyle was to be abhorred:

> As classical female bodies emblematic of a closed, regulated, homogenous social order, Miss Cass and Queen Victoria stood in stark contrast to the female grotesques of the street, those 'foreign' prostitutes, who with 'glaring colours' and 'wicked glances' endeavoured to arrest the attention of passersby.[67]

There were consistent problems with convincing magistrates to convict on the basis of uncorroborated police evidence alone.[68] This, according to the magistrates, was not because they were 'soft' on prostitution. As Magistrate Newton wrote to Sir James Ingham on 4 April 1889,

> I hope that you will assure the Secretary of State that it was not from any desire, on my part, that the Streets should not be freed from the Pest, which they are now subjected to, that I did not at once fall into the views of the Commissioner of Police.[69]

Very few men who had been solicited or had consorted with prostitutes were eager to describe those actions to a magistrate, and yet their evidence was crucial to ensuring conviction. Metropolitan Police Commissioner Sir Charles Warren issued directives to patrolling officers not to proceed against prostitutes unless corroborated evidence would be likely to be forthcoming.[70] In order to combat charges of police blackmail, Warren issued a police order on 19 July 1887 stating that

> the Commissioner considers it desirable that a Constable should not, himself, charge any woman for solicitation, but should only arrest when she is formally charged by the person annoyed or solicited, or by some inhabitant or passenger who can prove the annoyance.[71]

Police reluctance obviously enraged those trying to clamp down on prostitution. There certainly appears to have been an escalation in public interest and government response to the problem in the 1880s and 1890s. The Home Office was not impressed with the reluctance of the police and was not convinced that the Commissioner had the right to issue directives to his officers to ignore their duties.[72] Home Secretary Matthews did concede that 'arrest should be reserved for extreme cases where a woman will not move on'.[73] Various meetings with magistrates were held to overcome the impasse, with mixed success. The magistrates signalled their preparedness to accept police evidence, but clearly could not guarantee a conviction in each case.[74] Justice was supposed to be blind, and police pressure was not enough to tip the scales.

The law and its administration reflected the fact that prostitution was seen as a female vice, to which males could and did fall victim. By the late 1880s, with the ever-developing position of morality as a foundation stone of late-Victorian society, greater notice began to be taken of men's ability to escape prosecution for crimes of 'passion' in which they were at the very least equal participants. The case of Grace Blair in 1887 caused some consternation, because it resulted in a charge against her but none against the man with whom she had been engaging in offensive behaviour in public. On 19 July 1887, W. Booth J.P. wrote to Home Secretary Matthews about the case:

> Considering the man was equally guilty with the woman – did not deny the charge – but excused himself by saying she was introduced to him as a respectable person – that he was allowed to go free on giving his card. I very respectfully ask you Sir if this is not a partial and gross miscarriage of Justice? The girl is a prostitute because men are permitted to prostitute, but are never punished.[75]

Prostitutes had to be ostracised by the law because they represented uncontrollable passion. Their profession by its very nature seemed destined to undermine Victorian morality. Booth's comments were followed up by a similar question in Parliament by Henry Wilson, asking for the law to be amended to ensure that men and women were equally treated.[76]

Magistrate Vaughan was asked by the Home Office for his opinion on the case. His response indicates the wide gulf that had so long existed between men and women engaged in crimes against sexual morality:

> At the hearing before the Magistrates the various circumstances in the case viz the locality, the time, the publicity, & the probability of the act being witnessed by passers by, would all have formed subjects for their consideration, & if they had come to the conclusion that the case was not sufficiently established to justify them in committing the defendants for trial, they might

either have discharged the man absolutely, or bound him over in his own Recognizances or with Sureties for his good behaviour, & then have convicted the woman as a common prostitute to prison under the Statute.[77]

Wherever evidence was slight, women could always be convicted, but the man might have to be let go. The case came at an opportune time, because only a few months earlier the Metropolitan Police Commissioner had been sent a copy of the Vagrant Act Amendment Bill. According to the Memorandum accompanying the Bill, one of its objects was 'to assimilate the law as between the sexes. The present difference is a serious obstacle to the proper enforcement of the law.'[78]

The 1890s saw a further push, in the wake of the demise of the Contagious Diseases Acts, for new legislation to control public sexuality. The White Cross League, a Church of England society, wrote to the Home Office on 22 December 1893, with a number of suggested improvements to the law. They sought 'to have a Public Prosecutor in all large garrison Seaports to apply the laws against sexual immorality', a proposal reminiscent of the former Contagious Diseases Acts.[79] The League's proposals went further, to suggest 'that the words "female idiot or imbecile women" in s.5 of the Criminal Law Amendment Act should be deemed to include "women morally insane".'[80] On the front of the file a Home Office official has noted that, 'As examples of the "morally insane" they mention girls "who prostitute themselves, and molest men for that purpose, and are a source of great trouble and mischief".'[81] The dual Presidents of the White Cross League were the Archbishops of Canterbury and York. Although the relevant Home Office official described the idea as absurd because one would not be able to tell whether a girl was 'morally insane', the fact that a society with the support of the most powerful Churchmen in the land could put up such proposals reinforces how seriously late-Victorian Britain took its immorality.

The main corrupters of morals were still seen to be loose women, rather than the 'poor' and 'misguided' men who fell victim to them. The *Standard* of 4 May 1894 printed the story of an analysis done by Dr Lawson Tait of 70 cases of people charged under the Criminal Law

Amendment Act of 1885.[82] Tait alleged that the Act was allowing girls to falsely accuse men with impunity:

> Even where there is no pre-arranged conspiracy to extort money, it is easy enough to punish, with terribly undue severity, a person who has been guilty of a very minor offence, either in law or morals. Any precociously depraved servant girl who has 'gone wrong' has abundant facilities to fasten a charge upon some one who is not the real partner of her misadventure...[83]

As late as June 1896, the Archbishop of Canterbury was still seeking legislation to criminalise the spreading of a contagious disease.[84] The government, however, had been too badly burnt by the former Contagious Diseases Acts, and informed the Archbishop that legislation was unlikely.[85] In November 1894, the Executive Committee of 'those interested in the moral amelioration of the Garrison town of Dover' reported '... the necessity of a permanent official eg. an Inspector who would be charged with the duties of moral amelioration'.[86]

Contemporary chronicler Charles Booth argued that prostitutes relied on being easily spotted in public as being practitioners of their profession. He noted that, 'Even if for the moment they desire to hide their character, something in walk or manner is apt to betray them.'[87] He was not impressed with a sense that the majority of prostitutes were in fact seeking to be rescued from the clutches of their profession. He wrote that 'as a rule, it is rare to find any sense of sin, and if it can be aroused at all, it is very precarious'.[88] Booth put the blame for the evil on parents, employers and companions, a conglomerate who had all failed in their duty to provide correct guidance.[89] Booth's writings reflect the same underlying themes of individual responsibility for sin of earlier writers. They provided a fresh underpinning for prostitutes remaining outsiders. They were so clearly outsiders that just their walk or manner would be 'enough to betray them'. What is more, if they were generally not even sorry for their state of life, how could one consider them as representing anything other than 'un-British' values?

CHAPTER 9

CONTAINING DEVIANCE: THE LEGAL LIMITS OF MALE SEXUALITY

Of all the moral and sexual 'evils' that dominated the public mind in the late Victorian era, few aroused such passionate disgust as male homosexuality. In the words of the Attorney-General in 1871, sodomy was 'a crime held in peculiar detestation in this country'.[1] The idea that men could love men in a non-sexual sense was nothing new. It was a notion dating back to classical antiquity that was approvingly taught in the most esteemed universities. That this might develop into a sexual intimacy was what disturbed British lawmakers as they strove to protect the moral underpinnings of society from such 'un-British' behaviours.[2]

Moral uprightness was one of the foundations upon which British society supported itself in the late Victorian period. Homosexuality challenged it like no other vice. As Jeffrey Weeks has noted, prostitution was always tolerated to an extent. Homosexuality, at least after 1885, could be allowed no such freedom, at least publicly.[3] Within the upper class, there was perhaps a 'don't ask, don't tell' policy in relation to homosexual liaisons. What was vital was that all homosexual acts, and any alleged sexual attraction to men, were kept totally private, because their revelation would undermine the legitimacy of legislators as the protectors of society's morals. Prostitution was perhaps less of a threat, because it stemmed from male desires that 'British' men could understand. Homosexuality carried no such understanding for many of Britain's authorities. This became abundantly obvious in the way the Boulton and Park court case was run in 1870, which I'll come to shortly.

Sodomy did not become a secular crime in Britain until 1533, when it was legislated as a crime for which the penalty was death. Prior to this sodomy had been an ecclesiastical crime only, dealt with by the Church courts.[4] The transfer to a secular crime gave the state an interest in personal sexual behaviour it had previously not had. It was part of the broader move by the 'state', or the sixteenth-century equivalent of that entity, to increase the regulation of people's private lives following the English Reformation.

The crime of sodomy remained on the statute books, with the death penalty, until well into the nineteenth century. The death penalty was removed in 1828, and the crime itself abolished in 1861. It is perhaps pertinent here to draw a distinction between the crime of sodomy and the crime of unnatural practices between male persons that was to come. As Ed Cohen has pointed out, sodomy was a crime whether it was committed with a man, woman or animal, and reflected the Christian notion that the 'seed' of life should not be wasted.[5] The law against unnatural acts introduced in 1885 was aimed far more squarely at questions of public morality and the undesirability of an act seen as a perversion of true human sexual nature. As Porter and Weeks have noted, 'Homosexuality had scarcely been legal before then, but the new enactment represented a symbolic shift'.[6]

The debate over whether the State should indeed involve itself in the private sexual practices of its citizens was not an entirely new one in the 1880s. For example, in 1830 a surgeon serving with the 10th Cavalry in Bengal had written upon the subject:

> It always appears to me, that the punishment of this crime greatly exceeds the offence, and as we know there are many nations who think lightly of it, we may question, the justice of our own laws regarding it. If the crime must be noticed in our civil Courts, the

punishment should be ignominious and not capital; but I think it a question whether any notice should be taken of this offence, where violence is not offered. My reason for forming this opinion is, that I believe no bodily injury is sustained, nor is any injury done to the peace and happiness of civil society, as in the case of adultery.[7]

By the 1880s there was certainly widespread concern amongst lawmakers that questions of morality could have a very important impact indeed on the 'happiness of civil society'.[8] The 1885 Criminal Law Amendment Act arose out of the sensational revelations by W.T. Stead in the 'Maiden Tribute of Modern Babylon' articles alluded to earlier. The Act was aimed principally at raising the age of consent and trying to curtail the 'white slave' traffic. Henry Labouchere, a newspaper editor and MP, inserted an amendment dealing with unnatural practices between males. The fact that this was inserted as an individual afterthought rather than as government-sponsored legislation is itself a matter of interest, and will be discussed below.[9]

Before 1885, homosexuality was allegedly a largely unexplored phenomenon as far as the law was concerned Jeffrey Weeks has noted that:

> It is striking that as late as 1871 concepts both of homosexuality and of male prostitution were extremely undeveloped in the Metropolitan Police and in high medical and legal circles. Neither was there any comprehensive law relating to male homosexuality before 1885.[10]

Perhaps 1885 marked the critical point in the collective thought of the legislature. To have legislated prior to that might have been seen as giving credence to a vice that Parliament did not wish to acknowledge formally. Not to have legislated at that point would have provided no clear sanction to deal with a 'problem' that was increasingly seen to be undermining the sexual uprightness of Britons. However, the seemingly haphazard way the amendment was put forward militates against this view.

Homosexuality was not merely unknown to the law prior to 1885, it was in fact unknown to the language. The word itself and the concepts surrounding it only gained common currency in the 1890s and beyond, as writers like Edward Carpenter, Havelock Ellis and J.A. Symonds began to tackle this supposedly new subject matter.[11] Porter and Weeks have drawn attention to the fact that such writings could give solace to homosexuals, as well as the more negative results that unwelcome public discussion might bring: 'Writers such as these provided a vocabulary through which homosexually inclined people could give meaning to their feelings, and recognise that they were not the only such individuals in the world.'[12]

It was perhaps only after the passage of the 1885 Act that homosexuality became a dominant moral issue. There had been homosexual scandals before the Act, the Boulton and Park case in 1870 being the most prominent. But there was a 15-year gap between that case and the enactment of legislation directed specifically at that vice, and then thanks only to an individual amendment rather than to concerted government action. The reason for the 15-year gap is a matter for speculation. It seems likely, given the language used both by the judge and the Attorney-General in the Boulton and Park case, discussed below, that Britain did not wish to acknowledge the presence of a taint that it saw as belonging to other countries. To legislate against homosexual practices would constitute an admission that there were examples of this behaviour in Britain that necessitated legislation. The Attorney-General, appearing as the prosecuting counsel in the Boulton and Park case, applauded the fact that crimes of sexual perversion were little known in Britain.[13] As Ivan Crozier has argued, 'The ignorance of the doctors who tendered evidence at the trial essentially acted as a vindication of the morality of the English nation.'[14]

The Boulton and Park case of 1870 was one of the major homosexual scandals of the late nineteenth century.[15] Ernest Boulton and Frederick William Park had been arrested after being frequently found publicly wearing women's clothing. Like Oscar Wilde after them, they flaunted their disregard for accepted masculine behaviour in such a way that the authorities were goaded into action. Letters were seized and read at trial that suggested improper intimate relationships had been established amongst a group of men. One of the men, Lord Arthur Clinton, committed suicide before the trial.

The evidence presented in court seems on the whole to have been circumstantial and unconvincing, while the behaviour of the police was also brought into the spotlight. The judge hearing the case was displeased that a police surgeon had been allowed to carry out rectal examinations of the prisoners without judicial warrant.[16] Nonetheless, when the two men were acquitted, the judge made a point of urging Parliament to pass laws prohibiting men from dressing as women.[17] Pearsall has taken a rather positive view of the success of the defence in winning the case by praising the jury:

> It was an expression of live and let live, of the late nineteenth-century rejection of an outdated penal code, of the treadmill and the whip that Cockburn had promised for future offenders against public decency.[18]

While the jury may have been swayed by such considerations, it is perhaps a little optimistic to suggest that they saw the matter in those terms. It is far more likely that it was simply a case where the evidence was insufficient to procure a conviction for a crime that attracted a great deal of media publicity and condemnation of the defendants.

Certainly the Crown strove for a conviction, the Attorney-General himself taking on the task of prosecuting the case. The trial highlights the importance the government placed on protecting the moral foundations of society. In his opening speech, the Attorney-General suggested that he prosecuted with a 'peculiar reluctance when I see before me four Gentlemen, for such they are, well educated, and well connected'.[19] Why would the Attorney-General feel more reluctant to prosecute these men than any other? Because they were, by all appearances, 'British' types. Well educated and 'well connected', they would normally be pillars of British society, but the moral danger posed by their alleged crime outweighed their position. Only royalty and the upper aristocracy were high enough to warrant their protection from such a charge, as shall be discussed later. The judge was just as ready as the Attorney-General to play his part in protecting the edifice of the law. In his summing up, Lord Chief Justice Cockburn suggested:

> It would be fatal to the character of this country if guilt when detected were allowed to go unpunished and unscathed. The first and greatest attribute of a great nation is the moral character of its people. The second which is one of almost equal importance is the sacred cause of truth and justice.[20]

In essence, Cockburn provided a summary of the establishment position as it unfolded in late Victorian Britain. Morality was a foundation stone of society, which could only be protected by the rule of British 'truth and justice', allowing Britons to feel pride in the 'majesty of British Law' and in the moral uprightness of their country. To be homosexual was simply irreconcilable with being 'British'. On that basis, the defence could argue that the accused must be innocent because such immorality simply did not exist in England, and the prosecution could argue for conviction because such immorality must not be allowed to gain a foothold in England.[21] Such 'innocence' of course could not go on forever.[22] By 1895 and the trial of Oscar Wilde, British law could no longer claim that it knew nothing of crimes of homosexual passion.

As Oscar Wilde was to discover, societal disapproval in the later nineteenth century had moved from people's beliefs and cultural differences to a need to control their sexual actions. This was part of the greater shift from a concentration on the use of religion as a source of national unity to the use of morality as the stronger binding force. The 1885 Criminal Law Amendment Act does not perhaps mark the start of that change, but it is a significant part of it. The Contagious Diseases Acts had shown that governments were prepared to legislate on matters which in large part concerned people's morality. This trend was confirmed by the Criminal Law Amendment Act of 1885. The bulk of the Act deals with measures to inhibit child prostitution.

But one of the historically most important parts of the Act dealt with a seemingly totally unrelated area, that of homosexuality. The term 'homosexuality' was not used, and indeed was not yet in popular use in Britain, but aim was taken at the mischief of 'gross indecency' between males.[23]

It was the force of law that shaped public opinion. As Ed Cohen has argued through the title of his article 'Legislating the Norm', 1885 was a case of the Government shaping societal values through legislation. In the process it created an outsider group, consisting largely of people who would have remained 'respectable' but for the public revelation of their sexuality. Lord Arthur Somerset was equerry to the Prince of Wales prior to his disgrace in the Cleveland Street Scandal (discussed below). Lord Euston, although cleared in court in the same case, saw his prestige take a pounding. The general Victorian obsession with sexual morality at last had an outlet. Homosexuals as a group could take upon their shoulders the responsibility for the perversions of a nation. Along with prostitutes, homosexuals existed as an outsider group to make other people feel good about themselves and their status in society. The philandering husbands of all classes could console themselves with the thought that at least they were indulging in nothing unnatural. Theirs was an understandable 'British' passion, legitimised by the legislative provision of disease-free prostitutes to satisfy male desires. The concern over homosexuality was less about the sexuality of a deviant minority group than about the sexuality of the broader society which needed to be maintained.[24] As Jeffrey Weeks has noted, 'By creating the homosexual as a scapegoat you simultaneously bolster acceptable forms of behaviour and isolate the deviant.'[25]

What is historically puzzling is how little debate the 'indecent practices' section of the 1885 Act prompted in Parliament. It was an amendment proposed by Henry Labouchere, who gave little reason for introducing it. In a debate spanning many pages of *Hansard* on the 1885 Act, only one column is devoted to this amendment. Labouchere introduced it on 6 August 1885, to what can only be described as a warm reception. He did not seek to explain why the clause was necessary, or what popular evil it was aimed at. *Hansard* states:

> He did not think it necessary to discuss the proposal at any length, as he understood Her Majesty's Government were willing to accept it. He, therefore, left it for the House and the Government to deal with as might be thought best.[26]

Clearly there had been some Government consideration of the measure before its introduction on the floor of the House, and the Government had indicated its support. The depth of that support swiftly became apparent. No-one spoke against the amendment, and the only change was that Sir Henry James suggested that the period of imprisonment for the offence be altered to two years with hard labour. Apart from an inconsequential comment by Mr Hopwood, that was the entirety of the debate on the measure that was to have such consequences for Oscar Wilde ten years later.[27] In the Lords, the amendment was not even mentioned and the Bill was passed as amended by the Commons. It is undoubtedly a measure of the prevailing prejudices of the time that such a measure could pass without a single voice in either house of Parliament being raised to discuss it.

Henry Labouchere, the man responsible for the amendment which potentially criminalised thousands of his fellow Britons, provides another interesting case-study of the insider/outsider dichotomy. As already noted, he was a strong critic of the Salisbury Government over its treatment of Parnell. To all appearances, one would not consider him an 'insider'. He founded and edited the *Truth* newspaper, which was hardly seen as friendly towards the Establishment. According to Claire Hirshfield, 'His villains included the established church, the landed aristocracy, the imperial bureaucracy and the monarchy.'[28] Yet, while in appearance at least he was a political outsider, he was a supporter of British tradition. As the views of his newspaper readily confirmed, he was anti-Semitic, anti-feminist and anti-homosexual in outlook.[29] With the exception of the Irish, he showed an aversion to all the groups examined in this study as 'outsiders'.

The debate on the 1885 Criminal Law Amendment Act was also notable for the extent to which it reinforced the Government view of what were the twin foundations upon which society was built, namely religion and morality. To quote Earl Fortescue, 'Wherever they found a population destitute of religious principle or moral convictions, there they were sure to have a great deal of vice and immorality.[30] In no area was that societal attitude more prevalent than that of homosexuality. Sodomy and its overtones of perversion were seen in the late nineteenth century as the apex of sexual wrongdoing. Being a homosexual per se was not an offence. Being a practising homosexual was of course a different matter. Two events, with very different outcomes, indicate the ways in which the law in this period could be used as an agency to protect the British ruling class and exclude outsiders. These events were the Cleveland Street scandal of 1889 and the Oscar Wilde trials of 1895. These two spectacles of late Victorian Britain were part of a broader pattern of events that served to highlight the 'un-Britishness' of men engaging in homosexual acts.

The Cleveland Street Scandal

The details of the Cleveland Street scandal are now relatively well known.[31] An address in Cleveland Street was found to house a brothel where men would call to have sexual relations with young boys. The existence of this establishment was discovered when a young male postal worker of 15 years of age was questioned by police over why he was carrying such large sums of money. He indicated that it was payment he had received for prostituting himself. It was revealed that a man named Charles Hammond was the proprietor of the premises, where he was assisted by George Daniel Veck, who claimed to be a clergyman. A further figure, by the name of Henry Newlove, was a Post Office clerk who acted as a recruiting agent for the brothel.[32]

Newlove was arrested. His arrest led to the revelation that Lord Arthur Somerset and the Earl of Euston were reportedly amongst the clients who had attended the brothel.[33] The alleged involvement of Lord Somerset and Earl Euston was the subject of informed speculation in the press, which nonetheless declined to name the persons involved. The *Pall Mall Gazette* smelt high-level complicity in the air from the start:

> But the question which Sir Augustus Stephenson [the DPP] will have to answer is whether the two noble lords and other notable persons in society who were accused by the witnesses of having been the principals in the crime for which the man Veck was committed for trial are to be allowed to escape scot free. There has been much too much of that kind of thing in the past. The wretched agents are run in and sent to penal servitude; the lords and gentlemen who employ them swagger at large and are even welcomed as valuable allies of the Administration of the day.[34]

The greatest scandal of all, however, seems to have been averted. There is some suggestion that the eldest son of the Prince of Wales, and the second in line to the throne, Prince Albert Victor (Eddy), was also among the customers at this particular establishment. The same Salisbury Government that had been so keen to hold a special commission into the entire Irish parliamentary party now showed a marked reluctance to bring anything to do with Cleveland Street into the light of day.

The lack of information on the extent to which Prince Eddy was in fact involved in the Cleveland Street Scandal is mysterious. Theo Aronson, in his 1995 work *Prince Eddy and the Homosexual Underworld*, sets out to make a thorough examination of his topic.[35] The facts that Aronson puts forward suggest that Eddy may have been involved, but that is all. The accusations were sufficiently well-known for the press in the United States to notice them. The *New York Herald* defended Prince Albert Victor and attacked those members of the press who had dared to bring the Prince's name into the affair.[36] Despite a remarkable attempt, the Government of Lord Salisbury was not able to save Lord Somerset from exposure for his actions, and he was forced to flee to the Continent.

Radical newspapers of the day were quite free in implying the involvement of the Government in an attempt to protect well-connected fugitives from justice. On 25 November 1889 the *Star* stated that, 'Amid the whirlwind of ghoulish rumors...one hears of Cabinet Councils discussing all the details and actively intervening in the course of justice.'[37] The *Referee* of 24 November 1889 discussed the exposure the scandal was getting 'despite the desperate efforts that have been made by the Cabinet, the Premier, and the highest male representative of royalty to cover it up and keep it from the public knowledge'.[38]

The British Government was in the trenches defending its own. Labouchere, in his *Truth* newspaper, saw it in terms of class warfare:

> Very possibly our Government of the classes is of [the] opinion that the revelations which would ensue, were the criminals put on their trial, would deal a blow to the reign of the classes, and to the social influence of the aristocracy.[39]

Reynold's Newspaper, for one, drew the conclusion that British justice was indeed showing itself to be anything but blind:

> We are constantly assured, remarks our contemporary, the *North London Press*, that in this country all are equal before the law. There is no distinction of persons, rich and poor are treated alike, equal measure is meted out to peer and peasant, to millionaire and pauper. No statement could be wider of the truth, and these incidents serve to demonstrate the absurdity of the contention; serve to show that there *is* one law for the rich and another for the poor, let ignorant or interested people say what they may.[40]

The *Truth* of 6 February 1890 ventured:

> Were I Mr Newton's legal adviser, I should advise him to subpoena Lord Salisbury, Mr Matthews, Mr Munro, the Public Prosecutor, and the gentleman who appeared against Newlove and Veck for the Treasury when those two persons were prosecuted at the Old Bailey.[41]

However, even the *Truth* knew its limits, and went out of its way to defend the behaviour of the royal family during the affair. In an article applauding the Prince of Wales for his willingness to see a 'full and public investigation', the *Truth* reinforced the position that the values of royalty were beyond question. 'As the head of society he is determined that, so far as he is concerned, the malpractices shall be stamped out and the guilty be punished.'[42] Such rhetoric served to reassure the public that the majesty of law still prevailed and that the royal head of society would uphold the law.

Aronson argues that it was Lord Salisbury himself, inadvertently or otherwise, who leaked the information to Lord Somerset that he was in danger of arrest if he remained in England.[43] If this claim is true, it provides a useful illustration of the kind of informal channels that were available to Governments. But for his homosexuality, Lord Somerset was clearly an acceptable 'British' man. He was of aristocratic blood, an equerry of the Prince of Wales, in every sense a 'true born Englishman'. The publicity that had emerged about Somerset's involvement no longer allowed the Government to protect him as totally as they had Prince Albert Victor. Therefore they did what they could to keep him from the dock of British justice, where his very presence would have discredited the class from which he came.

Salisbury's most recent biographer, Andrew Roberts, seems to support this view. Roberts's conclusion on this point is worth quoting at length:

> If Salisbury had, via a courtier, warned Beaufort's son [Somerset] to flee the country before a warrant was even issued, and the circumstantial evidence suggests that he did, it would have been out of general class solidarity with Somerset, as well as a desire to protect Prince Albert Victor, who would have been embarrassed at the revelation of his friend's activities. *Technically, Salisbury probably conspired to pervert the course of justice* and committed misprision of felony, and he would not have done so without good reason. With so much of the power of the upper classes resting on their social prestige and the deference accorded them by the

rest of society, Salisbury was acutely conscious of how politically dangerous such 'West End Scandals'... could be.[44]

In other words, Salisbury used his position to deflect the arrows of the law, safe in the knowledge that the law was unlikely to be visited upon him for his actions. Again this was public knowledge at the time, with *The Times* of 1 March 1890 publishing the parliamentary debate of the previous day, which had focused on the legitimacy of Salisbury's actions.[45] It had in fact been Salisbury who had ultimately decided back in July 1889 not to seek the extradition of Charles Hammond from France, where he had fled as the scandal unfolded.[46] This was probably more in order to protect those whom Hammond might expose if brought back to give evidence than from any desire to protect Hammond himself.

Salisbury was convinced that he had in no way perverted the course of justice. He gave a speech in the House of Lords in his own defence, published in *The Times* on 4 March 1890. The Prime Minister claimed that he had merely indicated to Sir Dighton Probyn, equerry to the Prince of Wales, that he understood that there was insufficient evidence with which to charge Lord Arthur Somerset. 'I think I added – I am not quite certain – that rumours had reached me that further evidence had been obtained, but I did not know what its character was.'[47] Salisbury was adamant that he had not indicated that a warrant was to be issued.[48]

Who was to pay the ultimate price for the Cleveland Street Scandal was a matter of further press discussion in late 1889. There were rumours of a Cabinet re-shuffle in the air, and the most likely contender to be left out was Henry Matthews. There is no indication that it was his Roman Catholicism that created hostility towards him, although the *New York Herald* ventured that he had 'never been a favourite with the Conservative Party'.[49] Referring to the Cleveland Street Scandal, they suggested 'We do not believe that he is the Minister really responsible, although he may consent to be made the scapegoat.'[50]

It is somewhat ironic that it was with Salisbury as Prime Minister in 1888 that the Cabinet considered a measure to ban from Parliament those found to be involved in public scandals, as part of a package of reforms to the House of Lords. In his report to the Queen, Salisbury wrote that 'A general concurrence was expressed in the policy of eradicating from both Houses of Parliament, members who had become connected with any public scandal'.[51] There seems to be no further record in the cabinet files of what happened to the measure. Perhaps Salisbury was wise enough to see that such a measure could have unlooked-for effects on his Government in the near future.

The same official pressure which was six years later brought to bear to ensure Oscar Wilde was found guilty was exercised to ensure that Somerset suffered no legal sanction for his actions. Whether it was just in the provision of time to flee or whether it extended to encouraging him to flee, the Government was arguably successful in 'perverting' the course of justice by allowing Somerset to escape to the Continent. Speculation regarding the involvement of Prince Eddy appeared in print in France and the United States of America, while newspapers in Britain remained apprehensive of legal action that might result from publication.[52]

Veck, Hammond and Newlove were all, after some months, indicted for various indecency offences. Veck and Newlove were imprisoned with hard labour for nine and four months respectively. In his article on aspects of the scandal, Martin Dockray has pointed out that the solicitor for the defendants had his bill paid by Lord Arthur Somerset. He goes on to say of the defendants that 'they were almost certainly also paid to plead guilty and go to gaol quietly'.[53] The perceived inadequacies of the sentences handed down served only to fuel public suspicions that the objective workings of the law were being tampered with. The *North London Press*, whose editor was being charged with criminal libel by Lord Euston for bringing his name into the matter, noted the differentiation between the sentences and those of others charged with similar offences. They discovered that 'at a previous Sessions, a minister at Hackney had been condemned to penal servitude for life, with the special warning from the judge that he could have no hope of a mitigation of his dreadful doom'.[54] Newlove had been arrested on 7 July 1889. Somerset, despite the evidence of Newlove, remained free and left for France on 18 October. Henry Labouchere asked in the

House of Commons why no action had been taken against Somerset or Lord Euston, whose alleged involvement in the scandal was now public knowledge.[55]

Dockray's study reveals that the Director of Public Prosecutions was in fact supportive of bringing Somerset to court.[56] What, then, stopped that happening? The Home Secretary Henry Matthews, the Lord Chancellor and the Prime Minister Lord Salisbury were in contact with each other from 10 August in relation to the case. The crux of that contact seems to have been a case of 'pass the parcel' until it was decided, on two separate occasions, that there was insufficient evidence for a prosecution.[57] This showed the benefits that could flow from manipulating the technicalities of law enforcement. Those in positions of governmental power did not need Acts of Parliament to successfully interfere successfully in the course of justice. As this incident demonstrates, they had far more subtle means at their disposal.

While these three prominent Government members were procrastinating, Somerset made his move for freedom in France. It is hard to disagree with Dockray when he writes: 'Webster's [the Attorney General] denial that a titled suspect had received special treatment was absurd. The Prime Minister, The Home Secretary, the Law Officers and the DPP were not normally involved in prosecutions for gross indecency.'[58]

Webster was in fact in an excellent position to know that favourable treatment had been accorded to Somerset, because Webster himself had unsuccessfully encouraged his prosecution. As early as 10 August, Webster, the Solicitor-General Edward Clarke, and H.E. Avory had provided their legal opinion 'that proceedings should be taken against the man Veck alias Barber and also against Lord Arthur Somerset'.[59] Lord Arthur Somerset's name appears several times in that opinion, held in the DPP files, and on each occasion someone has attempted to paste a strip of cardboard over the name. A more literal cover-up would be difficult to find. Webster wrote his own legal opinion to the Solicitor to the Treasury along the same lines. That opinion too is dated 10 August 1889, but someone has afterwards indicated with a 'sic' that it should be 10 September.[60] The initials accompanying the change do not appear to be those of Webster. Nonetheless, whichever date is correct, it was still some time before a warrant was issued against Somerset. The delay occurred despite the fact that Webster expressly recommended prosecution of 'L.A.S.' under 'Section 11 of the Criminal Law Amendment Act 1885'.[61]

Webster was not the only one who was unhappy with the delay. The Commissioner of the Metropolitan Police, Munro, complained on a number of occasions that the police were being blamed in the press for inaction against Lord Arthur Somerset, when Munro's hands were tied by a lack of support from Government.[62] When Munro wrote on 5 October, alerting the Attorney-General that Lord Arthur Somerset was in London, Webster was unable to advise an arrest until the opinion of the Lord Chancellor was sought.[63] After a two-day delay caused by an inability to contact the Lord Chancellor in a remote Scottish hideaway, the Lord Chancellor eventually advised that no action should be taken unless more corroborative evidence against Somerset was available.[64] Hamilton Cuffe, the deputy Director of Public Prosecutions, expressed his frustration at this to Sir Augustus Stephenson, the Director of Public Prosecutions, suggesting that there was sufficient corroborative material available to substantiate a charge.[65] The extent to which those involved in the case knew that the Government was interfering is revealed by Munro's letter to Cuffe on 10 October, stating: 'I can only deplore the delay which is being made in high quarters abt [sic] this horrible case.'[66]

The Lord Chancellor, Lord Halsbury, claimed to be unsatisfied that there was sufficient corroboration of the allegations to justify charging Somerset.[67] However, he also stated:

> If, as is alleged in these papers, the social position of some of the parties will make a great sensation this will give very wide publicity, and consequently will spread very extensively matter of the most revolting and mischievous kind, the spread of which I am satisfied will produce enormous evil.[68]

Under Halsbury's reasoning, men of the British Establishment had to be kept from the dock because the publicity relating to their downfall would undermine the moral foundations upon which British society rested. The Director of Public Prosecutions was not in agreement with

Halsbury's reasoning, a fact he wished to make clear in a letter to the Attorney General of 15 September 1889. He set about 'distinctly disclaiming as I now do, most respectfully but most decidedly any agreement with the opinion that the evidence now in our possession does not justify or call for the prosecution of LAS'.[69] He went on later to deal specifically with Halsbury's reasoning:

> The public scandal involved in a criminal charge against a man in his position in society is undoubted – but... In my opinion the public scandal in declining to prefer such a charge – and in permitting such a man to hold Her Majesty's Commission & remain in English Society is much greater.[70]

A man in 'English society', particularly one linked to the royal head of society, should be beyond reproach, in Stephenson's view. Stephenson continued to express his disapproval to the Home Office during October, and also to Munro, telling the latter on 22 October that the matter had been 'entirely out of [his] hands' for some time.[71]

The extent of the Government's direct involvement in the case is revealed in the correspondence between Home Secretary Matthews and Stephenson, the Director of Public Prosecutions. A letter of 31 August 1889 from Stephenson to Matthews states, 'I have just returned from conference with Mr Avory, & he will conduct the case on Tuesday in strict accordance with your views as expressed in the last paragraph of your letter to me of the 29th.'[72] This was despite the fact that Stephenson himself felt that the evidence against Somerset 'is stronger than that against Veck against whom a charge has been preferred'.[73] In effect, the Ministers of the day were running criminal cases in the British courts. Montesquieu's theoretical separation of powers – already imperfectly embodied in the Westminster system – was sorely tested indeed. It was a prime example of the government exercising its ability to decide the rules of the legal game in order to protect one of its own number. Matthews himself would hardly have been considered a 'solid Briton' 50 years before, due to his Roman Catholicism, but now was sufficiently entrenched to take part in what was almost certainly a perversion of the course of justice. Stephenson wrote again on 2 September to assure Matthews, 'As far as the prosecution is concerned every precaution will be taken to prevent any name being mentioned.'[74] This behaviour was not lost on the magistrate, Mr Hannen, who nevertheless maintained solidarity with the Government. A report to the Attorney-General of the proceedings contained comments made by Hannen to the prosecutor:

> ... that if this had been an ordinary case before him ... or indeed a case of this character – not conducted by the Treasury – he should have felt it his duty to call for the disclosure of the names of the persons identified by description & had them brought before him by warrant & included in the charge.[75]

The magistrate effectively admitted that he had changed his behaviour and not called someone to account for criminal actions because it was a matter conducted by the Treasury. All sections of British authority, lawmakers and executors had combined to protect Lord Somerset, and with him the moral foundations of 'British' values.

In an intriguing postscript, the Liberal leader William Gladstone received a letter in 1890 in relation to the O'Shea divorce case, threatening to expose the hypocrisy of the Establishment in protecting its own moral deviants while persecuting those who happened to come from an 'outsider' group. The letter, from a correspondent named Clifton, included the following passage:

> If my cousin C.S. Parnell is driven from the House of Commons even for five minutes Sir William Marriot shall go too, upon the same charge that has proved fatal to two other scapegoat cousins of mine, Henty and Arthur Somerset. Lord Wolmer can tell you more. The Bendevells and Parnells have been persecuted long enough and it is time for me to make a [sic] example.[76]

The Trials of Oscar Wilde

Silhouetted against the curious outcomes of the Cleveland Street Scandal are the series of trials and tribulations that marked the downfall of Oscar Wilde.[77] Oscar Wilde was an Irishman by birth, and as such might at first glance fit more readily into the discussion of Irish outsiders in earlier chapters. However, Wilde was of that class and religion of Irishmen that generally found easy acceptance amongst Britons.[78] His parents were wealthy, allowing him to pursue an education first at the exclusive, Anglican Trinity College in Dublin, and then at Oxford. A literary artist of rare skill and wit, he was happily accepted into Victorian society as a gifted if somewhat irreverent literary larrikin. He was known and appreciated by the powerful in Britain by virtue of the renown that his work brought to the culture that had produced him. He toured the United States to popular acclaim in the 1880s, and his star seemed destined for an ever-continuing rise. Works such as *The Picture of Dorian Gray* and *The Ideal Husband* ensured his place as one of the pre-eminent Victorians. What ultimately brought about Wilde's downfall was not the irreverence of his work, but his willingness to challenge contemporary society with his behaviour. As Richard Dellamora has recognized, the Wilde trials 'touched the very centre of the establishment'.[79]

It is impossible to provide any meaningful statistical analysis of just how many practising homosexuals sheltered behind Victorian Britain's sexually moralistic veneer. However, events such as the Cleveland Street scandal can perhaps provide some indication. Aronson's graphic revelation of the details of the homosexual underworld does nothing to downplay those indications.[80] Oscar Wilde's crime, however, was not simply being homosexual. It was his willingness to flaunt his sexuality publicly that eventually brought him undone. In 1892, Wilde made the acquaintance of a man who had all the attractions that youth and energy could provide. Not only that, he was a titled member of the British aristocracy. Lord Alfred Douglas, third son of the Marquess of Queensberry, was also attracted to men. Douglas later married and had a child of his own, and renounced the 'bane' of the sexual love of men.[81] Douglas later wrote that he had merely '... permitted, against the grain, such familiarities as are common among boy friends in English public schools'.[82]

Youth, aristocracy and a sensual sexuality were more than Wilde could resist, and his letters of the time indicate that he was love-struck.[83]

The allegedly impetuous and ill-tempered Lord Alfred Douglas no doubt seems like a strange choice of companion for the urbane, witty Wilde, whose most treasured possession was his own genius.[84] Certainly, as he reflected back upon his infatuation from the cold reality of prison, Wilde, in a letter published under the title *De Profundis*, accused Douglas of having shown no respect for his need to work.[85] Douglas later passionately denied that claim, and labelled *De Profundis* a 'dreadful piece of cold-blooded, malignant malice, hypocrisy and lying'.[86]

Nevertheless, love was as ever an unpredictable thing, and for two or three crucial years it governed Wilde's life to the detriment firstly of his career and finally of his personal freedom. Wilde and Douglas were constant companions for months on end, with periods in between when Wilde later claimed he tried to end the relationship because of Douglas's ill-temper and insensitivity.[87] The Marquess of Queensberry had already made his name in history by drafting the Queensberry rules for boxing. He was to confirm it by his unrelenting pursuit of Wilde all the way to a prison cell.

Lord Alfred Douglas had long enjoyed at best, a cool relationship with a father who had been distant and cruel to him as a child. The Marquess was what might be called a 'man's man', and he was anything but accepting of his younger son's sexual tendencies.[88] The son may not have inherited his father's apparently strong heterosexuality, but he did possess the obstinacy and temper for which his father was equally famous.[89] Douglas was intent upon being seen in public wherever and whenever he pleased with Wilde, fully aware that this would enrage his father.

Interestingly, Douglas himself later displayed much the same attitude towards homosexuality as his father had, and labelled his former friend Robert Ross a sodomite, pleading justification in the subsequent libel case brought against him.[90] When writing of Ross in the 1920s, Douglas's language would have been difficult to differentiate from his father's against Wilde 30 years before:

> Ross...had become more and more obsessed with the dreadful vice which had been the bane of Oscar Wilde. The mantle of

Wilde in this respect had fallen on him. He was the High Priest of all the sodomites in London...[91]

In the Ross libel trial, Douglas was not entirely vindicated, as the hung jury produced no decision. In describing his disappointment at this, Douglas reiterated a strong belief in British justice; a belief which, in Douglas's case, was eroded by his experiences. 'The treatment I received at this time destroyed the last vestige of a belief in "British fair play" which had survived my former experiences.'[92]

The 'former experiences' to which Douglas referred had begun in 1894. In that year Queensberry's rage began to translate into action as he visited Oscar Wilde in his home to order him to stay away from his son (Douglas). Wilde responded by ordering his servants never to let Queensberry into his house again.[93] The Marquess went further, and tried to invade the theatre production of *The Importance of Being Earnest* on its opening night when Wilde appeared to receive his plaudits. The plot was discovered, and Queensberry was unsuccessful in his attempts to enter the building via various doors.[94]

The fatal final straw was the act of Queensberry in leaving a card for Wilde at Wilde's London club. The card was addressed to 'Oscar Wilde posing Somdomite [sic]'.[95] While the staff of the club were discreet, and it is unlikely that the presentation of the card to Wilde upon his arrival would have caused a great stir, Wilde was appalled. Queensberry had aired publicly the charge he had already made to Wilde in private. Wilde, rather uncharacteristically perhaps, took this insult to heart and decided to launch proceedings for criminal libel against the Marquess. To Lord Alfred Douglas, this was what he had been waiting for all his life. At last the chance presented itself for him to revenge himself upon the father who had never respected him. Lord Douglas himself unashamedly saw it in that light, and believed that Wilde would win in court if Douglas was allowed to testify as to his father's dark character.[96]

When Wilde wavered, Douglas, intent upon his father's destruction, pushed him into action. In a later publication Douglas defended his action in pushing Wilde forward, indicating that it was only an inexplicable change in legal tactics by Wilde's barrister, Sir Edward

Clarke, that resulted in the failure of the court case.[97] Douglas himself was perhaps also in some danger of facing criminal charges should the action fail. It is easy, with hindsight, to see that it was Wilde who was eventually to pay the price for Douglas's determination, but that was not necessarily clear at the outset.

Lord Douglas was prepared to testify at all the trials involving Wilde, and was only stopped from doing so by Wilde's pleadings that he did not wish to expose him to any danger. Douglas wrote letters to newspapers condemning the system that had condemned the man he claimed to adore. This is not to say that Douglas bears no blame for Wilde's downfall. He remains the chief instigator of the legal action that ultimately ended in Wilde's incarceration. Yet this was not without danger for Douglas himself. There is no indication that he was aware of the letter later sent from Charles Gill, Senior Treasury Council to Sir Hamilton Cuffe, DPP, indicating that no case could be proved against him and that he was best seen as 'one of Wildes [sic] victims'.[98]

The Marquess of Queensberry was arrested and charged with criminal libel on 1 March 1895, on the basis of Wilde's prosecution. Wilde was confident of his chances of success, and concerned above all with protecting Lord Douglas. 'I thought but to defend him from his father', he later lamented.[99] Perhaps Wilde underestimated Queensberry's determination, or perhaps he was over-confident in his own good fortune. Queensberry and his agents worked hard to procure evidence against Wilde, including witnesses who had worked as male prostitutes and were familiar with Wilde's movements.[100]

Oscar Wilde can perhaps be seen as the classic example of a man who overestimated his own degree of inclusion. He had been lauded and applauded by members of Britain's elite for his wit for so long that he could be excused for feeling that he was one of them. Wilde had long been too controversial and potentially scandalous a figure actually to be considered an 'Establishment man'. A jester may be allowed to entertain the court, but this does not make him a courtier. His homosexual practices had attracted too much publicity for him to be adequately protected, even if the political will had been there to do so.

British authorities had to protect the moral order they had put in place, a need that had already accounted for people closer to the centre of power than Oscar Wilde. According to one biographer, Wilde realised the truth of his outsiderness while in prison:

> Prison had taught Wilde much. It had taught him that he was not the centre of the universe; that he could not ride roughshod over the opinions and morals of others; above all, it had taught him pity. Pity for the poor and luckless, pity for his fellow outcasts.[101]

Prison was the graphic illustration to Wilde that he was indeed capable of being an 'outcast'. He could be a victim of the law because he did not make the law or control those who did. He merely, for a time, entertained them.

During the course of the libel trial it became clear that Wilde would not be able to sustain the charges he had made. This was also clear to contemporary commentators who followed proceedings through the press. Sir Edward Hamilton, former Private Secretary to Gladstone, noted the ongoing trial in his diary.

> The Oscar Wilde case is proceeding; and some horrible disclosures are being made. It seems impossible that a British Jury can do otherwise than acquit Queensberry of defaming O. Wilde's character by imputing to him the character of 'posing as' an unmentionable creature. The net seems to be closing round the brute: though he certainly is a very clever one, and has given utterance to many smart sayings in his cross-examination by Carson who is conducting the case for Queensberry with great skill.[102]

The 'British' jury agreed with Hamilton's interpretation and found against Wilde. The Director of Public Prosecutions also took an interest, and within a matter of days Wilde was arrested and charged under the 1885 Criminal Law Amendment Act for committing indecent acts.

The first criminal trial of Oscar Wilde was a close-run thing. That Wilde was guilty of the charge is difficult to deny. The evidence overall against him was, if not strong, then multifarious, and Wilde later admitted to having consistently perjured himself in the Queensberry trial as he denied any wrongdoing.[103] Lord Douglas later wrote, 'I knew that Oscar was guilty of what my father had accused him of'.[104] The jury on the first trial was unable to reach a verdict, and Wilde was released on bail.[105] Now the Government showed its determination to act by pursuing a retrial almost immediately. For 20 days of freedom, Wilde enjoyed the company of his old friend Ada Everson, with whom he stayed for the latter part of his bail.[106] Initially, upon being bailed, Wilde had attempted to find accommodation at various hotels, which refused him a room for fear of the disruption that would ensue.

The second trial, when it came, followed a similar pattern to the first, with only one or two rhetorical flourishes from Wilde adding colour to the proceedings. Lord Douglas records a different view, saying that Wilde 'was himself the worst witness I have ever heard give evidence'.[107] Wilde was found guilty and given the maximum available sentence of two years by a judge whose abhorrence of homosexuality was such that he decried his inability to impose a still harsher sentence.[108] Wilde's appeals from prison for a pardon or early commutation of his sentence were ignored.

There is little doubt that the Government had been determined to pursue Wilde's prosecution in so far as that was necessary to clear the names of Government members who had been mentioned during the libel action against Queensberry.[109] Chief amongst these was the former Foreign Secretary and then Prime Minister, Lord Rosebery.[110] Sir Edward Hamilton's diary suggests that Government members were indeed deeply interested in the outcome:

> The Oscar Wilde & Taylor cases have been brought forward again; & unless there is some cantankerous jury-man a verdict is confidently expected this time. A verdict of guilty would remove what appears to be a wide-felt impression that the Judge &

Jury were on the last occasion *got at*, in order to shield others of a higher status in life.[111]

The government had been keen to utilise the law to isolate a group whose behaviour seemed to threaten the moral foundation which held late Victorian society together. As the social divisions and economic inequalities of the age continued unabated, the Government was enthusiastically identifying the things that could unite Britons of all classes. And chief amongst those was the defence of British moral values. As Michael Foldy has suggested in his study of the symbolic importance of the Wilde trials, they were in various ways about the condition of Britain.[112] Oscar Wilde's trials provided a very public demonstration that British morals were not to be taken lightly.

It is possible to take this argument too far, however. In the Cleveland Street case, there had been ample time given to Lord Somerset to leave the country before any official charge was drawn up against him. Oscar Wilde clearly also had his chances to flee.[113] Some of his friends repeatedly urged him to do so, but Wilde chose to ignore them. He was determined to follow the advice both of his mother and of Douglas that he should stay and fight to clear his name. Arguably, this would have eventually happened to Lord Somerset had he not chosen to leave for the Continent. The political will to protect Oscar Wilde was certainly not great, but neither was the political will to prosecute him at all costs (at least to begin with). Sociologist Ari Adut has suggested that what Victorian governments were afraid of was scandal, rather than homosexuality per se.[114] Certainly the scandal could have been avoided had Wilde not been insistent on making it a matter for the courts. Trevor Fisher suggests that it was Oscar Wilde himself, rather than 'a homophobic government' that brought about his downfall.[115]

There is some support in Sir Edward Hamilton's diary for such a conclusion. Hamilton wrote of Wilde after the unsuccessful libel prosecution:

> He is said to have been aware that the Police has been watching him for some time, and that he took proceedings in the hope

that he would win in the action which he brought against so crack-brained a man as Queensberry, and that he would thus stave off Police proceedings.[116]

Whether Wilde took the action to protect himself or, as he claimed, to protect Lord Alfred Douglas, the result would have satisfied neither motivation. The great jester of late-Victorian Britain had sought to make a joke of British law, an institution that could not allow itself to share his sense of humour.

CHAPTER 10

CONCLUSION

As the cell door closed behind Oscar Wilde in 1895, it was pushed shut not merely by the judgement of a British court but by the moral disdain of the British state. He had broken not just a law but a moral code. He had been tested for his 'British' credentials by the objective judgement of a 'British' court – and had been found wanting. His literary wit had long been applauded. But his lack of moral values was a threat to the new foundation of 'Britishness'.

The law in nineteenth-century Britain was the mirror in which different minority groups could be reflected to their advantage or disadvantage. Governments had it in their power, through legislation and their rhetorical pulpit, to manufacture the images they wanted the mirror to show. By creating a special commission to try Parnell, for instance, the Salisbury Government could hide behind a seemingly judicial body, and yet portray a certain image of the Irish at the same time. Anti-Semitism was a reality of British society, yet it was a government choice whether such feelings should be encouraged or discouraged through the way the police dealt with Jewish people, or through the delaying of Jewish emancipation. Atheists were prevented by law from becoming Members of Parliament, not for any crime they had committed, but because of their beliefs.[1] Prostitutes were certainly not the only carriers of venereal disease in Victorian Britain, and yet the law targeted them because they could be targeted safely. Targeting them provided the rest of the society with an immoral 'other' against which to define itself.[2]

Outsider groups throughout the 1829–95 period were not universally condemned. All of the groups that have come under consideration here had their supporters in society as well as their detractors. What is noteworthy is that those in power who felt threatened by a particular outsider group often felt threatened by more than one. For instance, the letters of Queen Victoria and the writings of Goldwin Smith show equal concern over Roman Catholics and Jews.[3] Smith believed that both were potentially disloyal to Britain because they served international brotherhoods, whereas Queen Victoria saw both as a threat to the Protestant British hierarchy which it was her duty to protect.[4] Her letter to Gladstone on 20 January 1874 is proof enough of her views: 'Protestant to the very *heart's core* as the Queen is...'[5]

Similarly Arnold White, in his agitations about alien immigration at the end of the period, linked the arrival en masse of Jewish immigrants with Jewish involvement in prostitution.[6] Sir Robert Anderson, the Assistant Police Commissioner at the time of the Ripper murders, had expressed views against the Irish, the Jews and prostitutes during his tenure in the upper echelons of the Metropolitan Police.[7] If nothing else, the prejudices that were reflected in the thinking of those in positions of power indicated just how difficult it was to move from being a member of an outsider group to one of the more acceptable circles of society.

In the period under consideration, 1829–95, it is possible to discern broad shifts in levels of inclusion. By 1895, the positions of outsider groups had changed significantly. Roman Catholics had slowly clawed their way inwards during the period. Anti-Catholicism remained a distinct and powerful force throughout the Victorian era, yet gradually Roman Catholics began to ascend to those positions of power which were the traditional domain of 'true Britons'. Jews also moved inwards, and at a somewhat faster rate. Jews were only granted the right to sit in the Commons in 1858, and only achieved full removal of their legal disabilities in 1871, whereas Roman Catholics had achieved emancipation in 1829. Yet, not counting Disraeli, there were three Jewish British Cabinet ministers in the period, and only two Roman Catholics.[8] Perhaps this reflects the degree of threat traditionally associated with

Catholics and Jews in the British ruling mindset. Roman Catholics, since the Glorious Revolution of 1688, were the abiding enemy. Jews carried no such historical baggage in Britain. There may have been suspicion of them on cultural and racial/religious grounds, but this fell short of the deep historical hatred of Roman Catholicism that has dogged British politics to the present day.

In a sense, the strengthening of morality as a societal cornerstone provided a discourse in which all religious groups, even those formerly seen as 'un-British' outsiders, could be included. This was for instance recognised by A. Burgess, a Wesleyan Minister, writing to Gladstone to criticise the moral shortcomings of Parnell:

> You know well, Sir, that the religious public, including those who <u>respect</u> religion...Their support will infallibly be withdrawn in large part, if their most sacred feelings (shared in alike by Churchmen, Roman Catholics, Nonconformists, and Jews), are to be outraged.[9]

All religious groups could be united under the banner of morality, a fact which helped to redefine the nature of 'Britishness' in the closing years of Victoria's reign.

Atheists, riding the tide of religious liberalism that slowly wound its way through the nineteenth century, also found their path to inclusion less and less blocked by their unbelief. They had to fight long and hard for their representation in the House of Commons, at the heart of British lawmaking, following a similar pattern to that which Roman Catholics and Jews had faced. Just as Lord Rothschild had been elected for 11 years before he was allowed to take his seat, so Charles Bradlaugh had to be elected five times before he was finally accepted. But both finally made it. By the end of the period, religion was no longer a ground on which any recognised group could be legally banned from participating in the institutions of British government, excluding the monarchy.

David Feldman has emphasized that there was more to this shift than just liberalism: 'Jewish emancipation was an episode in the history of nationalism as well as of liberalism in England.'[10] R.W. Davis has characterised the string of limitations lifted from religious minorities from 1819 onwards as 'outsider' victories.[11] They were certainly a significant step forward for these groups. Yet, to characterise them as victories suggests that British governments were beaten, whereas they seem rather to have consistently made tactical withdrawals to higher ground. To allow Jews into Parliament after 1858 did not mean that Jews suddenly dominated parliamentary representation. The Parliament was secure enough in its power to allow another group to share it without any fear of domination. But in the process, it did change the boundaries that delineated contemporary conceptions of 'Britishness'.

If Roman Catholics, atheists and Jews were to some extent the winners in the nineteenth-century liberal process of inclusion, who were the losers? The Irish must be counted in that number. The fears and prejudices stirred up on account of Irish 'outrages' upon the British mainland and by the actions of the Land League in Ireland ensured that the Irish did not become any more accepted within Britain as the nineteenth century wore on. The Home Rule debates further crystallised the anomaly that Britain did not wish to let Ireland go, yet could not bring itself to regard its people as anything other than outsiders. The appearance of Parnell before the Special Commission and his later fall from grace at the hands of a divorce court did nothing to engender a greater acceptance of a people seen as disloyal to Britain.

Male homosexuals fared little better. They represented a threat not because they were socially powerful as an identifiable group, but because they threatened the moral order which underpinned late-Victorian society. Hence, they were ostracised more clearly than ever before by a specific law responding to that threat. By the 1890s homosexuality had become sufficiently dangerous to the social order that it could not be tolerated even from people who were in every other way good 'British' types. The rise in the importance of strong morals as a defining national characteristic meant that departures from the moral norm could no longer be given any latitude. The 1885 Criminal Law Amendment Act that criminalized indecent acts between males reflected that shift – and buttressed it with the force of 'British' law.

CONCLUSION

In a sense, at the beginning of the period, in 1829, homosexuals did not exist as a recognisable minority or outsider group. There was no open recognition of a homosexual culture or sub-culture in the sense that one emerged later in the century. As the Boulton and Park scandal revealed, the British authorities claimed to know very little about the vice that was soon to dominate the collective mind of late Victorian Britain. In that sense, homosexuals clearly lost out over the period. They were thrust from a kind of obscurity in 1829 into an unwanted limelight by 1895. The Criminal Law Amendment Act of 1885 marked the legally sanctioned 'otherness' of men who committed unacceptable acts with other men.

Amongst British lawmakers the emphasis had changed fully from highlighting religious difference to protecting British morality. Jeffrey Weeks has characterised it as a crusade:

> The undertones of imperialism had always been apparent in the debates over the Contagious Diseases Acts. Here they were being drawn together in a morality crusade against homosexuality and prostitution.[12]

Crusades – like all wars – work to unite people against a common enemy. For the British, the moral crusade helped to define what it meant to be 'British'. Crusades increasingly became moral rather than religious, and the attitudes of Britain's rulers both led and reflected that change.

Prostitutes were perhaps the one group that could be said to have remained static. They were the perpetual outsiders, always necessary within the fabric of society yet without any chance of ceasing to be a moral 'other'. Society could not live with them and society could not live without them. But in Victorian Britain, the nature of their 'otherness' was brought into sharper relief by the intensity of the focus on their moral degradation – a focus which stemmed from their embrace of values that were incompatible with the very idea of 'Britishness'. The repeal of the Contagious Diseases Acts can on one level be seen as a 'victory' for prostitutes, removing one of the legal factors ensuring their continued exclusion. Yet a reading of the sources confirms that it was a battle fought on other grounds. Those who believed in liberal England, in the right to freedom from official examination, did not necessarily hold any higher opinion of prostitutes than those who argued for the Contagious Diseases Acts. The argument over the Acts was an argument based on a moral high ground to which prostitutes were seen by neither side as having any claim.

The modern debate surrounding 'Britishness' rests on the foundations the Victorians built. It is a values-based identity. The values may have changed, but they continue to form the frame through which British identity is viewed. Britishness is no longer a question of external identifiers. It is not about race or religion or cultural heritage. Rather, it is a 'Britishness' based on internal values and how they manifest themselves in external behaviour. In the twenty-first century, one is 'British' if one exhibits tolerance towards others and an appreciation of fair play. It is 'British' to embrace liberty and cultural diversity.

In late Victorian Britain it was 'British' to show sexual propriety and to exclude those who did not. It was 'British' to decry the wretched moral choices that prostitutes had made. It was a values-based 'Britishness', but one based on a clear notion of who the 'other' was in terms of the people not displaying 'British' characteristics. British law was the tool that identified the 'other' by criminalising those who engaged in 'un-British' behaviour. The values that define twenty-first century 'Britishness' are expressed differently. They are couched in positive terms – and there is no commensurate body of British law to define clearly who the 'other' now is. In a more globalised world in which international standards are set through a discourse of human rights, these values are more difficult to define as peculiarly 'British'. Their power as values lies in their universalism, and by definition their utility as supports for national identity is therefore limited.

If the British 'project' is to continue successfully into this century, it needs to find a way to define itself that is uniquely identifiable as 'British'. At present, what is providing that differentiation is the old national borders. Scottishness, Welshness and Irishness all provide older cultural roots that can better sustain a unique identity. And all of them are sustained to some extent by seeing the 'English' as the 'other'. The notion of 'Britishness' no longer has a ready-made 'other' of that kind. In the Victorian era, governments were consistently able to use the force of law and political rhetoric to identify the 'other' – providing a lead to the nation. It remains to be seen whether 'Britishness' can remain a meaningful frame of identity in the twenty-first century without commensurate 'others' to define itself against.

The same tools are now being applied to that challenge as the Victorians used – legislation, rhetoric, and the courts. Values such as 'tolerance' and 'fair play' have boundaries even in the twenty-first century. We know what those boundaries are because legislation has given them definition. For example, successive pieces of anti-terror legislation have made it clear that forms of violence and association that can be labelled 'terrorist' are abhorrent to British values. They represent 'un-British' behaviour. Similarly, legislation such as the Racial and Religious Hatred Act 2006 helps to give definition to what tolerance means – in the process giving definition to the 'values' that are key components of modern 'Britishness'.

Those definitions are then backed up by political rhetoric. The speeches in Parliament of both those who support a Bill and its opponents help to test the boundaries that the Bill will create if it becomes legislation. For example, the Labour backbench revolt against the proposal to include a 90-day period in the Terrorism Act 2006 for terrorism suspects to be held without charge showed that, whilst 'British' tolerance did not extend to terrorist acts, 'British' justice required suspects not to be held without charge for any longer than absolutely necessary. Public speeches outside Parliament by political leaders – which are then often widely reported in the popular press – also help to give form and substance to the values that underpin new laws. Rhetoric is used to explain why laws are necessary to defend 'British' values.

Take Prime Minister Tony Blair in his 2006 Labour Conference speech: 'If we want our values to be the ones that govern global change, we have to show that they are fair, just and delivered with an even hand.' Fairness and justice – according to contemporary debates – are fundamentally 'British'. What then are the boundaries of such a 'British' fairness, How can we know when it is being applied? Well, the answer, given in the same speech by Blair, is that it doesn't stretch to allowing those who don't themselves display those values to strike out at their fellow citizens:

> When crimes go unpunished, that is a breach of the victim's liberty and human rights. When organised crime gangs are free to practise their evil, countless young people have their liberty and often their lives damaged.... When we can't deport foreign nationals even when inciting violence the country is at risk.[13]

The core problem is – as Blair himself frequently stated – that these are, or should be, universal values. They might be the modern delineators of what 'Britishness' is, but they do not act to show what is exceptional or unique about that 'Britishness'. The second major challenge raised by a 'Britishness' based on values is that it is an elusive identifier. In the early Victorian period there were clear ways to identify religious 'others' – if by nothing else than the houses of worship they frequented and the company they kept. A 'Britishness' that was muscularly Protestant had no shortage of internal 'others' against which to define itself. As the religious barriers to inclusion were progressively lifted during the nineteenth century, that identification of 'Britishness' became more difficult as the key characteristics changed to a values-based test of morals. How could one tell if a fellow citizen was a sexual 'deviant', displaying 'un-British' moral standards, unless high-profile court cases put them directly on trial? Such trials, when they did occur, helped the nation to understand and better define what was meant by 'British' values at the time.

As I write this in 2011, the content of 'British' morality has changed significantly since the Victorian age – and indisputably for the better. Where once it was defined by excluding those seen as sexually deviant, it now emphasises tolerance of difference. What 'British' values are has continually evolved, and no doubt will continue to evolve for as long as the concept of 'Britain' endures. But what has not changed since the late Victorian period is that 'Britishness' is values-based rather than being based on externally visible characteristics. In the modern United Kingdom, one is 'un-British' not because of being racially or religiously different, but because of the thoughts harboured in the mind that only become manifest when they emerge as intolerant action. As a result, it is much harder to tell in any meaningful way who is 'British' and who is not. And into that breach instead are stepping alternative, and often more destructive, identities that allow for a more marked sense of belonging. Whether that be in the embrace of criminal gangs and terrorist networks, or in the darker elements of more local nationalist sentiments, the search for identity goes on.

And the core problem remains that, for someone to be 'in', there must be people who can be 'out'. With no point of reference, there is no identity, and 'Britishness' becomes a 'grab-bag' of universal values that can no longer effectively bind the nation together. The devolution debate can ultimately be seen as the reaction that fills that gap. It immediately creates a well-defined 'other'. For the Scots and the Welsh, the English emerge as the 'other'. In response, the movement for an English Parliament continues to gather apace as Great Britain's largest national group also seeks the comfort of a more clearly defined 'other'. What these identities don't do – of course – is provide any comfort or support to the idea of 'Britishness'. Rather, 'Britishness' is sacrificed as a meaningful identifier and replaced with something more tangible and closer to home – like Scottishness, Welshness or Irishness.

So where to now for 'Britishness'? It was conceived in the age of empire, war and religious difference. 'Outsiders' were easily identified and easy to shun. The move in the late Victorian era to a values-based 'Britishness' has slowly hollowed out the meaning of that identity over the course of the last century. I in no way wish to be taken to be making a plea for any return to religious intolerance, moral judgements or anti-European sentiment in order to better bind together the British nation. Those intolerances belong in the past and have no rightful place in a modern conception of 'Britishness'. But they do provide the pointers for how it was done – how 'Britishness' was made. The question for policy-makers today becomes: How can 'Britishness' be re-made without jettisoning progressive universal values? What are the things that can be cast as uniquely British in opposition to an 'other' without unleashing all the intolerance that 'othering' is usually accompanied by?

My tentative suggestion would be that British institutions are the place to start looking for that missing ingredient. For instance, British law is a tie that still has the potential to bind. Law has a place in British life that is different to its place in the life of other nations. Both the English Common Law and Scots Law have a long and proud history that is not incompatible with their being seen as a binding agent for 'Britishness' as a whole.

Similarly, the British Parliament, and the Westminster system of government that underpins it, is a peculiarly British invention that now sustains the governance of much of the globe. While other nations have embraced the Westminster system, there is only one Parliament at Westminster itself that gave the 'system' life – and it is a peculiarly British one. And there are other institutions to be thought about in this context. The extraordinary national and international interest in the royal wedding of Prince William and Kate Middleton shows that the monarchy also retains a unifying power in a uniquely British way. When 'Britishness' is able to identify those things that remain uniquely 'British' in a globalised age, it may once more gain strength as an identity that has some genuine psychological purchase on how the British people see themselves.

NOTES

* Parts of this book include material first published by the author in article form in: D. Grube 'How can Britishness be re-made?', *The Political Quarterly*, Vol. 82, No. 4 (2011), pp. 628–635; and D. Grube 'Religion, Power and Parliament: Rothschild and Bradlaugh Revisited', *History*, Vol. 92, No. 1 (2007), pp. 21–38. The author thanks those publications for permission to reproduce the material here.

Chapter 1 Introduction: 'Britishness' and the 'Other'

1. This is a debate with a vast and rapidly developing literature. For a sample, see: *History, Nationhood and the Question of Britain*, eds H. Brocklehurst and R. Phillips (Basingstoke and New York, 2004); T. Nairn, *After Britain: New Labour and the Return of Scotland* (London, 2000); *Relocating Britishness*, eds S. Caunce et al. (Manchester and New York, 2004); C. Rojek, *Brit-Myth: Who Do the British Think They Are?* (London, 2007); K. Kumar, *The Making of English National Identity* (Cambridge, 2003); V. Ware, *Who Cares About Britishness? A Global View of the National Identity Debate* (London, 2007); *Debating Nationhood and Governance in Britain, 1885–1945: Perspectives from the 'Four Nations'*, eds D. Tanner et al. (Manchester, 2006); B. Crick, 'The Four Nations: Interrelations', *The Political Quarterly*, Vol. 79, No. 1 (2008), pp. 71–9; A. Aughey, 'Anxiety and injustice: the anatomy of contemporary English nationalism', *Nations and Nationalism*, Vol. 16, No. 3 (2010), pp. 506–24; A. Aughey, *The Politics of Englishness* (Manchester, 2007); C. Bryant, *The Nations of Britain* (Oxford, 2006); M. Keating, 'The Strange Death of Unionist Scotland', *Government and Opposition*, Vol. 45, No. 3 (2010), pp. 365–85; J. Burkett, 'Re-defining British Morality: "Britishness" and the Campaign for Nuclear Disarmament 1958–8', *Twentieth Century*

British History, Vol. 21, No. 2 (2010), pp. 184–205; G. Wemyss, 'The power to tolerate: contests over Britishness and belonging in East London', *Patterns of Prejudice*, Vol. 40, No. 3 (2006), pp. 215–36; K. Kumar, 'Negotiating English Identity: Englishness, Britishness and the Future of the United Kingdom', *Nations and Nationalism*, Vol. 16, No. 3 (2010), pp. 469–87. The journal *Parliamentary Affairs* (Vol. 63, No. 2, 2010) devoted a special issue to the *Politics of Britishness*, covering many contemporary perspectives.

2. G. Brown, 'Introduction', in M. d'Ancona, ed., *Being British: The Search for the Values that Bind the Nation* (Edinburgh and London, 2009), pp. 25–34.
3. See for example: *Britishness: Perspectives on the British Question*, eds A. Gamble and T. Wright (London, 2009); C. Julios, *Contemporary British Identity: English Language, Migrants and Public Discourse* (Aldershot, 2008).
4. For an argument that religion continues to be central to modern 'Britishness', see I. Bradley, *Believing in Britain: The Spiritual Identity of 'Britishness'* (London and New York, 2007).
5. L. Colley, *Britons: Forging the Nation 1707–1837* (New Haven and London, 1992). In acknowledging Colley's contribution, it is also important to acknowledge the earlier work of J. G. A. Pocock, who arguably began the new 'Britain' debate with his article 'British history: a plea for a new subject', *Journal of Modern History*, Vol. 47, No. 4 (1975), pp. 601–24. For a sample of the debate on the historical emergence of 'Britishness', see: M.G.H. Pittock, *Inventing and Resisting Britain: Cultural Identities in Britain and Ireland 1685–1789* (New York, 1997); A. Hastings, *The Construction of Nationhood: Ethnicity, Religion and Nationalism* (Cambridge, 1997); P. Readman, *Land and Nation in England: Patriotism, National Identity, and the Politics of Land, 1880–1914* (Woodbridge, 2008); K. Robbins, *Great Britain: Identities, Institutions, and the Idea of Britishness* (London, 1998); K. Robbins, *History, Religion and Identity in Modern Britain* (London, 1993); *A Union of Multiple Identities: The British Isles, c.1750–c.1850*, eds L. Brockliss and D. Eastwood (Manchester and New York, 1997); D. Powell, *Nationhood and Identity: The British State Since 1800* (London and New York, 2002).
6. For a discussion of how this criticism has evolved, see C. Harvie, 'Bad History', *The Political Quarterly*, Vol. 77, No. 4 (2006), pp. 439–47.
7. K. Robbins, 'An imperial and multinational polity: the "scene from the centre", 1832–1922', in A. Grant and K.J. Stringer, eds, *Uniting the Kingdom? The Making of British History* (London and New York, 1995), pp. 244–54.
8. H. Kearney, 'Four Nations History in Perspective', in Brocklehurst and Phillips, *History, Nationhood and the Question of Britain*, pp. 10–19.
9. A. Grant and K. Stringer, 'Introduction: The enigma of British History', in Grant and Stringer, *Uniting the Kingdom? The Making of British History*, pp. 3–11.

NOTES 165

10. P. Ward, 'Nationalism and National Identity in British Politics, c.1880s to 1914', in Brocklehurst and Phillips, *History, Nationhood and the Question of Britain*, pp. 213–26. See also Ward's larger work, *Britishness Since 1870* (London and New York, 2004).
11. P. Jupp, 'Government, parliament and politics in Ireland, 1801–41', in J. Hoppit, ed., *Parliaments, Nations and Identities in Britain and Ireland, 1660–1850* (Manchester, 2003), pp. 146–64. Marjorie Morgan has produced a very interesting analysis of how travellers from Victorian Britain saw themselves and their national identity as they travelled outside the British Isles. Her findings have suggested that the identity of 'British' could be superseded abroad by an all-encompassing title of 'English'. At home, the British still had very strong affiliations to the constituent nationalities of the United Kingdom – Scottish, Welsh, English – as well as the overarching 'British'. She concludes, 'In Victorian Britain, there was an ambiguity and elusiveness about national identity. Middle-class men and women exhibited a flexible repertoire of national identities rather than a single one as marked on their passports.' M. Morgan, *National Identities and Travel in Victorian Britain* (Basingstoke, 2001), p. 217.
12. Colley herself has already indicated that her concept extends to the Irish as an 'other': 'There is considerable evidence that at grass-roots level the Welsh, the Scottish, and the English saw (and often still see) the Irish as alien in a way that they did not regard each other as alien'. L. Colley, 'Britishness and otherness: an argument', *Journal of British Studies*, Vol. 31, No. 4 (1992), pp. 309–29, at p. 314. See also Colley, *Britons: Forging the Nation 1707–1837*. Her arguments are supported by the findings of Mary Hickman and D.G. Boyce. M.J. Hickman, 'Reconstructing and deconstructing "race": British political discourses about the Irish in Britain', *Ethnic and Racial Studies*, Vol. 21, No. 2 (1998), pp. 288–307, at p. 291; D.G. Boyce, *The Irish Question and British Politics 1868–1986* (New York, 1988), pp. 13–14. Stephen Conway suggests that the English saw England as being at the heart of Britain. S. Conway, 'War and national identity in the mid-eighteenth-century British Isles', *English Historical Review*, Vol. 116, No. 468 (2001), pp. 863–93.
13. For a discussion of how sociologists have sought to define the concept of a 'ruling elite', see: T. Bottomore, *Elites and Society*, 2nd edn (London, 1993); *Power in Societies*, ed. M.E. Olsen (New York, 1970). See also D. Sibley, *Outsiders in Urban Societies* (Oxford, 1981), and H.S. Becker, *Outsiders: Studies in the Sociology of Deviance* (New York, 1963). The question of which groups of people might be members of such a 'ruling elite' has been extensively researched elsewhere. See for example D. Cannadine, *The Decline and Fall of the British Aristocracy* (New Haven and London, 1990); A.J. Mayer,

The Persistence of the Old Regime (London, 1981); D. Cannadine, *Aspects of Aristocracy: Grandeur and Decline in Modern Britain* (New Haven and London, 1994); T. Nairn, 'The British political elite', *New Left Review*, Vol. 1, No. 23 (1964), pp. 19–25; P. Anderson, 'Origins of the present crisis', *New Left Review*, Vol. 1, No. 23 (1964), pp. 26–53; W.D. Rubinstein, *Elites and the Wealthy in Modern British History: Essays in Social and Economic History* (Sussex, 1987).

14. Prince Albert Victor, Duke of Clarence, was the eldest son of the Prince of Wales and, as such, second in line to the British throne.
15. For just a few examples of the vast literature in this area, see C. Emsley, *Crime and Society in England, 1750–1900*, 2nd edn. (London, 1996); D. Jones, *Crime, Protest, Community and Police in Nineteenth-Century Britain* (London, 1982); J.C. Wood, *Violence and Crime in Nineteenth-Century England: The Shadow of Our Refinement* (London and New York, 2004); V.A.C. Gatrell, 'Crime, authority and the policeman-state', in F.M.L. Thompson, ed., *The Cambridge Social History of Britain 1750–1950: Vol. 3: Social Agencies and Institutions* (Cambridge, 1990).
16. D. Hay, 'Property, authority and the criminal law', in D. Hay et al., *Albion's Fatal Tree: Crime and Society in Eighteenth-Century England* (London, 1975), p. 48.
17. Ibid.
18. Political participation and its relationship to national identity are well discussed by Hall, McClelland and Rendall in their study of the 1867 reform act. See C. Hall, K. McClelland and J. Rendall, *Defining the Victorian Nation: Class, Race, Gender and the Reform Act of 1867* (Cambridge, 2000).
19. The spread of religious emancipation is examined in a wider comparative European context in *The Emancipation of Catholics, Jews and Protestants: Minorities and the Nation State in Nineteenth-century Europe*, eds R. Liedtke and S. Wendehorst (Manchester and New York, 1999).
20. For a discussion of how the late nineteenth century was central to establishing what would subsequently come to be known as 'Victorian Values', see T. Fisher, *Scandal: The Sexual Politics of Late Victorian Britain* (Phoenix Mill, 1995).
21. For an introduction, see A. Mycock, 'British Citizenship and the Legacy of Empires', *Parliamentary Affairs*, Vol. 63, No. 2 (2010), pp. 339–55.
22. G. Stedman Jones, *Outcast London: A Study in the Relationship Between Classes in Victorian Society* (Harmondsworth, 1971).
23. The story of class struggle as a whole and the class antagonism that became increasingly apparent during the course of the nineteenth century has already been extensively studied. For a small sample over time, see H. Perkin,

The Origins of Modern English Society, 1780–1880 (London, 1969); F.M.L. Thompson, *The Rise of Respectable Society: A Social History of Victorian Britain 1830–1900* (London, 1988); E.P. Thompson, *The Making of the English Working Class* (Harmondsworth, 1968); and J. McCalman, 'Respectability and working-class politics in Late-Victorian London', *Historical Studies*, Vol. 19, No. 74 (1980–1), pp. 108–24.
24. Hall, McClelland and Rendall, *Defining the Victorian Nation: Class, Race, Gender and the Reform Act of 1867*, pp. 204–20.

Chapter 2 British Law and the Irish Other

1. For a discussion of the context of these challenges immediately after union, see R. English, *Irish Freedom: The History of Nationalism in Ireland* (Basingstoke and Oxford, 2006).
2. For a broad assessment of the political relationship between Ireland and the rest of Britain in the nineteenth century and beyond, see P. Bew, *Ireland: The Politics of Enmity 1789–2006* (Oxford, 2007). See also B. Girvin, *From Union to Union: Nationalism, Democracy and Religion in Ireland* (Dublin, 2002).
3. J. Ridden, 'Elite Power and the British Political Identity: The Irish Elite in the "British World"', in Brocklehurst and Phillips, *History, Nationhood and the Question of Britain*, pp. 197–212.
4. For an account of the importance of land to the nineteenth-century conflicts between Ireland and Britain, see P. Bull, *Land, Politics and Nationalism: A Study of the Irish Land Question* (Dublin, 1996); see also P. Bull, 'Land and Politics, 1879–1903', in D.G. Boyce, ed., *The Revolution in Ireland, 1879–1923* (Houndmills, 1988), pp. 23–46.
5. For an introduction to 'Ribbon societies' and 'Ribbonism', see T. Garvin, 'Defenders, Ribbonmen and others: underground political networks in pre-famine Ireland', in C.H.E. Philpin, ed., *Nationalism and Popular Protest in Ireland* (Cambridge, 1987), pp. 219–44, and M.R. Beames, 'The Ribbon societies: lower-class nationalism in pre-famine Ireland', in ibid., pp. 245–63.
6. T.P. O'Connor and R.M. McWade, *Gladstone–Parnell and the Great Irish Struggle* (Sydney, 1886), pp. 347–9.
7. 'An Act for the more effectual Suppression of local Disturbances and dangerous Associations in Ireland', Section 1, in *The Statutes of the United Kingdom of Great Britain and Ireland, 3 & 4 William IV, 1833* (London, 1833), p. 3.
8. Ibid., Section 4, p. 4.

9. Ibid., Section 9, pp. 5–6.
10. O'Connell to H. Sugden, 27 May 1843. *British Library*, Add. 40529, f. 236.
11. Ibid., f. 235.
12. Peel to Sugden, 31 May 1843, *British Library*, Add. 40529, ff. 239–40.
13. Gladstone Memorandum on O'Connell, 4 June 1841, *British Library*, Add. 44777, f. 77.
14. Memorandum of January, 1889, *British Library*, Add. 44702, f. 5.
15. This slow but steady shift in Gladstone's views is well traced in R. Jenkins, *Gladstone* (London, 1995).
16. O'Connell to Sturge, 13 October 1843, *British Library*, Add. 60753, f. 99.
17. 'An Act for the more effectual Suppression of local Disturbances and dangerous Associations in Ireland', Sections 13–14, in *3 & 4 William IV, 1833*, p. 7.
18. Ibid., p. 8. For a panel of nine judges, seven were required to convict, but this was lowered to five when the panel was less than nine strong.
19. Ibid., p. 11.
20. Ibid., Section 12, p. 11.
21. The onus was again placed on the absentee to show that he had good cause for being absent. Ibid., Section 23, pp. 11–12.
22. The sections allowing courts martial and the suppression of public meetings were repealed in 1834.
23. The Statutes of the United Kingdom of Great Britain and Ireland, 5 & 6 William IV, 1835 (London, 1833), p. 177.
24. Ibid., Section 11, p. 180.
25. Ibid., Section 13, p. 181.
26. *Hansard, Series 3*, Vol. 69, 9 March–15 June, 1843, p. 1001.
27. T. Holloway, 'O'Connell v. the Queen: a sesquicentennial remembrance', *Northern Ireland Legal Quarterly* 46 (1995), pp. 63–71, at p. 64.
28. O. MacDonagh, *The Emancipist: Daniel O'Connell 1830–47* (New York, 1989), p. 241.
29. *Hansard, Series 3*, Vol. 73, 22 February–2 April, 1844, p. 437.
30. Ibid., p. 458. For a discussion on the importance of religious toleration, especially of Catholics, to Lord John Russell and the Whig party after 1807, see R.W. Davis, 'The Whigs and religious issues, 1830–5', in R.W. Davis and R.J. Helmstadter, eds, *Religion and Irreligion in Victorian Society* (London and New York, 1992), pp. 29–50.
31. *Hansard, Series 3*, Vol. 69, 9 March–15 June, 1843, p. 1014.
32. *British Library*, Add. 40547, f. 257.
33. Ibid.

34. *HO* 119/18. Opinion delivered 15 September, 1843.
35. Ibid.
36. Ibid. This opinion was provided in response to a letter from Sir James Graham of 13 August 1843, and was delivered on 6 September 1843.
37. Holloway, 'O'Connell v. the Queen: a sesquicentennial remembrance', p. 64, citing *Sir Robert Peel from his Private Papers,* ed. Parker (1899), Vol. 3, p. 67.
38. Ibid., p. 65, quoting from *Greville*, Vol. 2, p. 228.
39. The 'Croker Papers': *The Correspondence and Diaries of the Right Honourable John Wilson Croker*, 3 Vols, Vol. 3, ed. L.J. Jennings (London, 1884), p. 20.
40. Whiteside to O'Connell, 5 September 1844. *Correspondence of Daniel O'Connell the Liberator*, ed. W.J. Fitzpatrick, 2 Vols., Vol. 2 (London, 1888), p. 327.
41. See for instance J. McEldowney, 'Crown Prosecutions in Nineteenth-Century Ireland', in D. Hay and F. Snyder, eds, *Policing and Prosecution in Britain 1750–1850* (Oxford, 1989), pp. 427–57, at p. 430.
42. A. Heesom, 'Ireland under the Union', *History Today*, Vol. 34, No. 1 (1984), pp. 31–5, at p. 35.
43. Ibid.
44. Ibid.
45. V. Crossman, *Politics, Law and Order in Nineteenth-Century Ireland* (New York, 1996), p. 1. For the role of the military in maintaining public confidence in the law, see V. Crossman, 'The army and law and order in the nineteenth century', in T. Bartlett and K. Jeffery, eds, *A Military History of Ireland* (Cambridge, 1996), pp. 358–78.
46. Du Cane Papers, undated, M.S. Eng. hist. c. 648, f. 128.
47. P. Bonsall, *The Irish RMs: The Resident Magistrates in the British Administration of Ireland* (Dublin, 1997), p. 13.
48. Ibid., p. 16.
49. W.E.H. Lecky, *The Leaders of Public Opinion in Ireland: Swift – Flood – Grattan – O'Connell* (London, 1871), p. 260.
50. Bonsall, *The Irish RMs*, p. 21.
51. E. Malcolm, 'The reign of terror in Carlow: the politics of policing Ireland in the late 1830s', *Irish Historical Studies*, Vol. 32, No. 125 (2000), pp. 59–74, at pp. 59–60.
52. Bonsall, *The Irish RMs*, p. 21.
53. Ibid., p. 32.
54. Bonsall, *The Irish RMs*, p. 39, quoting from *The Times*, 18 March 1889.
55. 'An Act to empower the Lord Lieutenant or other Chief Governor or Governors of *Ireland* to apprehend, and detain until the First Day of *March*

One thousand eight hundred and forty-nine, such Persons as he or they shall suspect of conspiring against Her Majesty's Person and Government', in *The Statutes of the United Kingdom of Great Britain and Ireland, 11 & 12 Victoria, 1847–8* (London, 1848), p. 165; 'An Act for the better Prevention of Crime and Outrage in certain Parts of *Ireland* until the First Day of *December* One thousand eight hundred and forty-nine, and to the End of the then next Session of Parliament', in *11 & 12 Victoria,* p. 12.
56. Ibid., Section 16, p. 19.
57. Ibid., Section 27, p. 20.
58. The Statutes of the United Kingdom of Great Britain and Ireland, 19 & 20 Victoria, 1856 (London, 1856), Section 2, p. 151.
59. Ibid., Section 4, p. 152.
60. 'The Public General Statutes passed in the Thirty-Third & Thirty-Fourth Years of the Reign of Her Majesty Queen Victoria, 1870' (London, 1870), Section 13, p. 134.
61. Ibid., Section 23, p. 137.
62. Ibid.
63. Ibid., Section 39, p. 146.
64. Ibid.
65. 'The Public General Statutes passed in the Thirty-Eighth & Thirty-Ninth Years of the Reign of Her Majesty Queen Victoria, 1875' (London, 1875), Section 3, p. 139
66. D. Johnson, 'Trial by jury in Ireland 1860–1914', *Journal of Legal History*, Vol. 17, No. 3 (1996), pp. 270–93.
67. Ibid., pp. 277–81.
68. Ibid., p. 278.
69. Chamberlain to Willie O'Shea, 17 April 1882. *British Library*, Add. 62114, f. 6.
70. Salisbury to Dilke, 15 December 1884, *British Library*, Add. 43876, f. 65.
71. Ibid.
72. Johnson, 'Trial by jury in Ireland 1860–1914', p. 285.
73. A. Macintyre, *The Liberator: Daniel O'Connell and the Irish Party 1830–1847* (London, 1965), p. 271. See also, S. O'Faolain, *King of the Beggars: A Life of Daniel O'Connell, the Irish Liberator in a Study of the Rise of the Modern Irish Democracy (1775–1847)* (New York, 1938), pp. 307–8.
74. *Hansard*, Series 3, Vol. 73, 22 February–2 April, 1844, p. 1068.
75. 'An Act for the better Protection of Person and Property in Ireland', in 'The Public General Statutes passed in the Forty-Fourth & Forty-Fifth Years of the Reign of Her Majesty Queen Victoria, 1881' (London, 1881), p. 3.
76. Ibid., Section 1, p. 3.

77. R. Kee, *The Laurel and the Ivy* (London, 1993), pp. 391–6.
78. St. J. Ervine, *Parnell* (London, 1925), p. 194.
79. J. Abels, *The Parnell Tragedy* (London, 1966), p. 172.
80. 'The Public General Statutes passed in the Forty-Fifth & Forty-Sixth Years of the Reign of Her Majesty Queen Victoria, 1882' (London, 1882), p. 54.
81. Ibid., p. 62.
82. On the famine, see C. Ó. Gráda, *The Great Irish Famine* (Cambridge and New York, 1995); *The Meaning of the Famine*, ed. P. O'Sullivan (London, 1997); and *The Great Famine: Studies in Irish History, 1845–52* R.D. Edwards and T.D. Williams, (Dublin, 1956).
83. For a detailed study of the Irish in Liverpool, see J. Belchem, *Irish, Catholic and Scouse: The History of the Liverpool-Irish, 1800–1939* (Liverpool, 2007).
84. R. Swift, 'The Outcast Irish in the British Victorian City: Problems and Perspectives', *Irish Historical Studies*, Vol. 25, No. 99 (1987), pp. 264–76, at p. 264.
85. F. D'arcy, 'St. Patrick's other island: the Irish invasion of Britain', *Eire – Ireland*, Vol. 28, No. 2 (1993), pp. 7–17, at pp. 9–10.
86. D.M. MacRaild, 'Irish immigration and the "condition of England" question: The roots of an historiographical tradition', *Immigrants & Minorities*, Vol. 14, No. 1 (1995), pp. 67–85, at p. 70.
87. Ibid., p. 71.
88. Ibid., p. 73.
89. The likes of Edward Freeman, Grant Allen and J.R. Green were prominent in these discussions. See B. Ward-Perkins, 'Why did the Anglo-Saxons not become more British?', *English Historical Review*, Vol. 155, No. 462 (2000), pp. 513–33; G. Allen, 'Are we Englishmen?', *Fortnightly Review*, 28 (1880), pp. 472–87, in M.D. Biddiss, ed., *Images of Race* (Leicester, 1979), pp. 237–56; R. Floyd, '449 and all that: Nineteenth- and Twentieth-Century Interpretations of the "Anglo-Saxon Invasion" of Britain', in Brocklehurst and Phillips, *History, Nationhood and the Question of Britain*, pp. 184–96.
90. See MacRaild, 'Irish immigration and the "condition of England" question', pp. 76–7. For a thorough assessment of Carlyle's writings on the Irish, see R. Swift, 'Thomas Carlyle and Ireland', in D.G. Boyce and R. Swift, eds, *Problems and Perspectives in Irish History Since 1800: Essays in Honour of Patrick Buckland* (Dublin, 2004), pp. 117–46.
91. H.F. Augstein, 'Aspects of philology and racial theory in nineteenth-century Celticism: the case of James Cowles Prichard', *Journal of European Studies*, Vol. 28, No. 4 (1998), pp. 355–71, at p. 366.

92. S. Gilley, 'English attitudes to the Irish in England, 1780–1900', in C. Holmes, ed., *Immigrants and Minorities in British Society* (London, 1978), pp. 81–110, at pp. 93 and 96.
93. P.B. Rich, 'Social Darwinism, anthropology and English perspectives of the Irish, 1867–1900', *History of European Ideas*, Vol. 19, Nos. 4–6 (1994), pp. 777–85, at p. 784.
94. R. Dye, 'Catholic protectionism or Irish nationalism? Religion and politics in Liverpool, 1829–1845', *Journal of British Studies*, Vol. 40, No. 3 (2001), pp. 357–90. For a useful overview of historical scholarship on the Irish in Britain, see R. Swift, 'Historians and the Irish: Recent writings on the Irish in nineteenth-century Britain', in D.M. MacRaild, ed., *The Great Famine and Beyond: Irish Migrants in Britain in the Nineteenth and Twentieth Centuries* (Dublin, 2000), pp. 14–39.
95. Swift, 'The outcast Irish in the British Victorian City: Problems and Perspectives', pp. 264–76.
96. Ibid., p. 274.
97. R. Swift, 'Heroes or villains?: The Irish, crime, and disorder in Victorian England', *Albion*, Vol. 29, No. 3 (1997), pp. 399–421.
98. K.T. Jeffes, 'The Irish in early Victorian Chester: an outcast community?' in R. Swift, ed., *Victorian Chester: Essays in Social History 1830–1900* (Liverpool, 1996), pp. 85–117. Modern scholarship has also reiterated the differences in overall Irish experiences based on the locality in which they settled in Britain. See *The Irish in Victorian Britain: The Local Dimension*, eds R. Swift and S. Gilley (Dublin, 1999). David Feldman has also emphasised that Irish immigrants were anything but homogenous. See D. Feldman, 'Migration', in M. Daunton, ed., *The Cambridge Urban History of Britain, Vol. 3* (Cambridge, 2000), pp. 185–206. For the counter-argument, suggesting that national factors overrode local ones in importance, see M.J. Hickman, 'Alternative historiographies of the Irish in Britain: a critique of the segregation/assimilation model', in Swift and Gilley, eds, *The Irish in Victorian Britain: The Local Dimension*, pp. 236–53.
99. On over-policing see R. Swift, 'Crime and the Irish in nineteenth-century Britain', in R. Swift and S. Gilley, eds, *The Irish in Britain 1815–1939* (London, 1989), pp. 163–82, at p. 169.
100. Swift, 'The outcast Irish in the British Victorian City', p. 268. See also Swift 'Heroes or villains?', pp. 409–410. For perceptions of the Irish in York, see R. Swift, *Police Reform in Early Victorian York, 1835–1856* (York, 1988), p. 5.
101. S. Gilley, 'Roman Catholicism and the Irish in England', in *Immigrants and Minorities*, Vol. 18, Nos. 2–3 (1999), pp. 147–67, at p. 158.

102. O. MacDonagh, *States of Mind: A Study of Anglo-Irish Conflict 1780–1980* (London, 1983), pp. 101–2.
103. Gilley, 'Roman Catholicism and the Irish in England', at pp. 151 and 155.
104. H. Mayhew, *London Labour and the London Poor*, Vol. I (London, 1967, first published 1851), p. 460.
105. Ibid., p. 126.
106. Swift, 'Heroes or villains?', pp. 401–2.
107. Swift, 'Crime and the Irish in nineteenth century Britain', p. 172.
108. As quoted in R. Swift, '"Another Stafford Street row": Law, order and the Irish presence in mid-Victorian Wolverhampton', in R. Swift and S. Gilley, eds, *The Irish in the Victorian City* (London, 1985), pp. 179–205, at p. 194.
109. *MEPO* 2/43.
110. Ibid.
111. Ibid.
112. F. D'arcy, 'St Patrick's other island: the Irish invasion of Britain', *Eire – Ireland*, Vol. 28, No. 2 (1993), pp. 7–17, at p. 11.
113. Van Duin, 'Ethnicity, race and labour, 1830s–1930s', p. 89, citing J.A. Jackson, *The Irish in Britain* (London, 1963), p. 191.
114. See ibid., p. 197.
115. See *HO* 45/3140.
116. *Catholic Standard*, Saturday 12 April 1851. *HO* 45/3140, f. 5.
117. Ibid., f. 12.
118. Ibid., f. 76.

Chapter 3 Ireland on Trial: The Parnell Experience

1. For a discussion of the different historical interpretations of these events, see C. Collins, 'Britain and Ireland 1880–1921: searching for the scapegoat', *Modern History Review*, Vol. 2, No. 4 (1991), pp. 1–4.
2. The group led by Chamberlain and another of Gladstone's previous supporters, Lord Hartington, came to be known as Liberal-Unionists. The Unionists commanded sufficient electoral support to keep the Liberal Party out of Government again until 1892, and they eventually became a part of the Conservative Party.
3. *Hansard, Series 3*, cciv, 1036–81, 8 April 1886, as cited in *Irish Political Documents 1869–1916*, eds A. Mitchell and P. O'Snodaigh (Dublin, 1989), p. 67.
4. Labouchere to Harcourt, 10 January 1893. Ms Harcourt, dep. 87, f. 89.
5. For a discussion of how Parnell has been symbolically cast as a hero by subsequent generations of writers, see R. Foster and A. Jackson, 'Men for All

Seasons? Carson, Parnell, and the Limits of Heroism in Modern Ireland', *European History Quarterly*, Vol. 39 (2009), pp. 414–38.
6. For an in-depth look at their relationship, see Kee, *The Laurel and the Ivy*.
7. Kee, *The Laurel and the Ivy*, p. 526.
8. K. O'Shea, *Charles Stewart Parnell: His Love Story and Political Life*, Vol. II (London, 1914), pp. 129–30.
9. Ibid., p. 130.
10. *Hansard. Series 3*, Vol. 329, 20 July–7 August, 1888, pp. 296 and 301.
11. *The Journal of John Wodehouse, First Earl of Kimberley, for 1862–1902*, eds A. Hawkins and J. Powell (London, 1997). Camden Fifth Series Vol. 9, p. 383.
12. *Hansard, Series 3*, Vol. 329, 20 July–7 August, 1888, p. 340.
13. Ibid., p. 350.
14. Ibid., p. 293.
15. Ibid., p. 270.
16. Ibid., p. 243.
17. Ibid., p. 382.
18. *British Library*, Add. 56371, ff. 33–4.
19. *Hansard, Series 3*, Vol. 329, 20 July–7 August, 1888, p. 335.
20. See *HO* 144/926/A49962.
21. Anderson's letter to *The Times*, 12 April 1910, ibid.
22. Ibid.
23. *Hansard, Series 3*, Vol. 329, 20 July–7 August, 1888, pp. 244 and 257.
24. Letter of 14 October 1882. Miss Harcourt, dep. 105, f. 14.
25. Anderson to Harcourt, 20 March 1883. Miss Harcourt, dep. 105, f. 30. The 'people' he refers to as having committed crimes are Walsh and Frank Byrne.
26. *Hansard, Series 3*: Vol. 333, 21 February–15 March, 1889, pp. 713–14.
27. Ibid., p. 714.
28. C. Russell, *The Parnell Commission: The Opening Speech for the Defence* (London, 1889), p. 4.
29. M. O'Callaghan, 'Parnellism and crime: constructing a Conservative strategy of containment 1887–91', in D. McCartney, ed., *Parnell: The Politics of Power* (Dublin, 1991), pp. 102–24, at p. 110.
30. Russell, *The Parnell Commission: The Opening Speech for the Defence*, p. 14.
31. *Hansard, Series 3*, Vol. 329, 20 July–7 August, 1888, p. 406.
32. J.L. Hammond, *Gladstone and the Irish Nation* (London, 1938), p. 583.
33. *Hansard, Series 3*, Vol. 329 – 20 July–7 August, 1888, pp. 241–426.
34. Ibid., p. 266.

35. Ibid., p. 266.
36. *Hammond, Gladstone and the Irish Nation*, p. 584.
37. Ibid., p. 587.
38. Russell, *The Parnell Commission: The Opening Speech for the Defence*, p. 15.
39. Ibid., pp. 15–16.
40. *Hansard, Series 3*, Vol. 333, 21 February–15 March, 1889, pp. 715–17.
41. Ibid., p. 717.
42. HO 144/222/A49553B.
43. Ibid. The answer in the Commons suggested that the visit was initiated by Daly, when in fact it was initiated by Pigott. Joseph Soames, solicitor for *The Times*, informed Matthews by letter on 20 March 1889 that Pigott did not act at the request of *The Times* in visiting Daly (ibid). *The Times* expressly repeated in their 21 March 1889 edition that 'Pigott's visit to the dynamiter Daly was in no way procured or furthered by *The Times*, whatever light other people might possibly be able to throw upon it if they chose.' *The Times*'s leading article, on 21 March 1889, contained in HO 144/926/A49962.
44. Kee, *The Laurel and the Ivy*, p. 528.
45. Ibid.
46. HO 144/477/X22687.
47. HO 144/926/A49962.
48. Ibid.
49. Ibid.
50. Anderson to Home Office, 22 March 1889, ibid.
51. Matthews to Anderson, 5 March 1890, ibid.
52. Mathews's Parliamentary answer as quoted in *The Standard*, 16 March 1889, ibid.
53. *The Times*, 21 March 1889, contained in HO 144/926/A49962.
54. Letter to *The Times*, 22 April 1910, contained in HO 144/926/A49962.
55. *Hansard, Series 3*, Vol. 329, 20 July–7 August, 1888, p. 365.
56. Ibid., p. 371.
57. Russell, *The Parnell Commission: The Opening Speech for the Defence*, p. 22.
58. T. Corfe, *The Phoenix Park Murders: Conflict, Compromise and Tragedy in Ireland, 1879–1882* (London, 1968), pp. 137–8.
59. O'Callaghan: 'Parnellism and crime: constructing a Conservative strategy of containment 1887–91', pp. 123–4.
60. A. Jackson, *Home Rule: An Irish History, 1800–2000* (Oxford, 2003), pp. 72–5.

61. O'Shea, *Charles Stewart Parnell*, Vol. II, pp. 140–1.
62. The belief that the letters were in fact a forgery seems to have been widely held when the first one was published in April 1887. Gladstone referred to it in his diary as 'the forged letter', and Justin McCarthy indicated that other members thought so to. He wrote in a letter of 18 April to Mrs Campbell Praed that the letter 'did not after all find much credence in the House even among our enemies – at all events among our intelligent enemies – and it will only hurt and disgrace *The Times* in the end'. J. McCarthy and C. Praed, *Our Book of Memories: Letters of Justin McCarthy to Mrs Campbell Praed* (London, 1912), p. 92.
63. E. Byrne, *Parnell: A Memoir*, ed. F. Callanan (Dublin, 1991), pp. 22–3.
64. Kee, *The Laurel and the Ivy*, pp. 534–5.
65. Ibid., p. 536.
66. Ervine, *Parnell*, p. 270.
67. Kee, *The Laurel and the Ivy*, p. 537.
68. Ervine, *Parnell*, p. 270.
69. Kee, *The Laurel and the Ivy*, pp. 537–8.
70. Ibid., pp. 537–55.
71. *The Journal of John Wodehouse*, eds Hawkins and Powell, p. 395.
72. For the split in the Irish Party which followed Parnell's disgrace in the divorce case, see P. Bull, 'The fall of Parnell: the political context of his intransigence', in D.G. Boyce and A. O'Day, eds, *Parnell in Perspective* (London and New York, 1991), pp. 129–47.
73. This recollection was made by Edward Byrne, Parnell supporter and editor of *Freeman's Journal*, in a memoir he wrote in 1898. Byrne: *Parnell: A Memoir*, p. 21.
74. Ms Harcourt, dep. 87, ff. 41–6, 24–5 November and 31 December, 1890.
75. *British Library*, Add. 56448, f. 110.
76. Ibid.
77. Ibid., f. 112.
78. Ibid., f. 117.
79. Memo of 21 November 1890, ibid., f. 46.
80. Gladstone's stand against Parnell's immorality was possibly hypocritical. Foster alleges that Gladstone was told in 1882 of the affair between Parnell and O'Shea. R.F. Foster, *Paddy and Mr Punch: Connections in Irish and English History* (London, 1993), p. 135.
81. Letter to Gladstone from Malcolm Macydr, 19 November 1890, *British Library*, Add. 56448, f. 22.
82. Letter of 22 November 1890, ibid., f. 77.
83. Letter of 26 November 1890, ibid., f. 144.

Chapter 4 British Jews: The Search for Equality

1. A.T. Carter, 'Changes in the Constitution', in *A Century of Law Reform: Twelve Lectures on the Changes in the Law of England During the Nineteenth Century* (South Hackensack, New Jersey, 1972), pp. 97–130, at p. 115. Legal barriers against Jews were buttressed also by the cultural barriers of popular perception, as embodied in works of fiction. See *Between 'Race and Culture': Representations of 'the Jew' in English and American Literature*, ed. B. Cheyette (Stanford, 1996); B. Cheyette, *Constructions of 'The Jew' in English Literature and Society* (Cambridge, 1993).
2. For an overview of the progression of the legislative changes that brought political rights to Britain's Jews, see G. Alderman, *The Jewish Community in British Politics* (Oxford, 1983).
3. Earl Halsbury, *The Laws of England: Being a Complete Statement of the Whole Law of England*, Vol. XI (31 Vols, London, 1910), p. 826.
4. Carter, 'Changes in the Constitution', p. 115.
5. Ibid.
6. Salomons to Russell, 1 August 1845, PRO 30/22/4D, f. 231.
7. Salomons to Russell, 2 July 1846, PRO 30/22/5B, ff. 33–4.
8. Salomons to Peel, 8 May 1849, *British Library*, Add. 40609, f. 340.
9. For a detailed study of Jewish history in the County of Hampshire – including in the emancipation period – see T. Kushner, *Anglo-Jewry Since 1066* (Manchester and New York, 2009).
10. Lord John Russell alludes to these in his speech on the Oaths Bill but does not detail which positions he means. *Hansard, Series 3*, Vol. 151, 13 July 1858, p. 1375.
11. For a very readable summary account of Rothschild's push for Parliament, see D. Wilson, *Rothschild: A Story of Wealth and Power* (1988), pp. 142–56.
12. See speech of Lord John Russell, *Hansard, Series 3*, Vol. 151, 13 July 1858, p. 1372.
13. Carter, 'Changes in the Constitution', pp. 116.
14. D.C. Itzkowitz, 'Cultural pluralism and the Board of Deputies of British Jews', in Davis and Helmstadter: *Religion and Irreligion in Victorian Society*, pp. 85–101, at p. 86.
15. Ibid., p. 89.
16. C. Holmes, *Anti-Semitism in British Society, 1876–1939* (London, 1979), p. 7.
17. D. Cesarani, *The Jewish Chronicle and Anglo-Jewry, 1841–1991* (Cambridge, 1994), p. 6.
18. C. Roth, *A History of the Jews in England* (Oxford, 1964), pp. 252–3.

19. D. Feldman: *Englishmen and Jews: Social Relations and Political Culture, 1840–1914* (New Haven and London, 1994), p. 13.
20. Ibid., p. 36. The links between Jewish identity and British identity in the period immediately following emancipation are examined in M. Clark, *Albion and Jerusalem: The Anglo-Jewish Community in the Post-Emancipation Era, 1858–1887* (Oxford, 2009).
21. D.J. Anderson, *Jewish Emancipation: A Voice from Israel* (London, 1857), p. 17.
22. Ibid., p. 4.
23. Ibid., p. 29.
24. *Jewish Emancipation*, by an Israelite (D. Nutt, 1845), p. 1.
25. Mayhew: *London Labour and the London Poor*, Vol.II, p. 126.
26. Ibid., p. 127.
27. Ibid.
28. For a discussion of the role of the Conservative Press in opposing emancipation in this period, see J. Sack, 'The British Conservative Press and Its Involvement in Antisemitic and Racial Discourse, Circa 1830–1895', *The Journal of the Historical Society*, Vol. 8, No. 4 (2008), pp. 567–83.
29. Quoted by Lord Russell in the House of Commons, referring to the rejection of the Oaths Bill in its original form by the Lords. *Hansard, Series 3*, Vol. 151, 13 July 1858, p. 1376.
30. D. Englander, 'Anglicized not Anglican: Jews and Judaism in Victorian Britain', in G. Parsons, ed. *Religion in Victorian Britain: Vol. 1 Traditions* (Manchester, 1988), pp. 235–73, at p. 239.
31. *Hansard, Series 3*, Vol. 151, 18 June–2 August 1858, p. 709.
32. Ibid., p. 722.
33. *Hansard, Series 3*, 9 February 1858, p. 978.
34. Ibid., p. 976.
35. *Hansard, Series 3*, 16 July 1858, p. 1614.
36. Ibid., p. 1616.
37. Ibid., p. 1618.
38. He proved every bit as obstinate in the 1880s as he was in 1858. A study of *Hansard* reveals that Newdegate tried unsuccessfully to stop the House releasing some papers that Bradlaugh required for his action before the Court of Queens Bench in 1882. *Hansard, Series 3*, Vol. 270, 5 June–21 June 1882, p. 1112. In fact, he strove long and hard to prevent Bradlaugh from taking his seat as a Member of the House. See D. Tribe, *President Charles Bradlaugh, M.P.* (London, 1971).
39. *The Parliamentary Diaries of Sir John Trelawny, 1858–1865*, ed. T.A. Jenkins (London, 1990). Camden Fourth Series Vol. 40, p. 41.

40. This was certainly the view of Lord Granville when proposing to the Queen ten years later that Rothschild should be made a Peer.
41. *Hansard, Series 3*, 19 July 1858, pp. 1754–5.
42. Salomons to Russell, 19 July 1851, PRO 30/22/9D, f. 267.
43. Ibid., f. 267.
44. Ibid., f. 268.
45. *Hansard, Series 3*, 26 July 1858, p. 2111.
46. Ibid., p. 2112.
47. Lord Granville to the Queen, 23 August 1869, quoted in Lord E. Fitzmaurice, *The Life of Granville George Leveson Gower, Second Earl Granville K.G. 1815–1891* (2 Vols, London, 1905), ii, p.17.
48. The Gladstone Government's policy of removing the obstacles to Jews playing a full part in political life was further illustrated by the passage of the Promissory Oaths Act 1871, which allowed Jews to hold office as Lord Chancellor. V.D. Lipman, *A History of the Jews in Britain since 1858* (Leicester, 1990), p. 11.
49. *The Political Correspondence of Mr Gladstone and Lord Granville 1868–1876*, ed. A. Ramm (2 vols, 1952) (hereafter *Corr., Glad–Gran*) i, p. 48, letter 112. Camden Third Series Vol. 81.
50. Ibid., p. 49, letter 113.
51. Ibid., p. 51, letter 117.
52. Holmes, *Anti-Semitism*, p. 227.
53. 22 August 1869. *The Queen and Mr Gladstone*, ed. P. Guedalla (New York, 1969, 1st pub. 1934), Letter 141, p 247.
54. Ibid., Letter 149, p. 253.
55. Ibid., Letter 151, p. 254.
56. Ibid.
57. See: Holmes, *Anti-Semitism*, pp. 83–7.
58. Ramm, *Corr, Glad-Gran*, ii, p. 403, letter 883.
59. Holmes, *Anti-Semitism*, pp. 83–4.
60. R.W. Davis, 'Disraeli, the Rothschilds, and Anti-Semitism', *Jewish History*, Vol. 10, No. 2 (1996), pp. 9–19, at p. 17.
61. Ibid., p. 10.
62. Ibid., p. 11.
63. Ibid., p. 15.
64. D. Sinclair, *The Pound: A Biography* (2000), p. 240.
65. T. Wemyss Reid, 'Lord Beaconsfield', in *Politicians of To-day: A Series of Personal Sketches* (1880), Vol. 1, pp. 38–9, as cited in A.S. Wohl, '"Dizzi-Ben-Dizzi": Disraeli as Alien', *Journal of British Studies,* Vol. 34, No. 3 (1995) (hereafter Wohl, 'Dizzi') pp. 375–411, at p. 395.

66. Lord Bryce, 'Lord Beaconsfield', *Century Magazine* (March 1882), pp. 733, 741, as cited in Wohl, 'Dizzi', p. 395.
67. P. Smith, *Disraeli: A Brief Life* (Cambridge, 1996), p. 46.
68. Wohl, 'Dizzi', p. 393.
69. That is not to say that his Jewishness was ignored. Richard Altick has suggested that Punch stressed Disraeli's Jewishness in a negative way in its early years. R. Altick, 'Punch's first ten years: the ingredients of success', *Journal of Newspaper and Periodical History*, Vol. 7, No. 2 (1991), pp. 5–16, at p. 14. See also A. Gilam, *The Emancipation of the Jews in England 1830–1860* (New York, 1982), p. 155; T.M. Endelman, '"A Hebrew to the end": the emergence of Disraeli's Jewishness', in C. Richmond and P. Smith eds, *The Self-Fashioning of Disraeli 1818–1851* (Cambridge, 1998), pp. 106–30; and E. Feuchtwanger, *Disraeli* (London, 2000), pp. 13–28.
70. See on this point A.S. Wohl, '"Ben JuJu": representations of Disraeli's Jewishness in the Victorian political cartoon', *Jewish History*, Vol. 19, No. 2 (1996), pp. 89–134.
71. Feldman, *Englishmen and Jews*, pp. 94–120.

Chapter 5 The Politics of Atheism

1. Notes partly used in a speech of 3 May 1883. *British Library*, *Additional Manuscript* (hereafter *BL Add. Ms.*) 50043, f. 257.
2. F.W. Maitland, *The Constitutional History of England* (Cambridge, 1908), p. 522.
3. Notes partly used in a speech of 3 May 1883. *BL Add. Ms.* 50043, f. 258.
4. G.J. Holyoake, *The History of the Last Trial by Jury for Atheism in England: A Fragment of Autobiography (1850)* (hereafter *Trial*).
5. Ibid., p. 63.
6. J. McCabe, *Life and Letters of George Jacob Holyoake* (2 Vols, 1908), Vol. I, pp. 62–7.
7. Holyoake, *Trial*, p. 9.
8. Ibid.
9. Ibid., p. 61.
10. For a good factual understanding of Bradlaugh's case, see W.L. Arnstein, *The Bradlaugh Case: A Study in Late Victorian Opinion and Politics* (Oxford, 1965). For a collection of Bradlaugh's political views, see *A Selection of the Political Pamphlets of Charles Bradlaugh*, prefaced by John Saville (New York, 1970).
11. *BL Add. Ms.* 56453 ff. 36–49.
12. Ibid., f. 46.

13. *BL Add. Ms.* 44111, f. 66.
14. Ibid.
15. Notes partly used in a speech of 3 May 1883. *BL Add. Ms.* 50043, f. 259. The part in italics seems to have been added as an afterthought and is written in blue pencil.
16. Ibid., f. 261.
17. These events are covered in detail in Tribe, *Bradlaugh*.
18. H. Bradlaugh Bonner, *Charles Bradlaugh: A Record of His Life and Work* (London, 1908), p. 203.
19. *Hansard, Series 3*, Vol. 270, 5 June–21 June 1882, p. 17.
20. An excellent short chronology of the events surrounding Bradlaugh's attempts to take his seat can be found in the biography published by his daughter: Bradlaugh Bonner, *Charles Bradlaugh*, pp. 203–8.
21. Letter of 4 March 1884. M.S. Eng. Lett. d. 180 (Bodleian), ff. 167–70.
22. See *The Gladstone Diaries*, Vols. ix, x, ed. H.C.G. Matthew (Oxford, 1986 and 1990).
23. Ibid., ix, p. 549.
24. Ibid., x, p. 58, fn 7.
25. *The Journal of John Wodehouse, First Earl of Kimberley, for 1862–1902*, eds A. Hawkins and J. Powell (1997). Camden Fifth Series Vol. 9, p. 317.
26. Matthew, *The Gladstone Diaries*, x, pp. 80–1.
27. Gladstone to Sir William Harcourt, 1 August 1881, ibid, p. 103.
28. Ibid., p. 208, fn 4.
29. Father Ignatius of Llauthaery Abbey to Bradlaugh, 13 July 1880. M.S. Eng. Lett. d. 180, f. 152.
30. *HO* 144/573/A62996.
31. R.K. Wilson, *History of Modern English Law* (London, 1875), p. 101.
32. W. Holdsworth, *A History of the English Law*, Vol. XV, eds A.L. Goodhart and H.G. Hanbury (London, 1965), p. 139.
33. Carter, 'Changes in the Constitution', p. 113.
34. Holdsworth, *A History of the English Law*, Vol. XV, p. 139.
35. Ibid.
36. *British Library*, Add. 50041, f. 9.
37. Ibid.
38. Ibid.
39. Bradlaugh to Northcote, 1 July 1881, ibid., f. 60.
40. Ibid.
41. Ibid., f. 61.
42. Bradlaugh to Gladstone, 6 May 1881, ibid., f. 88.
43. 5 August 1881. *British Library*, Add. 44111, f. 110.

44. S.J. Celestine-Edwards, *Political Atheism: A Lecture* (London, 1889), p. 1.
45. Ibid., p. 7.
46. G.W. Foote, *Atheism and Morality* (London, 1891), p. 2. See also *Atheism and its Bearing on Morals: A Debate between Annie Besant and the Rev. G.F. Handel Rowe* (London, 1887), p. 34.

Chapter 6 Roman Catholics: The Enduring 'Other'

1. *HO* 44/37, f. 212.
2. Ibid., f. 213.
3. *HO* 45/872.
4. Ibid.
5. Ibid.
6. *HO* 45/872.
7. Colley, 'Britishness and otherness: an argument', p. 320.
8. *HO* 44/19, 8 March 1830, ff. 239–40.
9. Ibid.
10. Ibid., f. 240.
11. *MEPO* 5/256.
12. Memorial of Rev. Thomas Griffiths, Catholic Bishop, 10 April 1840. *HO* 44/35, f. 278.
13. *HO* 45/1996.
14. *HO* 144/926/A49962. Catholic priests had been allowed into workhouses by the Poor Law Board in 1859. See E.R. Norman, *The English Catholic Church in the Nineteenth Century* (Oxford, 1984), p. 186.
15. *HO* 144/926/A49962.
16. *HO* 45/9737/A54570.
17. These were Lord Ripon in the short-lived Gladstone Government of 1886 and Henry Matthews in the Salisbury Government that replaced it.
18. For an overview of the continuing phenomenon of post-1829 anti-Catholicism, see G.F.A. Best, 'Popular Protestantism in Victorian Britain', in R. Robson, ed., *Ideas and Institutions of Victorian Britain* (London, 1967), pp. 115–42.
19. *The Political Correspondence of Mr Gladstone and Lord Granville 1868–1876*, ed. A. Ramm, Vol. I, p. 48, letter 112.
20. Granville's comments must be seen against the background of defections from the High Anglican Church to the Roman Catholic Church in Victorian England, led by the likes of John Newman and Henry Manning and influenced by the Oxford Movement. See O. Chadwick, *The Spirit of the*

Oxford Movement: Tractarian Essays (Cambridge, 1990); J. Newman, *Apologia Pro Vita Sua*, ed. M.J. Svaglic (Oxford, 1967).
21. Victoria to Granville, 24 August 1869. Guedalla, *The Queen and Mr Gladstone*, Letter 143, p. 250.
22. Victoria to Gladstone, 15 October 1869. Ibid., Letter 148, p. 252.
23. F.H. Wallis, *Popular Anti-Catholicism in Mid-Victorian Britain* (Lewiston, 1993), p. 1.
24. Victoria to Gladstone, 20 January 1874. Guedalla, *The Queen and Mr Gladstone*, Letter 499, p. 435.
25. 9 March 1873. Victoria to Granville, 24 August 1869. Ibid., Letter 443, p. 407.
26. For an overview see M. Whitehead, 'A view from the bridge: the Catholic school', in V.A. McClelland and M. Hodgetts, eds, *From Without the Flaminian Gate: 150 Years of Roman Catholicism in England and Wales 1850–2000* (London, 1999), pp. 217–44.
27. On the Maynooth question, see Wallis: *Popular Anti-Catholicism in Mid-Victorian Britain*, pp. 115–55; E.R. Norman, *Anti-Catholicism in Victorian England* (London, 1968), pp. 23–51.
28. D.G. Paz, *Popular Anti-Catholicism in Mid-Victorian England* (Stanford, 1992), p. 6.
29. Ibid., p. 16.
30. Wallis, *Popular Anti-Catholicism in Mid-Victorian Britain*, p. 157.
31. Paz, *Popular Anti-Catholicism in Mid-Victorian England*, pp. 13–14.
32. N. Hughes, 'The Tichbornes, the Doughtys, and Douglas Woodruff', *Recusant History*, Vol. 23, No. 4 (1997), pp. 602–21.
33. W.L. Arnstein, 'The Murphy riots: a Victorian dilemma', *Victorian Studies*, Vol. 19, No. 1 (1975), pp. 51–71, at p. 59. See also W.L. Arnstein, *Protestant versus Catholic in Mid-Victorian England: Mr Newdegate and the Nuns* (Columbia and London, 1982), p. 4.
34. Wallis, *Popular Anti-Catholicism in Mid-Victorian Britain*, p. 252.
35. A useful discussion of the riots can be found in Arnstein, *Protestant versus Catholic in Mid-Victorian England*, pp. 88–107.
36. Arnstein, 'The Murphy riots: a Victorian dilemma'.
37. Ibid.
38. Ibid., p. 71.
39. For a discussion of the possible causes for the strength of British reaction to the re-establishment of the Catholic hierarchy, see W. Ralls, 'The papal aggression of 1850: A study in Victorian anti-Catholicism', in G. Parsons, ed., *Religion in Victorian Britain, Vol. IV: Interpretations* (Manchester and

New York, 1988), pp. 115–34; J.P. von Arx, 'Catholics and politics', in V.A. McClelland and M. Hodgetts, eds, *From Without the Flaminian Gate: 150 Years of Roman Catholicism in England and Wales 1850–2000* (London, 1999), pp. 245–71; and G. Parsons, 'Victorian Roman Catholicism: emancipation, expansion and achievement', in Parsons, *Religion in Victorian Britain, Vol. 1: Traditions*, pp. 146–83. For a sympathetic although dated view of the Catholic position, see D. Gwynn, *A Hundred Years of Catholic Emancipation (1829–1929)* (London, 1929), pp. 78–92.
40. See Wallis, *Popular Anti-Catholicism in Mid-Victorian Britain*, pp. 53–83; Norman, *Anti-Catholicism in Victorian England*, pp. 52–79. For the text of the 'Durham letter' see ibid. pp. 159–61.
41. Quoted in Wallis, *Popular Anti-Catholicism in Mid-Victorian Britain*, pp. 159–60.
42. See letters to Lord Palmerston of November and December, 1850. *HO* 45/3235.
43. Perriers to Palmerston, 30 November 1850. Ibid.
44. J. Wolffe, *God and Greater Britain: Religion and National Life in Britain and Ireland 1843–1945* (London and New York, 1994), p. 114.
45. *PRO* 30/22/9B, ff. 121–2.
46. Ibid., f. 127.
47. D. Newsome, *The Convert Cardinals: John Henry Newman and Henry Edward Manning* (London, 1993), pp. 193–4.
48. *HO* 45/3988.
49. Ibid.
50. Ibid.
51. Legal opinion of 2 December 1850. *HO* 45/3235.
52. Ibid.
53. Legal opinion of 2 December 1850. *HO* 45/3235.
54. Ibid.
55. *HO* 45/4238, letter of 18 June 1852.
56. Letter of 1 May 1852. *British Library, Add.* 44138, f. 30.
57. *CAB* 41/2/17, 27 April 1870.
58. *CAB* 41/1/51, 9 December 1869.
59. *CAB* 41/2/18, 7 May 1870.
60. J.L. Altholz, 'The Vatican decrees controversy, 1874–1875', *Catholic Historical Review*, Vol. 57, No. 4 (1972), pp. 593–605.
61. E.R. Norman, *The English Catholic Church in the Nineteenth Century* (Oxford, 1984), p. 311.
62. Altholz, 'The Vatican decrees controversy, 1874–1875', p. 593.
63. W.E. Gladstone, 'The Vatican decrees in their bearing on civil allegiance: a political expostulation', in W.E. Gladstone, *Rome and the Newest Fashions*

in Religion – Three Tracts: The Vatican Decrees; Vaticanism; Speeches of the Pope (London, 1875), p. xxiv.
64. Ibid., p. xli
65. Ibid., p. l.
66. Ibid., p. lxxii.
67. Quoted in *Religion in Victorian Britain Vol. III Sources*, ed. G. Parsons (Manchester and New York, 1988), p. 115.
68. Altholz, 'The Vatican decrees controversy, 1874–1875', p. 604.
69. *The Times*, 5 September 1874, quoted in D. Quinn, *Patronage and Piety: The Politics of English Roman Catholicism 1850–1900* (Stanford, 1993), p. 91.
70. *Vaticanism: A Full Report of the Great Public Meeting – In Relation to the Present Attitude of the Papacy, and its bearings on Civil Allegiance and National Prosperity and Freedom* (Glasgow, 1875); *Papalism: A Full Report of the Great Public Meeting, In Exposition of the Principles that Respectively Distinguish the Papal System and the Protestant Religion, and their Influences on Individual Well-being and National Prosperity, held Wednesday, 15 November 1876* (Glasgow, 1876).
71. *Vaticanism: A Full Report of the Great Public Meeting*, p. 14.
72. W.E. Gladstone, *Vaticanism: An Answer to Replies and Reproofs* (London, 1875), p. 118.
73. M.I. Friedland, *The Trials of Israel Lipski* (London, 1984), p. 105.
74. D. Quinn, *Patronage and Piety: The Politics of English Roman Catholicism 1850–1900* (Stanford, 1993), pp. 148–9.
75. *HO* 144/485/X37824.
76. Ibid.
77. The petition is contained in *HO* 45/9861/B13251.
78. Ibid.
79. Ibid.
80. Ibid.
81. *HO* 45/10077/B7918.
82. Letter of 4 February 1891. Ibid.
83. Notes on questions raised in Parliament, dated 4 February 1891. Ibid.
84. Ibid.
85. Ibid.
86. Petition of 14 March 1890. Ibid.
87. Dated 2 February 1891. Ibid.
88. Ibid.
89. 23 November 1890? (The date is unclear on the original document). *British Library Add.* 56371, ff. 41–6.

Chapter 7 The New Jewish Threat

1. See C. Bermant, *Point of Arrival: A Study of London's East End* (London, 1975), pp. 31–6. See also A. Davies, *The East End Nobody Knows: A History, A Guide, An Exploration* (London, 1990), pp. 32–4.
2. Bermant, *Point of Arrival*, p. xi.
3. See J.P. May, 'The Chinese in Britain, 1860–1914', in Holmes, *Immigrants and Minorities in British Society*, pp. 111–24.
4. Ng Kwee Choo, *The Chinese in London* (London, 1968), pp. 5–14.
5. For a comparative assessment of how immigration policy can buttress particular perceptions of national identity, see M.M. Ngai, *Impossible Subjects: Illegal Aliens and the Making of Modern America* (Princeton, 2004). For the British context, see R. Cohen, *Frontiers of Identity: The British and the Others* (London, 1994). Lauren McLaren and Mark Johnson have also undertaken contemporary research which shows modern British immigration is opposed by some because of its challenge to British customs and values, rather than for reasons of self-interest. L. McLaren and M. Johnson, 'Resources, Group Conflict and Symbols: Explaining Anti-Immigration Hostility in Britain', *Political Studies*, Vol. 55 (2007), pp. 709–32.
6. Holmes, *Anti-Semitism*, p. 103.
7. Ibid.
8. Ibid., p. 5.
9. Anderson, *Jewish Emancipation: A Voice from Israel*, p. 18.
10. Mayhew, *London Labour and the London Poor*, Vol. I, p. 117.
11. Ibid.
12. Ibid., p. 125.
13. Ibid.
14. Bermant, *Point of Arrival*, p. 140.
15. Ibid., pp. 136–7. For a discussion of Jewish educational accomplishment in the period, see I. Osborne, 'Achievers of the ghetto: the education of Jewish immigrants' children in Tower Hamlets, 1870–1914', in A. Newman, ed., *The Jewish East End 1840–1939* (London, 1981), pp. 163–72. For the Jews' Free School in particular, see M. Michaels, 'Memories of the Jews' Free School, Bell Lane', in Newman, *The Jewish East End 1840–1939*, pp. 155–61.
16. Van Duin, 'Ethnicity, race and labour, 1830s–1930s', p. 91.
17. Cited in D. Feldman, 'There was an Englishman, an Irishman and a Jew...: immigrants and minorities in Britain', *Historical Journal*, Vol. 26, No. 1 (1983), pp. 185–99, at p. 185.

18. Feldman, *Englishmen and Jews*, p. 4. Feldman has emphasised that Jewish integration had periods of great success as well as periods of friction. See D. Feldman, 'Jews and the State in Britain', in M. Brenner et al., eds, *Two Nations: British and German Jews in Comparative Perspective* (Tübingen, 1999), pp. 141–61.
19. For a discussion of the anarchism link, see P. Knepper, 'The Other Invisible Hand: Jews and Anarchists in London before the First World War', *Jewish History*, Vol. 22, No. 3 (2008), pp. 295–315.
20. See generally Holmes, *Anti-Semitism*, pp. 36–48.
21. Ibid., pp. 64–5, relating mainly in this case to the late 1890s and early 1900s.
22. T.M. Endelman, 'Native Jews and foreign Jews in London, 1870–1914', in D. Berger, ed., *The Legacy of Jewish Migration: 1881 and Its Impact* (Brooklyn, 1983), pp. 109–29, at p. 121.
23. Ibid.
24. W.D. Rubinstein, *A History of the Jews in the English-Speaking World: Great Britain* (Basingstoke and London, 1996), p. 5.
25. M. Ragussis, 'The "secret" of English anti-Semitism: Anglo-Jewish studies and Victorian studies', *Victorian Studies*, Vol. 40, No. 2 (1997), pp. 295–307, at p. 296.
26. A.L. Shane, 'The Dreyfus Affair: could it have happened in England?', *Jewish Historical Studies*, Vol. 30 (1987–88), pp. 135–48.
27. S.A. Hochberg, 'The repatriation of Eastern European Jews from Great Britain, 1881–1914', *Jewish Social Studies*, Vol. 50, Nos. 1–2 (1988–92), pp. 49–62, at p. 50.
28. Endelman, 'Native Jews and foreign Jews in London, 1870–1914', p. 113.
29. Hochberg, 'The repatriation of Eastern European Jews from Great Britain: 1881–1914', p. 57.
30. For an introduction to anti-alienism in the 1880s, see W.J. Fishman, *East End Jewish Radicals 1875–1914* (London, 1975), pp. 61–93.
31. For an overview of Judaism in Britain in this period, see E.C. Black, *The Social Politics of Anglo-Jewry 1880–1920* (Oxford, 1988).
32. Bermant, *Point of Arrival*, p. 138.
33. For a discussion of the attitude towards new immigrants, see D. Feldman, 'The importance of being English: Jewish immigration and the decay of liberal England', in D. Feldman and G. Stedman Jones, eds, *Metropolis London: Histories and Representations Since 1800* (London, 1989), pp. 56–84.
34. The case is briefly discussed in C. Holmes, 'East End crime and the Jewish community 1887–1911', in Newman, *The Jewish East End 1840–1939*,

pp. 109–23. For greater depth, see M.I. Friedland, *The Trials of Israel Lipski* (London, 1984).
35. The details of the case are contained in the reports in *The Times* at the time of Lipski's trial. See *The Times*, Saturday 30 July 1887, p. 7, and Monday 1 August 1887, p. 10.
36. *Hansard, Series 3*, 19 August 1887, pp. 1102–3. Cunninghame Graham took a strong interest in the matter, questioning the Home Secretary on other occasions. *Hansard, Series 3*, 12 August 1887, p. 253; 13 August 1887, p. 364; 15 August 1887, p. 449.
37. *Hansard, Series 3*, 3 September 1887, pp. 1071–2.
38. Ibid., pp. 1072.
39. Sir Henry Tyler, asking a question in Parliament, referred to the 'considerable doubt and difficulty in the case'. *Hansard, Series 3*, 15 August 1887, p. 448.
40. 27 August 1887. Madame Olga Novikoff Collection, Bodleian Library, Oxford, MSS. Eng. Misc. D. 182, as quoted in Friedland, *The Trials of Israel Lipski*, p. 183.
41. Friedland, *The Trials of Israel Lipski*, pp. 204–5.
42. *The Times*, Tuesday 23 August 1887, p. 9.
43. *Hansard, Series 3*, 1 September 1887, p. 718.
44. Ibid., p. 719.
45. L. Perry Curtis, *Jack the Ripper and the London Press* (New Haven and London, 2001), pp. 170–1.
46. Wallis, *Popular Anti-Catholicism in Mid-Victorian Britain*, p. 178.
47. D. Cesarani, *The Jewish Chronicle and Anglo-Jewry, 1841–1991* (Cambridge, 1994), p. 39.
48. D. Englander, 'Anglicized not Anglican: Jews and Judaism in Victorian Britain', in Parsons, *Religion in Victorian Britain Vol. 1 Traditions*, pp. 235–73, at p. 243.
49. See S. Knight, *Jack the Ripper: The Final Solution* (London, 1976); P. Begg, M. Fido and K. Skinner, *Jack the Ripper A to Z* (London, 1991); B. Paley, *Jack the Ripper: The Simple Truth* (London, 1995); P. Sugden, *The Complete History of Jack the Ripper* (London, 1995); A.P. Wolf, *Jack the Myth: A New Look at the Ripper* (London, 1993); D. Abrahamsen, *Murder and Madness: The Secret Life of Jack the Ripper* (London, 1992); S.P. Evans and P. Gainey, *The Lodger: The Arrest and Escape of Jack the Ripper* (London, 1995); J. Tully, *The Secret of Prisoner 1167: Was This Man Jack the Ripper?* (London, 1997); P. Begg, *Jack the Ripper: The Uncensored Facts* (London, 1988); M. Fairclough, *The Ripper and the Royals* (London, 1991); M. Howells and K. Skinner, *The Ripper Legacy: The Life and Death of Jack the Ripper* (London, 1987).
50. See p. 191, n. 19.

NOTES

51. For an excellent discussion of the impact of the Jack the Ripper murders on London, see J.R. Walkowitz, *City of Dreadful Delight: Narratives of Sexual Danger in Late-Victorian London* (London, 1992), pp. 191–228.
52. The range of suspects, including those who were Jewish, is well covered in Begg et al., *Jack the Ripper A to Z*.
53. W.J. Fishman has noted the 'Judophobia' brought about by the murders: Fishman, *East End Jewish Radicals 1875–1914*, p. 73.
54. Cesarani, *The Jewish Chronicle and Anglo-Jewry, 1841–1991*, p. 81.
55. *MEPO* 3/140 fol. 238. Report of Inspector Helson, 7 September 1888, as quoted in Begg, *Jack the Ripper: The Uncensored Facts*, p. 83.
56. For details on John Pizer, see Sugden, *The Complete History of Jack the Ripper*, pp. 141–7; Paley, *Jack the Ripper: The Simple Truth*, pp. 47–8; Begg, *Jack the Ripper: The Uncensored Facts*, pp. 80–5.
57. Begg, *Jack the Ripper: The Uncensored Facts*, p. 126.
58. Warren explained his actions to the Home Office. *HO* 144/221/A49301C 8c, as cited in Begg, *Jack the Ripper: The Uncensored Facts*, p. 127.
59. Knight, *Jack the Ripper: The Final Solution*, pp. 177–8.
60. *HO* 144/221/A49301C 8c, 6 November 1888, as cited in Begg, *Jack the Ripper: The Uncensored Facts*, p. 126.
61. Holmes, *Anti-Semitism*, pp. 5–6.
62. Ibid., pp. 49–62.
63. Ibid., p. 55.
64. Ibid., p. 56.
65. As cited in Begg et al., *Jack the Ripper A to Z*, pp. 14–15.
66. Ibid.
67. Ibid., p. 15.
68. Ibid.
69. Eye-witness evidence has long been looked upon with suspicion. In 1895 a man by the name of Adolf Beck was convicted on the evidence of 12 women who testified that Beck was 'the man who had inveigled each of them into an intimate relationship and then persuaded them to hand over various valuables before disappearing'. M. Aronson and J. Hunter, *Litigation: Evidence and Procedure*, 5th edn (Sydney, 1995), p. 721. Beck served seven years imprisonment and was being held on another charge when the real culprit was caught red-handed. The English Court of Appeal in *R v Turnbull* has since decided that a caution to a jury is mandatory when witness identification is a factor. L. Re, 'Eyewitness identification: why so many mistakes?', *Australian Law Journal*, Vol. 58 (1984), pp. 509–20, at p. 517.
70. For the view that Cutbush is actually a likely Ripper suspect, see Wolf, *Jack the Myth*.

71. For details on the Memorandum, see Begg et al., *Jack the Ripper A to Z*.
72. See for instance ibid., pp. 149–52.
73. Ibid., p. 150.
74. R. Anderson, *The Lighter Side of My Official Life* (London, 1910), pp. 135–6, as quoted in Begg, *Jack the Ripper: The Uncensored Facts*, p. 138.

Chapter 8 'Un-British' Women: The 'Problem' of Prostitution

1. Mrs Butler's third letter, from Kent, *Shield*, 9 March 1870, as quoted in *Women in Public 1850–1900: Documents of the Victorian Women's Movement*, ed. P. Hollis (London, 1979), p. 212.
2. For a broad-ranging discussion of Victorian prostitution – including the debates on who held the moral blame for the vice – see P. Bartley, *Prostitution: Prevention and Reform in England, 1860–1914* (London and New York, 2000).
3. H.J. Self, *Prostitution, Women and Misuse of the Law* (London, 2003).
4. C. Booth, *Life and Labour of the People in London, Final Volume: Notes on Social Influences and Conclusion* (London, 1902), p. 123.
5. D. Crow, *The Victorian Woman* (London, 1971), p. 215.
6. Ibid., p. 216.
7. Ibid., p. 218.
8. D. MacAndrew, '"Skittles": the darling of London', in G. Alexander, ed., *The Mammoth Book of Heroic and Outrageous Women* (London, 1999), pp. 295–311, at p. 297.
9. T. Fisher, *Prostitution and the Victorians* (New York, 1997), p. viii.
10. Ibid.
11. Ibid., pp. 29–79.
12. See ibid., pp. 17–23.
13. These concerns were given voice during a period in which the British State was showing an increasing willingness to impact more directly on people's lives in the name of public health. See for instance, B. Harris, *The Origins of the British Welfare State: Society, State and Social Welfare in England and Wales, 1800–1945* (Basingstoke and New York, 2004), pp. 104–24.
14. W. Acton, *Prostitution*, ed. P. Fryer (London, 1968, 1st pub. 1857).
15. Paula Bartley has suggested that this picture changed so that, by the end of the nineteenth century, poverty was overwhelmingly recognised as the main cause of prostitution. P. Bartley, *Prostitution: Prevention and Reform in England, 1860–1914* (London and New York, 2000), p. 6.
16. F. Harrison, *The Dark Angel: Aspects of Victorian Sexuality* (New York, 1978), p. 229.

17. Mayhew, *London Labour and the London Poor*, Vol. I, p. 459.
18. Ibid., p. 458.
19. Booth, *Life and Labour of the People in London*, Final Volume, p. 123.
20. For a table of the number of prostitutes arrested between 1870 and 1914, see S. Petrow, *Policing Morals: The Metropolitan Police and the Home Office 1870–1914* (Oxford, 1994), p. 15.
21. Mayhew, *London Labour and the London Poor*, Vol. IV, p. 263.
22. J.R. Walkowitz, *Prostitution and Victorian Society: Women, Class and the State* (Cambridge, 1980), pp. 14–15.
23. Jones, *Crime, Protest, Community and Police in Nineteenth-Century Britain*, p. 25.
24. Walkowitz, *City of Dreadful Delight*, p. 6.
25. *MEPO 3/36*. The file includes contemporary press coverage from the *Morning Advertiser*.
26. Letter of 17 December 1860 from Wandsworth Division. *MEPO 3/35*.
27. Mayhew, *London Labour and the London Poor*, Vol. IV, p. 263.
28. Petrow, *Policing Morals*, p. 122.
29. For a discussion of white slavery and measures taken against it, see Walkowitz, *City of Dreadful Delight*, pp. 81–134. See also Petrow, *Policing Morals*, pp. 158–75.
30. E.M. Sigsworth and T.J. Wyke, 'A study of Victorian prostitution and venereal disease', in *Suffer and Be Still: Women in the Victorian Age*, ed. M. Vicinus (Bloomington and London, 1972), pp. 77–99, at p. 93.
31. For a detailed discussion of these Acts and the events surrounding them, see P. McHugh, *Prostitution and Victorian Social Reform* (London, 1980), and Walkowitz, *Prostitution and Victorian Society*.
32. An Act for the Prevention of Contagious Diseases at Certain Naval and Military Stations, 1864, Section 17, as cited in Fisher, *Prostitution and the Victorians*, p. 86.
33. J. Walkowitz, 'The making of an outcast group: prostitutes and working women in nineteenth-century Plymouth and Southampton', in Vicinus, ed., *A Widening Sphere: Changing Roles of Victorian Women*, pp. 72–93. For a Scottish perspective on the 'othering' of prostitutes, see L. Mahood, *The Magdalenes: Prostitution in the Nineteenth Century* (London and New York, 1990).
34. Walkowitz, 'The making of an outcast group', pp. 72–93, at p. 72.
35. Ogborn, 'Law and discipline in nineteenth century English state formation: the Contagious Diseases Acts of 1864, 1866 and 1869', *Journal of Historical Sociology*, Vol. 6, No. 1 (1993), pp. 28–55, at p. 38.
36. For some of the contemporary views on prostitution and the Contagious Diseases Acts, see *Prostitution in the Victorian Age: Debates on the Issue from*

19th Century Critical Journals, introduction by K. Nield (Farnborough (Hants), 1973).

37. An in-depth appreciation of Josephine Butler's role can be gained from her own writings and a number of biographies. See for example J.E. Butler, *Personal Reminiscences of a Great Crusade* (London, 1911); M.G. Fawcett and E.M. Turner, *Josephine Butler: Her Work and Principles, and Their Meaning for the Twentieth Century* (London, 1927); E. Moberly Bell, *Josephine Butler: Flame of Fire* (London, 1962).
38. Petrow, *Policing Morals*, p. 125.
39. *HO* 144/78/A4010.
40. Ibid.
41. Acton, *Prostitution*, p. 21.
42. Sigsworth and Wyke, 'A study of Victorian prostitution and venereal disease', p. 96.
43. Acton, *Prostitution*, p. 22.
44. Ibid., p. 26.
45. Ibid., p. 27.
46. WO 33/27, ff. 298 onwards.
47. Ibid.
48. WO 33/41.
49. Ibid.
50. Sigsworth and Wyke, 'A study of Victorian prostitution and venereal disease', pp. 96–7.
51. Walkowitz, 'The making of an outcast group', p. 81, quoting from *Shield*, 17 December 1870.
52. J. Lewis, 'The working-class wife and mother and State intervention, 1870–1918', in J. Lewis, ed., *Labour and Love: Women's Experience of Home and Family, 1850–1940* (Oxford, 1986), pp. 99–120, at p. 105–6.
53. Sigsworth and Wyke, 'A study of Victorian prostitution and venereal disease', pp. 96–7.
54. Petrow, *Policing Morals*, p. 122.
55. Ibid., pp. 123–4.
56. For a scholarly edition of the text of the series of articles, see W.T. Stead, *The Maiden Tribute of Modern Babylon: The Report of the Secret Commission*, ed. A.E. Simpson (Lambertville, NJ, 2007).
57. Petrow, *Policing Morals*, pp. 122–3.
58. Walkowitz has argued that Stead's reporting distorted the truth by suggesting that women and girls were entrapped into prostitution, when economic imperatives played by far the greater role. J.R. Walkowitz, 'Male vice and feminist virtue: feminism and the politics of prostitution in nineteenth-

century Britain', *History Workshop Journal*, Vol. 13 (1982), pp. 79–93, at p. 83.
59. Mayhew, *London Labour and the London Poor*, Vol. IV, pp. 269–72.
60. *HO* 144/154/A40202C.
61. Police report on Stead allegations, ibid.
62. *HO* 144/154/A40202F
63. Ibid. Report written 19 October 1885.
64. Fisher, *Prostitution and the Victorians*, p. 157.
65. Ibid., p. 133.
66. Walkowitz, *City of Dreadful Delight*, p. 128.
67. J.R. Walkowitz, 'Going public: shopping, street harassment, and street-walking in Late Victorian London', *Representations*, Vol. 62 (1998), pp. 1–30, at p. 18.
68. Petrow, *Policing Morals*, p. 130.
69. *HO* 45/9964/X15663.
70. Petrow, *Policing Morals*, p. 134.
71. *HO* 45/9964/X15663.
72. Petrow, *Policing Morals*, pp. 134–5. Sir Charles Warren's insistence on his independence of action ultimately resulted in his resignation when he was criticised by the Home Secretary for an article he published in *Murray's Magazine*. See *Hansard, Series 3*, 13 November 1888, pp. 1036–8.
73. Notes on file, 18 March 1889. *HO* 45/9964/X15663.
74. Petrow, *Policing Morals*, p. 136.
75. *HO* 144/472/X15501.
76. Ibid.
77. Vaughan to Godfrey Lushington, Home Office, 13 August 1887. *HO* 144/472/X15501.
78. *MEPO* 2/209.
79. *HO* 45/9740/A55536.
80. Ibid.
81. Ibid.
82. Extract contained in *HO* 45/9740/A55536/3.
83. Ibid.
84. *HO* 45/9740/A55536/15.
85. Letter from Local Government Board to the Archbishop of Canterbury, 20 July 1896. *HO* 45/9740/A55536/16.
86. *HO* 45/9740/A55536/6.
87. Booth, *Life and Labour of the People in London*, Final Volume, p. 121.
88. Ibid., p. 126.
89. Ibid., p. 127.

Chapter 9 Containing Deviance: The Legal Limits of Male Sexuality

1. Opening Speech in the case of Boulton et al., 9 May 1871. *DPP* 4/6, f. 4.
2. H.G. Cocks has noted that, despite official protestations that the crime was almost 'unknown' in England, there were in fact thousands of prosecutions undertaken through the nineteenth century against men engaged in homosexual acts. See H.G. Cocks, 'Secrets, Crimes and Diseases, 1800–1914', in M. Cook, ed., *A Gay History of Britain: Love and Sex Between Men Since the Middle Ages* (Oxford and Westport, CT, 2007).
3. J. Weeks, *Against Nature: Essays on History, Sexuality and Identity* (London, 1991), p. 52. See also H.G. Cocks, *Nameless Offences: Homosexual Desire in the Nineteenth Century* (London and New York, 2003). For a detailed examination of the criminalisation of homosexuals in the first half of the nineteenth century, see C. Upchurch, *Before Wilde: Sex Between Men in Britain's Age of Reform* (Berkely, 2009).
4. E. Cohen, 'Legislating the norm: from sodomy to gross indecency', *South Atlantic Quarterly,* Vol. 88, No. 1 (1989), pp. 181–217, at pp. 185–6.
5. Ibid.
6. *Between the Acts: Lives of Homosexual Men 1885–1967*, K. Porter and J. Weeks, eds, (London, 1991), p. 1.
7. J.E. Baker to Mr Malwah, 26 May 1830, *HO* 44/20, ff. 205–7.
8. There was a particular fear of urban areas – predominantly London – as places that could effectively hide sexual 'perversion'. See M. Cook, *London and the Culture of Homosexuality, 1885–1914* (Cambridge, 2003).
9. For a summary of how perceptions of homosexual behaviour moved from 'sin' to 'crime' over this period, see J. Weeks, *Coming Out: Homosexual Politics in Britain, from the Nineteenth Century to the Present* (London, 1977), pp. 11–22.
10. Weeks, *Against Nature*, p. 50.
11. The pervasive official silence about homosexuality was supported by the structures of the criminal law through the court system, which discouraged discussion of the topic in open court. See H.G. Cocks, 'Making the Sodomite Speak: Voices of the Accused in English Sodomy Trials, c. 1800–98', *Gender & History*, Vol. 18, No. 1 (2006), pp. 87–107.
12. Porter and Weeks, *Between the Acts*, p. 3.
13. I.D. Crozier, 'The medical construction of homosexuality and its relation to the law in nineteenth-century England', *Medical History*, Vol. 45, No. 1 (2001), pp. 61–83.
14. Ibid.

15. For a useful discussion of the case, see W.A. Cohen, *Sex Scandal: The Private Parts of Victorian Fiction* (Durham and London, 1996). See also M.B. Kaplan, *Sodom on the Thames: Sex, Love, and Scandal in Wilde Times* (Ithaca and London, 2005).
16. R. Pearsall, *The Worm in the Bud: The World of Victorian Sexuality* (London, 1969), p. 464. The results of rectal examinations by medical practitioners were extensively discussed in court. See Crozier, 'The medical construction of homosexuality and its relation to the law in nineteenth-century England', pp. 61–83.
17. Pearsall, *The Worm in the Bud*, p. 465–6.
18. Ibid., p. 466.
19. DPP 4/6, f. 3.
20. Ibid., f. 1003.
21. Cohen: *Sex Scandal: The Private Parts of Victorian Fiction*, pp. 97–110.
22. For a discussion on the validity of the claims regarding the alleged ignorance of homosexuality displayed in the Boulton and Park case, see J. Bristow, 'Remapping the Sites of Modern Gay History: Legal Reform, Medico-Legal Thought, Homosexual Scandal, Erotic Geography', *Journal of British Studies*, Vol. 46, No. 1 (2007), pp. 116–42.
23. The Criminal Law Amendment Act, 1885, in The Statutes of the United Kingdom of Great Britain and Ireland, 48 & 49 Victoria, Section 11, p. 362.
24. See J. Weeks, '"Sins and diseases": some notes on homosexuality in the nineteenth century', *History Workshop Journal*, Vol. 1, No. 1 (1976), pp. 211–19, at p. 215.
25. Ibid., p. 212.
26. *Hansard, Series 3*, Vol. 300, p. 1397.
27. For an assessment of the degree to which Labouchere's amendment was merely an ill-considered individual act, see H. Montgomery Hyde, *The Other Love: An Historical and Contemporary Survey of Homosexuality in Britain* (London, 1970), pp. 134–7. For a more recent discussion of Labouchere's motivations, see N. McKenna, *The Secret Life of Oscar Wilde* (New York, 2005), pp. 77–81.
28. C. Hirshfield, 'The tenacity of tradition: *Truth* and the Jews 1877–1957', *Patterns of Prejudice*, Vol. 28, Nos. 3–4 (1994), pp. 67–85, at p. 69.
29. C. Hirshfield, 'Labouchere, Truth and the uses of Anti-Semitism', *Victorian Periodicals Review*, Vol. 26, No. 3 (1993), pp. 134–42, at p. 135.
30. *Hansard, Series 3*, Vol. 300, p. 1552.
31. For a useful synopsis of the case, see DPP 1/95/1, f. 332–5. For a secondary study, see C. Simpson et al., *The Cleveland Street Affair* (Boston and Toronto, 1976).

32. M. Dockray, 'The Cleveland Street scandal 1889–90: the conduct of the defence', *Journal of Legal History*, Vol. 17, No. 1 (1996), pp. 1–16, at pp. 2–3.
33. Ibid.
34. *Pall Mall Gazette*, 12 September 1889, DPP 1/95/2, f. 8.
35. T. Aronson, *Prince Eddy and the Homosexual Underworld* (London, 1994).
36. *New York Herald*, 22 December 1889, see DPP 1/95/2.
37. *The Star*, 25 November 1889, contained in DPP 1/95/2, f. 40.
38. *The Referee*, 24 November 1889, contained in DPP 1/95/2, f. 36.
39. *Truth*, 14 November 1889, contained in DPP 1/95/2, f. 22.
40. *Reynold's Newspaper*, 29 September 1889, contained in DPP 1/95/2, f. 12.
41. *Truth*, 6 February 1890, contained in DPP 1/95/2, f. 108.
42. *Truth*, 2 January 1890, contained in DPP 1/95/2, f. 69.
43. Aronson, *Prince Eddy and the Homosexual Underworld*, p. 142.
44. A. Roberts, *Salisbury: Victorian Titan* (London, 1999), p. 546.
45. Cuttings contained in DPP 1/95/2.
46. Letter from Foreign Office informing Home Office of Salisbury's decision, 24 July 1889. DPP 1/95/1, f. 13.
47. DPP 1/95/2, f. 175.
48. Ibid
49. *New York Herald*, 22 December 1889. ibid., f. 61.
50. Ibid.
51. *CAB* 41/21/1, 10 March 1888.
52. Aronson, *Prince Eddy and the Homosexual Underworld*, p. 146.
53. Dockray, 'The Cleveland Street scandal 1889–90: the conduct of the defence', p. 3.
54. *North London Press*, 23 November 1889, contained in DPP 1/95/2, f. 29.
55. Dockray, 'The Cleveland Street scandal 1889–90: the conduct of the defence', p. 3–8.
56. Ibid.
57. Ibid., pp. 8–9.
58. Ibid., p. 11.
59. DPP 1/95/3.
60. Ibid., f. 8.
61. Ibid.
62. 1 October 1889 to *DPP*; 2 October 1889 to the Treasury Solicitor. DPP 1/95/1.
63. Ibid., ff. 233–46.
64. Ibid., f. 247.

65. Ibid., ff. 253–4.
66. Ibid., f. 255.
67. DPP 1/95/3/4, f. 25.
68. Ibid., f. 23.
69. DPP 1/95/7, f. 42.
70. Ibid., f. 47.
71. Letter of 19 October 1889. *DPP* 1/95/1, folios. 291 & 307.
72. DPP 1/95/7.
73. Ibid.
74. Ibid.
75. Ibid., ff. 23–30.
76. Letter of 27 November 1890. *British Library*, Add. 56448, f. 240.
77. For a sense of the literary and historiographical battles that continue over how scholars have written about the trials, see L.J. Moran, 'Transcripts and Truth: Writing the Trials of Oscar Wilde', in J. Bristow, ed., *Oscar Wilde and Modern Culture* (Athens, OH, 2008), pp. 234–58.
78. For an overview of Wilde's life, see B. Belford, *Oscar Wilde: A Certain Genius* (London, 2000). See also McKenna, *The Secret Life of Oscar Wilde*.
79. R. Dellamora, *Masculine Desire: The Sexual Politics of Victorian Aestheticism* (Chapel Hill, 1990), p. 194.
80. Aronson, *Prince Eddy and the Homosexual Underworld*, pp. 7–34.
81. F. Harris and Lord A. Douglas, *New Preface to the 'Life and Confessions of Oscar Wilde'* (London, 1925), p. 38.
82. Ibid., p. 49.
83. H. Pearson, *The Life of Oscar Wilde* (Harmondsworth, 1960, 1st published 1946 by Methuen), p. 265. See also *The Letters of Oscar Wilde*, ed. R. Hart-Davis (London, 1963).
84. In *De Profundis* Wilde wrote: 'The gods had given me almost everything. I had genius, a distinguished name, high social position, brilliancy, intellectual daring...'. *The Complete Letters of Oscar Wilde*, eds M. Holland and R. Hart-Davis (London, 2000), p. 729.
85. Hart-Davis and Holland, *The Letters of Oscar Wilde*, pp. 425–6. *De Profundis* is published in full on pp. 423–511.
86. Harris and Douglas, *New Preface to the 'Life and Confessions of Oscar Wilde'*, p. 34.
87. See Hart-Davis and Holland, *De Profundis* in *The Letters of Oscar Wilde*, pp. 423–511.
88. See Belford, *Oscar Wilde*, pp. 225–6.
89. Pearson, *The Life of Oscar Wilde*, p. 267.

90. Harris and Douglas, *New Preface to the 'Life and Confessions of Oscar Wilde'*, pp. 38–42.
91. Ibid., p. 38.
92. Ibid., p. 43.
93. S. Morley, *Oscar Wilde* (New York, 1976), pp. 95–6.
94. Pearson, *The Life of Oscar Wilde*, p. 277.
95. R. Ellman, *Oscar Wilde* (London, 1988, 1st pub. 1987), p. 412.
96. Harris and Douglas: *New Preface to the 'Life and Confessions of Oscar Wilde'*, pp. 21–8.
97. Ibid., pp. 20–1.
98. Letter of 19 April 1895. DPP 1/96, p. 2.
99. Wilde to Ada and Ernest Leverson, 9 April 1895. Hart-Davis and Holland: *The Letters of Oscar Wilde*, pp. 389–90.
100. Ellman, *Oscar Wilde*, p. 415.
101. Marquess of Queensberry, *Oscar Wilde and the Black Douglas* (London, 1949), p. 74.
102. *The Destruction of Lord Rosebery: From the Diary of Sir Edward Hamilton 1894–1895*, ed. D. Brooks (London, 1986), p. 236, Entry for Thursday 4 April 1895.
103. Pearson, *The Life of Oscar Wilde*, p. 286.
104. Harris and Douglas, *New Preface to the 'Life and Confessions of Oscar Wilde'*, p. 29.
105. J. Pearce, *The Unmasking of Oscar Wilde* (London, 2000), p. 239.
106. Holland and Hart-Davis, *The Letters of Oscar Wilde*, p. 649n.
107. Harris and Douglas, *New Preface to the 'Life and Confessions of Oscar Wilde'*, pp. 29–30.
108. Ellman, *Oscar Wilde*, p. 449.
109. Pearson, *The Life of Oscar Wilde*, pp. 306–7.
110. H. Montgomery Hyde, *Oscar Wilde* (London, 1976), p. 205.
111. Brooks, *The Destruction of Lord Rosebery*, p. 250. Entry for Tuesday 21 May 1895.
112. M.S. Foldy, *The Trials of Oscar Wilde: Deviance, Morality, and Late Victorian Society* (New Haven and London, 1997).
113. For a discussion of Wilde's partial responsibility for his own downfall, see G. Robb, *Strangers: Homosexual Love in the 19th Century* (London, 2003), pp. 37–8.
114. A. Adut, 'A Theory of Scandal: Victorians, Homosexuality, and the Fall of Oscar Wilde', *American Journal of Sociology*, Vol. 111, No. 1 (2005), pp. 213–48.

115. T. Fisher, 'The mysteries of Oscar Wilde', *History Today*, Vol. 50, No. 12 (2000), pp. 18–20, at p. 18.
116. Brooks, *The Destruction of Lord Rosebery*, p. 236. Entry for Friday, 5 April 1895.

Chapter 10 Conclusion

1. For a discussion of the progress of atheism through the period, see F.B. Smith, 'The atheist mission: 1840–1900', in Robson, *Ideas and Institutions of Victorian Britain*, pp. 205–35.
2. For a sense of the 'stages' that Victorian society went through in its approach to questions of sexual deviance, see F. Mort, *Dangerous Sexualities: Medico-Moral Politics in England Since 1830* (London and New York, 2000).
3. On Smith's views, see Holmes, *Anti-Semitism*, pp. 11–12 and footnote 19.
4. Ibid.
5. Guedalla, *The Queen and Mr Gladstone*, Letter 499, p. 435.
6. Holmes, *Anti-Semitism*, p. 45.
7. Ibid., p. 43. Holmes suggests that the views were mostly anti-alien rather than anti-Jewish in particular.
8. The Jewish ministers were G.J. Goschen, Farrer Herschell, and Sir George Jessel, who was not actually in the Cabinet but was the first Jewish minister. Holmes, *Anti-Semitism*, p. 109.
9. The letter seems to be undated, but is included with others from November 1890 relating to the Parnell divorce. *British Library*, Add. 56448, f. 100.
10. Feldman: *Englishmen and Jews*, p. 47.
11. Davis, 'Disraeli, the Rothschilds, and Anti-Semitism', pp. 9–19, at p. 18.
12. Weeks, 'Sins and diseases', p. 214.
13. T. Blair, Prepared text for the Labour Party conference speech, 2006. http://news.bbc.co.uk/2/hi/uk_news/politics/5382590.stm accessed 23 June 2011.

BIBLIOGRAPHY

Primary Sources

Manuscript

A. Official

The National Archives, Kew

Cabinet Papers (CAB) 41
Director of Public Prosecutions (DPP) 1
Director of Public Prosecutions (DPP) 4
Metropolitan Police (*MEPO*) 3
Metropolitan Police (*MEPO*) 2
Metropolitan Police (*MEPO*) 5
Criminal Records (CRIM) 1
Foreign Office (*FO*) 881
Home Office (*HO*) 144
Home Office (*HO*) 119/18
Home Office (*HO*) 44
Home Office (*HO*) 45
The National Archives (PRO) 30 (Lord John Russell Papers)
War Office (WO) 33

B. Private

Bodleian Library, Oxford

Asquith Papers
Disraeli Papers
Ducane Papers
W.V. Harcourt Papers
Sandars Papers

British Library, London

Carnarvon Papers
Cross Papers
Sir Charles Dilke Papers
Viscount (Herbert) Gladstone Papers
W.E. Gladstone Papers
Gordon Papers
Halsbury Papers
William Hazlitt Correspondence
Iddesleigh Papers
William Morris Papers
Sir Robert Peel Papers

Documentary

C. Booth, *Life and Labour of the People in London, Final Volume: Notes on Social Influences and Conclusion*, London: MacMillan and Co., Ltd., 1902.
Correspondence of Daniel O'Connell the Liberator, ed. W.J. Fitzpatrick, 2 Vols, Vol. 2, London: John Murray, 1888.
Hansard's Parliamentary Debates: Third Series, London: Cornelius Buck & Son, various years.
Women in Public 1850–1900: Documents of the Victorian Women's Movement, ed. P. Hollis, London: George Allen & Unwin, 1979.
Irish Political Documents 1869–1916, eds A. Mitchell & P. O'Snodaigh, Dublin: Irish Academic Press, 1989.
Religion in Victorian Britain Vol. III Sources, ed. G. Parsons, Manchester & New York: Manchester University Press, 1988.
The Political Correspondence of Mr Gladstone and Lord Granville 1868–1876, ed. A. Ramm, Vol. I, London: 1952. Camden Thirds Series Vol. LXXXI.
The Public General Statutes: Reign of Her Majesty Queen Victoria, London: Eyre & Spottiswoode, 1848–82.
The Statutes of the United Kingdom of Great Britain and Ireland, Reign of His Majesty William IV, 1833 – Vol. 3 & 4, London: Eyre & Spottiswoode, 1833.

The Queen and Mr Gladstone, ed. P. Guedalla, New York: Kraus Reprint Co., 1969, 1st pub. 1934.

Literary

W. Acton, *Prostitution*, ed. P. Fryer, London: Macgibbon & Kee Ltd, 1968, 1st pub. 1857.
G. Allen, 'Are we Englishmen?', *Fortnightly Review*, Vol. 28 (1880), pp. 472–87, in M.D. Biddiss, ed., *Images of Race*, Leicester: Leicester University Press, 1979, pp. 237–56.
D.J. Anderson, *Jewish Emancipation: A Voice from Israel*, London, 1857.
A. Besant and G.F. Handel Rowe, *Atheism and its Bearing on Morals: A Debate between Annie Besant and the Rev. G.F. Handel Rowe*, London: Freethought Publishing Company, 1887.
Images of Race, ed. M.D. Biddiss, Leicester: Leicester University Press, 1979.
J.E. Butler, *Personal Reminiscences of a Great Crusade*, London: Horace Marshall & Son, 1911.
E. Byrne, *Parnell: A Memoir*, ed. F. Callanan, Dublin: The Lilliput Press Ltd, 1991.
A.T. Carter, 'Changes in the Constitution', in *A Century of Law Reform: Twelve Lectures on the Changes in the Law of England During the Nineteenth Century*, South Hackensack, New Jersey: Rothman Reprints Inc., 1972, pp. 97–130.
S.J. Celestine-Edwards, *Political Atheism: A Lecture*, London: John Kensit, 1889.
The Complete Letters of Oscar Wilde, eds M. Holland and R. Hart-Davis, London: Fourth Estate, 2000.
'The Croker Papers': *The Correspondence and Diaries of the Right Honourable John Wilson Croker*, 3 Vols, ed. L.J. Jennings, London: John Murray, 1884.
The Destruction of Lord Rosebery: From the Diary of Sir Edward Hamilton 1894–1895, ed. D. Brooks, London: Historians Press, 1986.
G.W. Foote, *Atheism and Morality*, London: Progressive Publishing Company, 1891.
The Gladstone Diaries, Volume 1. 1825–32, ed. M.R.D. Foot, Oxford: Clarendon Press, 1968.
W.E. Gladstone, 'The Vatican Decrees in their Bearing on Civil Allegiance: A Political Expostulation', in *Rome and the Newest Fashions in Religion: Three Tracts: The Vatican Decrees; Vaticanism; Speeches of the Pope*, London: John Murray, 1875.
W.E. Gladstone, *Vaticanism: An Answer to Replies and Reproofs*, London: John Murray, 1875.
F. Harris and Lord A. Douglas, *New Preface to the 'Life and Confessions of Oscar Wilde'*, London: Fortune Press, 1925.
G.J. Holyoake, *The History of the Last Trial by Jury for Atheism in England: A Fragment of Autobiography*, London: James Watson, 1850.

Jewish Emancipation, by an Israelite, London: D. Nutt, 1845.
The Journal of John Wodehouse, First Earl of Kimberley, for 1862–1902, eds A. Hawkins and J. Powell, London: Royal Historical Society, 1997. Camden Fifth Series Vol. 9.
The Letters of Oscar Wilde, ed. R. Hart-Davis, London: Rupert Hart-Davis, 1963.
W.E.H. Lecky, *The Leaders of Public Opinion in Ireland: Swift – Flood – Grattan – O'Connell*, London: Longmans, Green, & Co., 1871.
J. McCarthy and C. Praed, *Our Book of Memories: Letters of Justin McCarthy to Mrs Campbell Praed*, London: Chatto & Windus, 1912.
F.W. Maitland, *The Constitutional History of England*, Cambridge: Cambridge University Press, 1908.
H. Mayhew, *London Labour and the London Poor*, Volume I, London: Frank Cass & Co. Ltd, 1967, 1st published 1851.
J. Newman, *Apologia Pro Vita Sua*, ed. M. J. Svaglic, Oxford: Oxford University Press, 1967.
T.P. O'Connor & R.M. McWade, *Gladstone–Parnell and the Great Irish Struggle*, Sydney: McNeill & Coffee, Publishers, 1886.
K. O'Shea, *Charles Stewart Parnell: His Love Story and Political Life*, Vol. II, London: Cassell and Co., Ltd, 1914.
Papalism: A Full Report of the Great Public Meeting, In Exposition of the Principles that Respectively Distinguish the Papal System and the Protestant Religion, and their Influences on Individual Well-being and National Prosperity, held on Wednesday, 15 November 1876. Glasgow: West Scotland Protestant Association, 1876.
The Parliamentary Diaries of Sir John Trelawny, 1858–1865, ed. T.A. Jenkins, London, 1990. Camden Fourth Series Vol. 40.
Prostitution in the Victorian Age: Debates on the Issue from 19th Century Critical Journals, introduction by K. Nield, Farnborough, Hants: Gregg International Publishers, 1973.
C. Russell, *The Parnell Commission: The Opening Speech for the Defence*, London: Macmillan & Co, 1889.
A Selection of the Political Pamphlets of Charles Bradlaugh, prefaced by John Saville, New York: Augustus M. Kelley, 1970.
W.T. Stead, *The Maiden Tribute of Modern Babylon: The Report of the Secret Commission*, ed. A.E. Simpson, Lambertville, New Jersey: True Bill Press, 2007.
Vaticanism: A Full Report of the Great Public Meeting – In Relation to the Present Attitude of the Papacy, and its bearings on Civil Allegiance and National Prosperity and Freedom, Glasgow: West of Scotland Protestant Association, 1875.
R.K. Wilson, *History of Modern English Law*, London: Rivingtons, 1875.

Newspapers

The Times
North London Press

The Star
The Pall Mall Gazette
Reynolds's Newspaper
Truth
The New York Herald
The Referee

Secondary Sources

General Reference

Earl Halsbury, *The Laws of England: Being a Complete Statement of the Whole Law of England*, Vol. XI, London: Butterworth & Co., 1910.

W. Holdsworth, *A History of the English Law*, Vol. XV, eds A.L. Goodhart and H. G. Hanbury, London: Methuen & Co. Ltd, Sweet and Maxwell, 1965.

Books

J. Abels, *The Parnell Tragedy*, London: The Bodley Head, 1966.

D. Abrahamsen, *Murder and Madness: The Secret Life of Jack the Ripper*, London: Robson Books, 1992.

G. Alderman, *The Jewish Community in British Politics*, Oxford: Clarendon Press, 1983.

W.L. Arnstein, *The Bradlaugh Case: A Study in Late Victorian Opinion and Politics*, Oxford: Clarendon Press, 1965.

W.L. Arnstein, *Protestant versus Catholic in Mid-Victorian England: Mr Newdegate and the Nuns*, Columbia & London: University of Missouri Press, 1982.

M. Aronson and J. Hunter, *Litigation: Evidence and Procedure*, 5th edn, Sydney: 1995.

T. Aronson, *Prince Eddy and the Homosexual Underworld*, London: John Murray, 1994.

A. Aughey, *The Politics of Englishness*, Manchester: Manchester University Press, 2007.

P. Bartley, *Prostitution: Prevention and Reform in England, 1860–1914*, London & New York: Routledge, 2000.

H.S. Becker, *Outsiders: Studies in the Sociology of Deviance*, New York: The Free Press, 1963.

P. Begg, M. Fido, and K. Skinner, *Jack the Ripper A to Z*, London: Headline Book Publishing, 1991.

P. Begg, *Jack the Ripper: The Uncensored Facts: A Documented History of the Whitechapel Murders of 1888*, London: Robson Books, 1988.

J. Belchem, *Irish, Catholic and Scouse: The History of the Liverpool-Irish, 1800–1939*, Liverpool: Liverpool University Press, 2007.

B. Belford, *Oscar Wilde: A Certain Genius*, London: Bloomsbury, 2000.
E. Moberly Bell, *Josephine Butler: Flame of Fire*, London: Constable & Co., 1962.
C. Bermant, *Point of Arrival: A Study of London's East End*, London: Eyre Methuen, 1975.
P. Bew, *Ireland: The Politics of Enmity 1789–2006*, Oxford, Oxford University Press, 2007.
E.C. Black, *The Social Politics of Anglo-Jewry 1880–1920*, Oxford: Basil Blackwell, 1988.
P. Bonsall, *The Irish RMs: The Resident Magistrates in the British Administration of Ireland*, Dublin: Four Courts Press, 1997.
T. Bottomore, *Elites and Society*, 2nd edn, London: Routledge, 1993.
D.G. Boyce, *The Irish Question and British Politics 1868–1986*, New York: St Martin's Press, 1988.
H. Bradlaugh Bonner, *Charles Bradlaugh: A Record of His Life and Work*, London; T. Fisher, 1908.
I. Bradley, *Believing in Britain: The Spiritual Identity of 'Britishness'*, London/New York: I.B. Tauris, 2007.
A Union of Multiple Identities: The British Isles, c. 1750–c.1850, eds L. Brockliss and D. Eastwood, Manchester and New York: Manchester University Press, 1997.
C. Bryant, *The Nations of Britain*, Oxford: Oxford University Press, 2006.
P. Bull, *Land, Politics and Nationalism: A Study of the Irish land Question*, Dublin: Gill & MacMillan, 1996.
D. Cannadine, *Aspects of Aristocracy: Grandeur and Decline in Modern Britain*, New Haven and London: Yale University Press, 1994.
D. Cannadine, *The Decline and Fall of the British Aristocracy*, New Haven and London: Yale University Press, 1990.
Relocating Britishness, eds S. Caunce et al., Manchester and New York: Manchester University Press, 2004
D. Cesarani, *The Jewish Chronicle and Anglo-Jewry, 1841–1991*, Cambridge: Cambridge University Press, 1994.
O. Chadwick, *The Spirit of the Oxford Movement: Tractarian Essays*, Cambridge: Cambridge University Press, 1990.
Between 'Race and Culture' – Representations of 'the Jew' in English and American Literature, ed. B. Cheyette, Stanford: Stanford University Press, 1996.
B. Cheyette, *Constructions of 'The Jew' in English Literature and Society*, Cambridge: Cambridge University Press, 1993.
M. Clark, *Albion and Jerusalem: The Anglo-Jewish Community in the Post-Emancipation Era, 1858–1887*, Oxford: Oxford University Press, 2009.
H.G. Cocks, *Nameless Offences: Homosexual Desire in the Nineteenth Century*, London/ New York: I.B.Tauris Publishers, 2003.
R. Cohen, *Frontiers of Identity: The British and the Others*, London: Longman, 1994.

W.A. Cohen, *Sex Scandal: The Private Parts of Victorian Fiction*, Durham and London: Duke University Press, 1996.
L. Colley, *Britons: Forging the Nation 1707–1837*, New Haven and London: Yale University Press, 1992.
M. Cook, *London and the Culture of Homosexuality, 1885–1914*, Cambridge: Cambridge University Press, 2003.
T. Corfe, *The Phoenix Park Murders: Conflict, Compromise and Tragedy in Ireland, 1879–1882*, London: Hodder & Stoughton, 1968.
V. Crossman, *Politics, Law and Order in Nineteenth-Century Ireland*, New York: St Martin's Press, 1996.
D. Crow, *The Victorian Woman*, London: George Allen & Unwin, 1971.
L. Perry Curtis Jr, *Jack the Ripper and the London Press*, New Haven and London: Yale University Press, 2001.
Being British: The Search for the Values that Bind the Nation, ed. M. d'Ancona, Edinburgh/London: Mainstream Publishing, 2009.
A. Davies, *The East End Nobody Knows: A History, A Guide, An Exploration*, London: Macmillan, 1990.
R. Dellamora, *Masculine Desire: The Sexual Politics of Victorian Aestheticism*, Chapel Hill: University of North Carolina Press, 1990.
The Great Famine: Studies in Irish History, 1845–52, eds R.D. Edwards and T.D. Williams, Dublin: Published for the Irish Committee of Historical Sciences by Browne and Nolan, 1956.
C. Emsley, *Crime and Society in England*, 1750–1900, 2nd edn, London: Longman, 1996.
R. English, *Irish Freedom: The History of Nationalism in Ireland*, Basingstoke/Oxford: Macmillan, 2006.
St J. Ervine, *Parnell*, London: Ernest Benn Limited, 1925.
S.P. Evans and P. Gainey, *The Lodger: The Arrest and Escape of Jack the Ripper*, London: Century, 1995.
M. Fairclough, *The Ripper and the Royals*, London: Duckworth, 1991.
M.G. Fawcett and E.M. Turner, *Josephine Butler: Her Work and Principles, and their meaning for the Twentieth Century*, London: Association for Moral and Social Hygiene, 1927.
D. Feldman, *Englishmen and Jews: Social Relations and Political Culture, 1840–1914*, New Haven/London: Yale University Press, 1994.
E. Feuchtwanger, *Disraeli*, London: Arnold, 2000.
T. Fisher, *Scandal: The Sexual Politics of Late Victorian Britain*, Phoenix Mill: Alan Sutton Publishing, 1995.
T. Fisher, *Prostitution and the Victorians*, New York: St Martin's Press, 1997.
W.J. Fishman, *East End Jewish Radicals 1875–1914*, London: Duckworth, 1975.
Lord E. Fitzmaurice, *The Life of Granville George Leveson Gower, Second Earl Granville K.G. 1815–1891*, 2 Vols, London: Longmans, Green & Co., 1905.
M.S. Foldy, *The Trials of Oscar Wilde: Deviance, Morality, and Late Victorian Society*, New Haven/London: Yale University Press, 1997.

R.F. Foster, *Paddy and Mr Punch: Connections in Irish and English History*, London: Allen Lane, The Penguin Press, 1993.
M.I. Friedland, *The Trials of Israel Lipski*, London: Macmillan, 1984.
Britishness: Perspectives on the British Question, eds A. Gamble and T. Wright, London: Wiley Blackwell, 2009.
A. Gilam, *The Emancipation of the Jews in England 1830–1860*, New York: Garland Publishing, Inc., 1982.
The Irish in Britain 1815–1939, eds S. Gilley and R. Swift, London: Pinter Publishers, 1989.
B. Girvin, *From Union to Union: Nationalism, Democracy and Religion in Ireland*, Dublin: Gill & Macmillan, 2002.
P. Gray, *Famine, Land and Politics: British Government and Irish Society 1843–1850*, Dublin: Irish Academic Press, 1999.
D. Gwynn, *A Hundred Years of Catholic Emancipation (1829–1929)*, London: Longmans Green & Co., 1929.
C. Hall, K. McClelland and J. Rendall, *Defining the Victorian Nation: Class, Race, Gender and the Reform Act of 1867*, Cambridge: Cambridge University Press, 2000.
J.L. Hammond, *Gladstone and the Irish Nation*, London: Longmans, Green & Co., 1938.
B. Harris, *The Origins of the British Welfare State: Society, State and Social Welfare in England and Wales, 1800–1945*, Basingstoke/New York: Palgrave Macmillan, 2004.
F. Harrison, *The Dark Angel: Aspects of Victorian Sexuality*, New York: Universe Books, 1978.
A. Hastings, *The Construction of Nationhood: Ethnicity, Religion and Nationalism*, Cambridge: Cambridge University Press, 1997.
C. Holmes, *Anti-Semitism in British Society, 1876–1939*, London: Edward Arnold, 1979.
M. Howells and K. Skinner, *The Ripper Legacy: The Life and Death of Jack the Ripper*, London: Sidgwick & Jackson, 1987.
A. Jackson, *Home Rule: An Irish History, 1800–2000*, Oxford: Oxford University Press, 2003.
R. Jenkins, *Gladstone*, London: Papermac, 1995.
D. Jones, *Crime, Protest, Community and Police in Nineteenth-Century Britain*, London: Routledge & Kegan Paul, 1982.
C. Julios, *Contemporary British Identity: English Language, Migrants and Public Discourse*, Aldershot: Ashgate, 2008.
M.B. Kaplan, *Sodom on the Thames: Sex, Love, and Scandal in Wilde Times*, Ithaca/London: Cornell University Press, 2005.
R. Kee, *The Laurel and the Ivy*, London: Hamish Hamilton, 1993.
S. Knight, *Jack the Ripper: The Final Solution*, London: HarperCollins, 1976.
K. Kumar, *The Making of English National Identity*, Cambridge: Cambridge University Press, 2003.

T. Kushner, *Anglo-Jewry Since 1066*, Manchester/New York: Manchester University Press, 2009.

The Emancipation of Catholics, Jews and Protestants: Minorities and the Nation State in Nineteenth-Century Europe, eds R. Liedtke and S. Wendehorst, Manchester/New York: Manchester University Press, 1999.

V. D. Lipman, *A History of the Jews in Britain since 1858*, Leicester/London: Leicester University Press, 1990.

O. MacDonagh, *The Emancipist: Daniel O'Connell 1830–47*, New York: St Martin's Press, 1989.

O. MacDonagh, *States of Mind: A Study of Anglo-Irish Conflict 1780–1980*, London: George Allen & Unwin, 1983.

P. McHugh, *Prostitution and Victorian Social Reform*, London: Croom Helm, 1980.

A. Macintyre, *The Liberator: Daniel O'Connell and the Irish Party 1830–1847*, London: Hamish Hamilton, 1965.

N. McKenna, *The Secret Life of Oscar Wilde*, New York: Basic Books, 2005.

A.J. Mayer, *The Persistence of the Old Regime*, London: Croom Helm, 1981.

H. Montgomery Hyde, *Oscar Wilde*, London: Eyre Methuen, 1976.

H. Montgomery Hyde, *The Other Love: An Historical and Contemporary Survey of Homosexuality in Britain*, London: Heinemann, 1970.

M. Morgan, *National Identities and Travel in Victorian Britain*, Basingstoke: Palgrave MacMillan, 2001.

S. Morley, *Oscar Wilde*, New York: Holt, Rinehart & Winston, 1976.

F. Mort, *Dangerous Sexualities: Medico-Moral Politics in England Since 1830*, London/New York: Routledge, 2000.

T. Nairn, *After Britain: New Labour and the Return of Scotland*, London: Granta, 2000.

D. Newsome, *The Convert Cardinals: John Henry Newman and Henry Edward Manning*, London: John Murray, 1993.

M.M. Ngai, *Impossible Subjects: Illegal Aliens and the Making of Modern America*, Princeton: Princeton University Press, 2004.

Ng Kwee Choo, *The Chinese in London*, London: Oxford University Press, 1968.

E.R. Norman, *Anti-Catholicism in Victorian England*, London: George Allen & Unwin, 1968.

E.R. Norman, *The English Catholic Church in the Nineteenth Century*, Oxford: Clarendon Press, 1984.

S. O'Faolain, *King of the Beggars: A Life of Daniel O'Connell, the Irish Liberator in a Study of the Rise of the Modern Irish Democracy (1775–1847)*, New York: Viking Press, 1938.

C.Ó. Gráda, *The Great Irish Famine*, Cambridge/New York: Cambridge University Press, 1995.

Power in Societies, ed. M.E. Olsen, New York: Macmillan, 1970.

L. Mahood, *The Magdalenes: Prostitution in the Nineteenth Century*, London/New York: Routledge, 1990.

The Meaning of the Famine, ed. P. O'Sullivan, London: Leicester University Press, 1997.
B. Paley, *Jack the Ripper: The Simple Truth*, London: Headline Book Publishing, 1995.
D.G. Paz, *Popular Anti-Catholicism in Mid-Victorian England*, Stanford: Stanford University Press, 1992.
J. Pearce, *The Unmasking of Oscar Wilde*, London: Harper Collins Publishers, 2000.
R. Pearsall, *The Worm in the Bud: The World of Victorian Sexuality*, London: Weidenfeld & Nicolson, 1969.
H. Pearson, *The Life of Oscar Wilde*, Harmondsworth: Penguin Books, 1960, 1st published 1946 by Methuen.
H. Perkin, *The Origins of Modern English Society, 1780–1880*, London: Routledge & Kegan Paul, 1969.
S. Petrow, *Policing Morals: The Metropolitan Police and the Home Office 1870–1914*, Oxford: Clarendon Press, 1994.
M.G.H. Pittock, *Inventing and Resisting Britain: Cultural Identities in Britain and Ireland 1685–1789*, New York: St Martin's Press, 1997.
Between the Acts: Lives of Homosexual Men 1885–1967, eds K. Porter and J. Weeks, London: Routledge, 1991.
D. Powell, *Nationhood and Identity: The British State Since 1800*, London/New York: I.B. Tauris, 2002.
Marquess of Queensberry, *Oscar Wilde and the Black Douglas*, London: Hutchinson & Co., 1949.
D. Quinn, *Patronage and Piety: The Politics of English Roman Catholicism 1850–1900*, Stanford: Stanford University Press, 1993.
P. Readman, *Land and Nation in England: Patriotism, National Identity, and the Politics of Land, 1880–1914*, Woodbridge: Royal Historical Society, 2008.
G. Robb, *Strangers: Homosexual Love in the 19th Century*, London: Picador, 2003.
K. Robbins, *Great Britain: Identities, Institutions, and the Idea of Britishness*, London: Longman, 1998.
K. Robbins, *History, Religion and Identity in Modern Britain*, London: Hambledon Press, 1993.
A. Roberts, *Salisbury: Victorian Titan*, London: Weidenfeld & Nicolson, 1999.
C. Rojek, *Brit-Myth: Who Do the British Think They Are?* London: Reaktion Books, 2007.
C. Roth, *A History of the Jews in England*, Oxford: Clarendon Press, 1964.
W.D. Rubinstein, *Elites and the Wealthy in Modern British History: Essays in Social and Economic History*, Sussex: Harvester Press, 1987.
W.D. Rubinstein, *A History of the Jews in the English-Speaking World: Great Britain*, Basingstoke/London: MacMillan Press, 1996.
H.J. Self, *Prostitution, Women and Misuse of the Law*, London/Portland: Frank Cass, 2003.

D. Sibley, *Outsiders in Urban Societies*, Oxford: Basil Blackwell, 1981.
C. Simpson et al., *The Cleveland Street Affair*, Boston and Toronto: Little, Brown & Co., 1976.
D. Sinclair, *The Pound: A Biography*, London: Century, 2000.
P. Smith, *Disraeli: A Brief Life*, Cambridge: Cambridge University Press, 1996.
G. Stedman Jones, *Outcast London: A Study in the Relationship Between Classes in Victorian Society*, Harmondsworth: Penguin Books, 1971.
P. Sugden, *The Complete History of Jack the Ripper*, London: Robinson, 1995.
R. Swift, *Police Reform in Early Victorian York, 1835–1856*, York: University of York, 1988. University of York Borthwick Paper No. 73.
The Irish in Victorian Britain: The Local Dimension, eds R. Swift and S. Gilley, Dublin: Four Courts Press, 1999.
Debating Nationhood and Governance in Britain, 1885–1945: Perspectives from the 'Four Nations', eds D. Tanner et al., Manchester: Manchester University Press, 2006.
E.P. Thompson, *The Making of the English Working Class*, Harmondsworth: Penguin, 1968.
F.M.L. Thompson, *The Rise of Respectable Society: A Social History of Victorian Britain 1830–1900*, London: Fontana Press, 1988.
D. Tribe, *President Charles Bradlaugh, MP*, London: Archon Books, 1971.
J. Tully, *The Secret of Prisoner 1167: Was This Man Jack the Ripper?* London: Robinson, 1997.
C. Upchurch, *Before Wilde: Sex Between Men in Britain's Age of Reform*, Berkely: University of California Press, 2009.
J.R. Walkowitz, *City of Dreadful Delight: Narratives of Sexual Danger in Late-Victorian London*, London: Virago Press, 1992.
J.R. Walkowitz, *Prostitution and Victorian Society: Women, Class and the State*, Cambridge: Cambridge University Press, 1980.
F.H. Wallis, *Popular Anti-Catholicism in Mid-Victorian Britain*, Lewiston/Queenstown/Lampeter: Edwin Mellen Press, 1993. Texts and Studies in Religion Series Vol. 60.
P. Ward, *Britishness Since 1870*, London/New York: Routledge, 2004.
V. Ware, *Who Cares About Britishness? A Global View of the National Identity Debate*, London: Arcadia Books, 2007
J. Weeks, *Against Nature: Essays on History, Sexuality and Identity*, London: Rivers Oram Press, 1991.
J. Weeks, *Coming Out: Homosexual Politics in Britain, from the Nineteenth Century to the Present*, London: Quartet Books, 1977.
A.P. Wolf, *Jack the Myth: A New Look at the Ripper*, London: Robert Hale, 1993.
J. Wolffe, *God and Greater Britain – Religion and National Life in Britain and Ireland 1843–1945*, London/New York: Routledge, 1994.
J.C. Wood, *Violence and Crime in Nineteenth-Century England: The Shadow of Our Refinement*, London/New York: Routledge, 2004

Chapters from Books

J.P. von Arx, 'Catholics and politics', in V.A. McClelland and M. Hodgetts, eds, *From Without the Flaminian Gate: 150 Years of Roman Catholicism in England and Wales 1850–2000*, London: Darton, Longman & Todd, 1999, pp. 245–71.

M.R. Beames, 'The Ribbon societies: lower-class nationalism in pre-famine Ireland', in C.H.E. Philpin, ed., *Nationalism and Popular Protest in Ireland*, Cambridge: Cambridge University Press, pp. 245–63.

G.F.A. Best, 'Popular Protestantism in Victorian Britain', in R. Robson, ed., *Ideas and Institutions of Victorian Britain*, London: G. Bell & Sons, 1967, pp. 115–42.

G. Brown, 'Introduction', in M. d'Ancona, ed., *Being British: The Search for the Values that Bind the Nation*, Edinburgh and London: Mainstream Publishing, 2009, pp. 25–34.

P. Bull, 'The fall of Parnell: the political context of his intransigence', in D.G. Boyce and A. O'Day, eds, *Parnell in Perspective*, London/New York: Routledge, 1991, pp. 129–47.

P. Bull, 'Land and Politics, 1879–1903', in D.G. Boyce, ed., *The Revolution in Ireland, 1879–1923*, Houndmills: Macmillan Education, 1988, pp. 23–46.

H.G. Cocks, 'Secrets, Crimes and Diseases, 1800–1914', in M. Cook, ed., *A Gay History of Britain: Love and Sex Between Men Since the Middle Ages*, Oxford/Westport, CT: Greenwood World Publishing, 2007.

V. Crossman, 'The army and law and order in the nineteenth century', in T. Bartlett and K. Jeffery, eds, *A Military History of Ireland*, Cambridge: Cambridge University Press, 1996, pp. 358–78.

R.W. Davis, 'The Whigs and religious issues, 1830–5', in R.W. Davis and R.J. Helmstadter, eds, *Religion and Irreligion in Victorian Society*, London/New York: Routledge, 1992, pp. 29–50.

T.M. Endelman, ' "A Hebrew to the end": the emergence of Disraeli's Jewishness', in C. Richmond and P. Smith, eds, *The Self-Fashioning of Disraeli 1818–1851*, Cambridge: Cambridge University Press, 1998, pp. 106–30.

T.M. Endelman, 'Native Jews and foreign Jews in London, 1870–1914', in D. Berger, ed., *The Legacy of Jewish Migration: 1881 and its Impact*, Brooklyn: Brooklyn College Press, 1983, pp. 109–29.

D. Englander, 'Anglicized not Anglican: Jews and Judaism in Victorian Britain', in G. Parsons, ed., *Religion in Victorian Britain Vol. 1 Traditions*, Manchester: Manchester University Press, 1988, pp. 235–73.

D. Feldman, 'The importance of being English: Jewish immigration and the decay of liberal England', in D. Feldman and G. Stedman Jones, eds, *Metropolis London: Histories and Representations Since 1800*, London: Routledge, 1989.

D. Feldman, 'Jews and the State in Britain', in M Brenner et al., eds, *Two Nations: British and German Jews in Comparative Perspective*, Tübingen: Mohr Siebeck, 1999, pp. 141–61.

D. Feldman, 'Migration', in M. Daunton, ed., *The Cambridge Urban History of Britain, Vol. 3*, Cambridge: Cambridge University Press, 2000, pp. 185–206.

R. Floyd, '449 and All That: Nineteenth-and Twentieth-Century Interpretations of the "Anglo-Saxon Invasion" of Britain', in H. Brocklehurst and R. Phillips, eds, *History, Nationhood and the Question of Britain*, Basingstoke/New York: Palgrave Macmillan, 2004, pp. 184–96.

T. Garvin, 'Defenders, Ribbonmen and others: underground political networks in pre-famine Ireland', in C.H.E. Philpin, ed., *Nationalism and Popular Protest in Ireland*, Cambridge: Cambridge University Press, 1987, pp. 219–44.

V.A.C. Gatrell, 'Crime, authority and the policeman-state', in F.M.L. Thompson, ed., *The Cambridge Social History of Britain 1750–1950: Vol. 3: Social Agencies and Institutions*, Cambridge: Cambridge University Press, 1990, pp. 243–310.

S. Gilley, 'English attitudes to the Irish in England, 1780–1900', in C. Holmes, ed., *Immigrants and Minorities in British Society*, London: George Allen & Unwin, 1978, pp. 81–110.

A. Grant and K Stringer, 'Introduction: The enigma of British History', in A. Grant and K. Stringer, eds, *Uniting the Kingdom? The Making of British History*, London and New York, 1995, pp. 3–11.

D. Hay, 'Property, authority and the criminal law', in D. Hay et al., *Albion's Fatal Tree: Crime and Society in Eighteenth-Century England*, London: Allen Lane, 1975.

M.J. Hickman, 'Alternative historiographies of the Irish in Britain: a critique of the segregation/assimilation model', in R. Swift and S. Gilley, eds, *The Irish in Victorian Britain: The Local Dimension*, Dublin: Four Courts Press, 1999, pp. 236–53.

C. Holmes, 'East End crime and the Jewish community 1887–1911', in A. Newman, ed., *The Jewish East End 1840–1939*, London: The Jewish Historical Society of England, 1981, pp. 109–23.

D.C. Itzkowitz, 'Cultural pluralism and the Board of Deputies of British Jews', in R.W. Davis and R.J. Helmstadter, eds, *Religion and Irreligion in Victorian Society*, London and New York: Routledge, 1992, pp. 85–101.

K.T. Jeffes, 'The Irish in early Victorian Chester: an outcast community?' in R. Swift, ed., *Victorian Chester: Essays in Social History 1830–1900*, Liverpool: Liverpool University Press, 1996, pp. 85–117.

P. Jupp, 'Government, parliament and politics in Ireland, 1801–41', in J. Hoppit, ed., *Parliaments, Nations and Identities in Britain and Ireland, 1660–1850*, Manchester: Manchester University Press, 2003, pp. 146–64.

H. Kearney, 'Four Nations History in Perspective', in H. Brocklehurst and R. Phillips, eds, *History, Nationhood and the Question of Britain*, Basingstoke/New York: Palgrave Macmillan, 2004, pp. 10–19.

J. Lewis, 'The working-class wife and mother and State intervention, 1870–1918', in J. Lewis, ed., *Labour and Love: Women's Experience of Home and Family, 1850–1940*, Oxford: Basil Blackwell, 1986, pp. 99–120.

D. MacAndrew, ' "Skittles": the darling of London', in G. Alexander, ed., *The Mammoth Book of Heroic and Outrageous Women*, London: Robinson, 1999, pp. 295–311.

L. McLaren and M. Johnson, 'Resources, Group Conflict and Symbols: Explaining Anti-Immigration Hostility in Britain', *Political Studies*, Vol. 55, 2007, pp. 709–32.

J. McEldowney, 'Crown Prosecutions in Nineteenth-Century Ireland', in D. Hay and F. Snyder, eds, *Policing and Prosecution in Britain 1750–1850*, Oxford: Clarendon Press, 1989, pp. 427–57.

J.P. May, 'The Chinese in Britain, 1860–1914', in C. Holmes, ed., *Immigrants and Minorities in British Society*, London: George Allen & Unwin, 1978, pp. 111–24.

M. Michaels, 'Memories of the Jews' Free School, Bell Lane', in A. Newman, ed., *The Jewish East End 1840–1939*, London: Jewish Historical Society of England, 1981, pp. 155–61.

L.J. Moran, 'Transcripts and Truth: Writing the Trials of Oscar Wilde', in J. Bristow, ed., *Oscar Wilde and Modern Culture*, Athens, OH: Ohio University Press, 2008, pp. 234–58.

M. O'Callaghan, 'Parnellism and crime: constructing a Conservative strategy of containment 1887–91', in D. McCartney, ed., *Parnell: The Politics of Power*, Dublin: Wolfhound Press, 1991, pp. 102–24.

I. Osborne, 'Achievers of the ghetto: the education of Jewish immigrants' children in Tower Hamlets, 1870–1914', in A. Newman, ed., *The Jewish East End 1840–1939*, London: Jewish Historical Society of England, 1981, pp. 163–72.

G. Parsons, 'Victorian Roman Catholicism: emancipation, expansion and achievement', in G. Parsons, ed., *Religion in Victorian Britain, Vol. 1: Traditions*, Manchester: Manchester University Press, 1988, pp. 146–83.

W. Ralls, 'The papal aggression of 1850: A study in Victorian anti-Catholicism', in G. Parsons, ed., *Religion in Victorian Britain, Vol. IV: Interpretations*, Manchester New York: Manchester University Press, 1988, pp. 115–34.

J. Ridden, 'Elite Power and the British Political Identity: The Irish Elite in the "British World"', in H. Brocklehurst and R. Phillips, eds, *History, Nationhood and the Question of Britain*, Basingstoke/New York: Palgrave Macmillan, 2004, pp. 197–212.

K. Robbins, 'An imperial and multinational polity: The 'scene from the centre', 1832–1922', in *Uniting the Kingdom? The Making of British History*, A. Grant and K.J. Stringer, London/New York: Routledge, 1995, pp. 244–54.

E.M. Sigsworth and T.J. Wyke, 'A study of Victorian prostitution and venereal disease', in *Suffer and Be Still – Women in the Victorian Age*, M. Vicinus, ed., Bloomington and London: Indiana University Press, 1972, pp. 77–99.

F.B. Smith, 'The atheist mission: 1840–1900', in R. Robson, ed., *Ideas and Institutions of Victorian Britain*, London: G. Bell & Sons, 1967, pp. 205–35.

R. Swift, '"Another Stafford Street row": Law, order and the Irish presence in mid-Victorian Wolverhampton', in R. Swift and S. Gilley, eds, *The Irish in the Victorian City*, London: Croom Helm, 1985, pp. 179–205.

R. Swift, 'Crime and the Irish in nineteenth century Britain', in R. Swift and S. Gilley, eds, *The Irish in Britain 1815–1939*, London: Pinter Publishers, 1989, pp. 163–82.

R. Swift, 'Historians and the Irish: Recent writings on the Irish in nineteenth-century Britain', in D.M. MacRaild, ed., *The Great Famine and Beyond: Irish Migrants in Britain in the Nineteenth and Twentieth Centuries*, Dublin: Irish Academic Press, 2000, pp. 14–39.

R. Swift, 'Thomas Carlyle and Ireland', in D.G. Boyce and R. Swift, eds, *Problems and Perspectives in Irish History Since 1800 – Essays in Honour of Patrick Buckland*, Dublin: Four Courts Press, 2004, pp. 117–46.

J. Walkowitz, 'The making of an outcast group: prostitutes and working women in nineteenth-century Plymouth and Southampton', in M. Vicinus, ed., *A Widening Sphere: Changing Roles of Victorian Women*, Bloomington: Indiana University Press, 1977, pp. 72–93.

P. Ward, 'Nationalism and National Identity in British Politics, c. 1880s to 1914', in H. Brocklehurst and R. Phillips, eds, *History, Nationhood and the Question of Britain*, Basingstoke New York: Palgrave Macmillan, 2004, pp. 213–26.

M. Whitehead, 'A view from the bridge: the Catholic school', in V.A. McClelland and M. Hodgetts, eds, *From Without the Flaminian Gate: 150 Years of Roman Catholicism in England and Wales 1850–2000*, London: Darton, Longman & Todd, 1999, pp. 217–44.

Articles

J.L. Altholz, 'The Vatican decrees controversy, 1874–1875', *Catholic Historical Review*, Vol. 57, No. 4 (1972), pp. 593–605.

R. Altick, 'Punch's first ten years: the ingredients of success', *Journal of Newspaper and Periodical History*, Vol. 7, No. 2 (1991), pp. 5–16.

P. Anderson, 'Origins of the present crisis', *New Left Review*, Vol. 1, No. 23 (1964), pp. 26–53.

W.L. Arnstein, 'The Murphy riots: a Victorian dilemma', *Victorian Studies*, Vol. 19, No. 1 (1975), pp. 51–71.

A. Aughey, 'Anxiety and injustice: the anatomy of contemporary English nationalism', *Nations and Nationalism*, Vol. 16, No. 3 (2010), pp. 506–24.

H.F. Augstein, 'Aspects of philology and racial theory in nineteenth-century Celticism – the case of James Cowles Prichard', *Journal of European Studies*, Vol. 28, No. 4 (1998), pp. 355–71.

J. Bristow, 'Remapping the Sites of Modern Gay History: Legal Reform, Medico-Legal Thought, Homosexual Scandal, Erotic Geography', *Journal of British Studies*, Vol. 46, No. 1 (2007), pp. 116–42.

J. Burkett, 'Re-defining British Morality: "Britishness" and the Campaign for Nuclear Disarmament 1958–68', *Twentieth Century British History*, Vol. 21, No. 2 (2010), pp. 184–205.

E. Cohen, 'Legislating the norm: from sodomy to gross indecency', *South Atlantic Quarterly*, Vol. 88, No. 1 (1989), pp. 181–217.

L. Colley, 'Britishness and otherness: an argument', *Journal of British Studies*, Vol. 31, No. 4 (1992), pp. 309–29.

C. Collins, 'Britain and Ireland 1880–1921: searching for the scapegoat', *Modern History Review*, Vol. 2, No. 4 (1991), pp. 1–4.

S. Conway, 'War and national identity in the mid-eighteenth-century British Isles', *English Historical Review*, Vol. 116, No. 468 (2001), pp. 863–93.

B. Crick, 'The Four Nations: Interrelations', *Political Quarterly*, Vol. 79, No. 1 (2008), pp. 71–9.

I.D. Crozier, 'The medical construction of homosexuality and its relation to the law in nineteenth-century England', *Medical History*, Vol. 45, No. 1 (2001), pp. 61–83.

F. D'arcy, 'St Patrick's other island: the Irish invasion of Britain', *Eire – Ireland*, Vol. 28, No. 2 (1993), pp. 7–17.

R.W. Davis, 'Disraeli, the Rothschilds, and Anti-Semitism', *Jewish History*, Vol. 10, No. 2 (1996), pp. 9–19.

M. Dockray, 'The Cleveland Street scandal 1889–90: the conduct of the defence', *Journal of Legal History*, Vol. 17, No. 1 (1996), pp. 1–16.

P. Van Duin, 'Ethnicity, race and labour, 1830s–1930s: some Irish and international perspectives', *Saothar*, 19 (1994), pp. 86–103.

R. Dye, 'Catholic protectionism or Irish nationalism? Religion and politics in Liverpool, 1829–1845', *Journal of British Studies*, Vol. 40, No. 3 (2001), pp. 357–90.

D. Feldman, 'There was an Englishman, an Irishman and a Jew…: immigrants and minorities in Britain', *Historical Journal*, Vol. 26, No. 1 (1983), pp. 185–99.

T. Fisher, 'The mysteries of Oscar Wilde', *History Today*, Vol. 50, No. 12 (2000), pp. 18–20.

R. Foster and A. Jackson, 'Men for All Seasons? Carson, Parnell, and the Limits of Heroism in Modern Ireland', *European History Quarterly*, Vol. 39 (2009), pp. 414–38.

S. Gilley, 'Roman Catholicism and the Irish in England', *Immigrants and Minorities*, Vol. 18, Nos. 2–3 (1999), pp. 147–67.

A. Heesom, 'Ireland under the Union', *History Today*, Vol. 34, No. 1 (1984), pp. 31–5.

M.J. Hickman, 'Reconstructing and deconstructing "race": British political discourses about the Irish in Britain', *Ethnic and Racial Studies*, Vol. 21, No. 2 (1998), pp. 288–307.

C. Hirshfield, 'Labouchere, *Truth* and the uses of Anti-Semitism', *Victorian Periodicals Review*, Vol. 26, No. 3 (1993), pp. 134–42.

C. Hirshfield, 'The tenacity of tradition: *Truth* and the Jews 1877–1957', *Patterns of Prejudice*, Vol. 28, Nos. 3–4 (1994), pp. 67–85.
S.A. Hochberg, 'The repatriation of Eastern European Jews from Great Britain: 1881–1914', *Jewish Social Studies*, Vol. 50, Nos. 1–2 (1988–92), pp. 49–62.
T. Holloway, 'O'Connell and the Queen: a sesquicentennial remembrance', *Northern Ireland Legal Quarterly*, 46 (1995), pp. 63–71.
N. Hughes, 'The Tichbornes, the Doughtys, and Douglas Woodruff', *Recusant History*, Vol. 23, No. 4 (1997), pp. 602–21.
D. Johnson, 'Trial by jury in Ireland 1860–1914,' *Journal of Legal History*, Vol. 17, No. 3 (1996), pp. 270–93.
M. Keating, 'The Strange Death of Unionist Scotland', *Government and Opposition*, Vol. 45, No. 3 (2010), pp. 365–85.
P. Knepper, 'The Other Invisible Hand: Jews and Anarchists in London before the First World War', *Jewish History*, Vol. 22, No. 3 (2008), pp. 295–315.
K. Kumar, 'Negotiating English Identity: Englishness, Britishness and the Future of the United Kingdom', *Nations and Nationalism*, Vol. 16, No. 3 (2010), pp. 469–87.
J. McCalman, 'Respectability and working-class politics in Late-Victorian London', *Historical Studies*, Vol. 19, No. 74 (1980–1), pp. 108–24.
D.M. MacRaild, 'Irish immigration and the "Condition of England" question: The roots of an historiographical tradition', *Immigrants and Minorities*, Vol. 14, No. 1 (1995), pp. 67–85.
E. Malcolm, 'The reign of terror in Carlow: the politics of policing Ireland in the late 1830s', *Irish Historical Studies*, Vol. 32, No. 125 (2000), pp. 59–74.
A. Mycock, 'British Citizenship and the Legacy of Empires', *Parliamentary Affairs*, Vol. 63, No. 2 (2010), pp. 339–55.
T. Nairn, 'The British political elite', *New Left Review*, Vol. 1, No. 23 (1964), pp. 19–25.
M. Ogborn, 'Law and discipline in nineteenth century English state formation: the Contagious Diseases Acts of 1864, 1866 and 1869', *Journal of Historical Sociology*, Vol. 6, No. 1 (1993), pp. 28–55.
J.G.A. Pocock, 'British history: a plea for a new subject', *Journal of Modern History*, Vol. 47, No. 4 (1975), pp. 601–24.
M. Ragussis, 'The "secret" of English anti-Semitism: Anglo-Jewish studies and Victorian studies', *Victorian Studies*, Vol. 40 No. 2 (1997), pp. 295–307.
L. Re, 'Eyewitness identification: why so many mistakes?', *Australian Law Journal*, 58 (1984), pp. 509–20.
P.B. Rich, 'Social Darwinism, anthropology and English perspectives of the Irish, 1867–1900', *History of European Ideas*, Vol. 19, Nos. 4–6 (1994), pp. 777–85.
J. Sack, 'The British Conservative Press and Its Involvement in Antisemitic and Racial Discourse, Circa 1830–1895', *Journal of the Historical Society*, Vol. 8, No. 4 (2008), pp. 567–83.

A.L. Shane, 'The Dreyfus Affair: could it have happened in England?', *Jewish Historical Studies*, Vol. 30 (1987–88), pp. 135–48.
R. Swift, 'Heroes or villains? The Irish, crime, and disorder in Victorian England', *Albion*, Vol. 29, No. 3 (1997), pp. 399–421.
R. Swift, 'The outcast Irish in the British Victorian City: Problems and Perspectives', *Irish Historical Studies*, Vol. 25, No. 99 (1987), pp. 264–76.
J.R. Walkowitz, 'Going public: shopping, street harassment, and streetwalking in Late Victorian London', *Representations*, Vol. 62 (1998), pp. 1–30.
J.R. Walkowitz, 'Male vice and feminist virtue: feminism and the politics of prostitution in nineteenth-century Britain', *History Workshop Journal*, Vol. 13 (1982), pp. 79–93.
B. Ward-Perkins, 'Why did the Anglo-Saxons not become more British?', *English Historical Review*, Vol. 155, No. 462 (2000), pp. 513–33.
J. Weeks, ' "Sins and diseases": some notes on homosexuality in the nineteenth century', *History Workshop Journal*, Vol. 1 (1976), p. 211–19.
G. Wemyss, 'The power to tolerate: contests over Britishness and belonging in East London', *Patterns of Prejudice*, Vol. 40, No. 3 (2006), pp. 215–36.
A.S. Wohl, ' "Ben JuJu": representations of Disraeli's Jewishness in the Victorian Political Cartoon', *Jewish History*, Vol. 19, No. 2 (1996), pp. 89–134.
A.S. Wohl, ' "Dizzi-Ben-Dizzi": Disraeli as Alien', *Journal of British Studies*, Vol. 34, No. 3 (1995), pp. 375–411.

INDEX

Aberdeen, Lord George Hamilton-Gordon, Earl of, 87
Act for the better Prevention and more speedy Punishment of Offences endangering the Public Peace in Ireland (1835), 14
Act of Union, 10–11
Acton, William, 111, 117
Adler, Chief Rabbi, 98
Adut, Ari, 151
Albert Victor (Eddy), Prince, 136, 138
Aliens Act of 1905, the, 99-100
Altholz, Josef L., 91
Anderson, David John, 59, 98
Anderson, Sir Robert, 38–39, 40, 44–45, 104–107, 154
 and the Jack the Ripper murders, 104–107
 and Fenianism, 40
 and Parnellism and Crime articles, 38–39, 44–45
 and Pigott, 44
anti-catholicism, 28, 30, 81–84, 88, 92, 154
 and Anti-Popery Association, 92
 and appointments to the peerage, 82
 and the courts, 84
 and Murphy riots 1867, 85
 and Queen Victoria, 82–84
 and the Metropolitan Police, 81

anti-Semitism, 65–66, 68, 99–101, 103, 153
 and the Jack the Ripper murders, 102–107
Arnstein, Walter, 85
Aronson, Theo, 136, 138, 145
Association for the Extension of the Contagious Diseases Act, the, 117, 119
Atheism, 70–71, 73, 76–77
 history of restrictions against, 75
Avory, H.E., 141, 143

Beach, Michael Hicks, MP, 19
Bell, Laura, 110
Bellew, Thomas MP, 23
Bermant, Chaim, 97
Birkenhead disturbances, 1850, 30–31
Blair, Tony, 159–160
Bonsall, Penny, 19–20
Booth, Charles, 103, 112, 125
Boulton and Park court case, 128, 130, 157
Bradlaugh, Charles, 8, 61, 69–78, 155
 affirmation in House of Commons, 73
 'Appeal to the electors of Northampton', 71–72
 background, 71
 hostility towards Whiggism, 72
 and rights as an Englishman, 76

Bright, John, MP, 74
Britishness, 1–4, 8, 28, 65, 67, 78, 85–86, 135, 153, 155–162
Brown, Gordon, 1
Bryce, Lord, 67
Burgess, A., 155
Burke, T.H, as Under-Secretary for Ireland 24
Burton, Sir Richard, 104
Butler, Josephine, 109, 116
Byrne, Edward, 49

Carlyle, Thomas, 26
Carpenter, Edward, 130
Carter, A.T., 55
Cavendish, Lord Frederick, 24
Celestine Edwards, S.J., 77
Celts, 26–27
  and Anglo-Saxons, 26
Cesarani, David, 58, 102–103
Chamberlain, Joseph, MP, 22–23, 33, 36
Chambers, Sir Thomas, MP, 91
Clancarty, Earl of, 60
Clarence, Duke of, 5
Clark, Annie, 119
Clarke, Sir Edward, 36–37, 141, 148
Cleveland Street Scandal, 5, 78, 133, 135–144, 145, 151
Clinton, Lord Arthur, 131
Cobb, Henry, MP, 43
Cockburn, A.E., 88, 132
Cohen, Ed, 128, 133
Coleridge, Chief Justice, 89
Colquhoun, Patrick, 111
Coote, William, 120
Corfe, Thomas, 47
Colley, Linda, 3, 4, 7, 80
Contagious Diseases Acts, 5, 78, 109–110, 112, 114–119, 124–125, 132, 157–158
Criminal Law Amendment Act 1885, the, 120, 124, 129, 132, 135, 142, 149, 156–157
Croker, John Wilson, MP, 17

Crossman, Virginia, 19
Crozier, Ivan, 130
Cuffe, Hamilton, 142, 148
Cunninghame-Grahame, Robert, MP, 101
Curtis, L.Perry, 27, 102

Daly, John, 43
Dangerous Disturbances Act 1833, 11
D'arcy, Fergus, 26, 29
Dellamora, Richard, 145
Denman, Lord Thomas, 18
Dilke, Sir Charles, MP, 23
Dillon, John, 24
Disraeli, Benjamin, Earl of Beaconsfield, 1, 66–68, 92, 104, 154
  and Jewish 'otherness', 67–68
Dockray, Martin, 140–141
Douglas, Lord Alfred, 145–148, 150–152
Dover, 116, 118, 125
  and Contagious Diseases Acts, 116
Duin, Peter van, 29, 99
Duncombe, Thomas, MP, 15, 61
Dye, Ryan, 27

Ecclesiastical Titles affair, the, 30, 79, 86–92
Edinburgh, magistrates of, 16
Edinburgh Review, 30
Eliot, Lord Edward, 14, 24
Ellis, Havelock, 130
Endelman, Todd, 99–100
Englander, David, 102
Erskine, Mr Justice, 70
Establishment, the, 5, 10, 34–35, 50, 56, 63, 73, 77, 85–86, 95, 110, 134, 142, 144–145, 148
Euston, Lord Henry James FitzRoy, Earl of, 133, 135, 140–141

Feldman, David, 58, 68, 99, 155
Fenianism, 10–11, 29–30, 40, 45, 83
Fisher, Trevor, 111, 121, 151
Flynn, J.C., MP, 43

Index

Foldy, Michael, 151
Forster, W.E., MP, 24
Fortescue, Earl of, 135
Foucault, Michel, 5
Friedland, Martin, 92, 101

Garibaldi riots, 30
Gill, Charles, 148
Gilley, Sheridan, 27
   and Home Rule for Ireland, 33–34
   and Charles Stewart Parnell, 24, 39, 52–53, 144, 155
   and Queen Victoria, 64–66, 83, 89–90, 154
Graham, George, 29
Graham, Sir James MP, 17–18, 80, 87
Grant, Alexander, 4
Granville, George Leveson Gower, 2nd Earl of, 64–66, 82
Great Reform Act, the, 6
Greg, William R., 111
Greville, Charles, 17
Grey, Sir George, 29, 31, 87, 113
habeas corpus, writ of, 18, 20

Hall, Catherine, 7
Halsbury, Lord Giffard Hardinge, 1st Earl of, 37, 95, 142–143
Hamilton, Sir Edward, 149–151
Hammond, Charles, *see* Cleveland Street Scandal
Hammond, John Lawrence, 42
Hampden, Henry the Viscount, 71
Harcourt, Sir William, MP, 40, 43, 45–46, 51, 74, 116
Harrison, Fraser, 112
Hartington, Spencer Compton Cavendish, Marquess of, 24, 53
Hay, Douglas, 6
Healy, Timothy M., Irish MP, 37, 43, 51
Heesom, Alan, 18
Hirshfield, Claire, 134
Hochberg, S.A., 100
Holmes, Colin, 58, 65, 97, 99, 104

Holyoake, George Jacob, 70
Home Rule, *see* Ireland
Homosexuality, 110, 127–130, 133, 135, 138, 146, 150–151, 156–157
Homosexual(s), 2, 3, 5, 7, 78, 91, 110, 127, 130, 132–133, 135–136, 145, 148, 156–157
House of Commons, 6, 14–15, 26, 57–59, 61–62, 64–65, 69, 72–75, 90, 141, 144, 155
House of Lords, 5, 16–18, 56–59, 62–64, 67, 71, 77, 83, 139, 140

Ignatius, Father, of Llauthaery Abbey, 74
Ireland, 4, 9–26, 28, 33–35, 37–38, 40, 42–43, 48–49, 51–52, 54, 67, 80, 83, 88–89, 94–95, 107, 156
   disestablishment of Irish Church, 89
   Home Rule, 13, 31, 33–34, 51, 156
   Resident Magistrates, 19
Irish, 2–4,6–7, 9–35, 37, 39, 41–43, 46–54, 63, 78, 83, 85, 93, 97–99, 102, 112, 134, 136, 145, 153–154, 156, 158, 161
   and alleged criminality, 2, 11, 14–15, 21, 23, 25, 28–29, 35, 47, 48, 54, 78
   and illegal public meetings, 12, 25
   duty to join in 'Search and Pursuit', 20–21
   and jury acquittal rates, 22
   as 'priest-ridden', 20
Itzkowitz, David, 58

Jackson, Alvin, 48
Jack the Ripper murders, the, 100, 102–107, 112, 154
James, Sir Henry, MP, 134
Jeffes, Kristina, 27
Jewish Chronicle, the, 103
   Asher Myers as editor, 103
Jew(s), 2–3, 5–7, 23, 28–29, 55–67, 69, 78, 91–92, 97–107, 153–156
   legal position at start of nineteenth century, 55

Jew(s), *(cont.)*
  immigration to Britain following pogroms, 1881–1905, 97
  and alleged criminality, 100, 102
Jupp, Peter, 4

Kearney, Hugh, 4
Kilmainham Treaty, 24
Kimberley, Earl of, 35–36, 51, 74
Knight, Stephen, 104
Knightley, Rainald, MP, 62
Knill, Stuart, Roman Catholic Lord Mayor of London, 92–93

Labouchere, Henry, MP, 34, 36–38, 44, 51, 129, 133–134, 137, 141
Ladies National Association, the, 116
Land League, the (Ireland), 24, 156
Lecky, William E., 19
Lewis, Jane, 119
Lipski, Israel, 100–102
Lloyd, Clifford, 20
London, 26, 28, 57, 62, 67, 92–93, 97–98, 100, 102, 105, 110, 112, 115, 142, 147
  East End as point of arrival for immigrants 97
  Gazette, 88
Luddite disturbances, 18

MacAndrew, Donald, 111
MacDonagh, Oliver, 15, 28
MacNaughten, Sir Melville, 106
MacRaild, Donald, 26
Maitland, Frederic, 70
Malcolm, Elizabeth, 20
Manning, Henry, Roman Catholic Archbishop of Westminster, 90
Marx, Karl, 5
Matthews, Henry, MP, 37, 40, 43, 45, 92, 94, 102, 122–123, 137, 139, 141, 143–144
Mayne, Sir Richard, Metropolitan Police Commissioner, 81, 113

Maynooth, Roman Catholic Seminary, 84
McWade, R.M. 11
Middleton, Kate, 162
Morgan, George R., 81
Murphy, William, 85

National Vigilance Association, the, 120
Nevins, Dr Birkbeck, 118
Newdegate, Charles, MP, 61–62
Newlove, Henry, *see* Cleveland Street Scandal
Newman, John, 88
Newsome, David, 87
New York Herald, the (newspaper), 136, 139
Northcote, Sir Stafford, MP, 69–70, 72–73, 75–76
North London Press (newspaper), 137, 140

O'Brien, William, 24
O'Callaghan, Margaret, 41, 48
O'Connell, Daniel, 6, 10, 12–13, 15–18, 23–24, 80
O'Connor, T.P., 11, 35
O'Donnell v Walter court case, 35, 42
Ogborn, Miles, 115
O'Kelly, J.J., 24
O'Shea, Katherine, 34–35, 44, 49–52, 144
O'Shea, Captain William, 34, 50
Oxford, Bishop of, 61

Pall Mall Gazette, the, 101, 120–121, 136
Palmerston, Viscount, Henry John Temple, 10, 86
Parker, Francis, MP, 102
Parnell, Charles Stewart, 8–11, 15, 24, 32, 34–36, 38–54, 106, 134, 144, 153, 155–156
  and Katherine O'Shea, *see* O'Shea, Katherine
  and The Special Commission, 35–50
Paz, Denis G., 84

INDEX 223

Peace Preservation (Ireland) Act, the
   of 1856, 21
   of 1870, 21
   of 1875, 22
Pearsall, Ronald, 131
Peel, Robert, MP, 12, 16–17, 56–57, 102
Phoenix Park Murders, 24, 35, 47, 50, 52, 78, 107
Pigott, Richard, 43–44, 47, 49, 52
Pilot, The (Irish newspaper), 17
Pollock, Fred, 17
Porter, K., 128, 130
Portsmouth Protestant Institute, 95
Prevention of Crime Act 1882, the, 24–25
Prichard, James Cowles, 26
Prostitution, 103, 110–115, 117–123, 127, 129, 133, 154, 157
   Grace Blair case 1887, 123
   numbers of prostitutes, 112–113
   policing and magistrates, 113, 121–122
Protestant, 3, 5, 7, 10–11, 17, 19–20, 23, 30, 34, 62, 74, 79, 82–83, 85–87, 89, 91–95, 154, 160
   and Ascendancy, 10

Queensberry, the Marquess of, 145–150, 152

Racial and Religious Hatred Act 2006, 159
Ragussis, Michael, 100
Referee, The (newspaper), 137
Reid, T. Wemyss, 67
Reynold's Newspaper, 137
Ribbonism, 10
Rich, Paul B., 27
Ridden, Jennifer, 10
Ripon, Marquess of, George Frederick Samuel Robinson, 92
Robbins, Keith, 3
Roberts, Andrew, 138
Roman Catholicism, 2–3, 5–7, 9–10, 16, 20, 24, 27–28, 31, 56, 66, 69, 78–95, 139, 143, 154–156

Emancipation, 2, 6, 19, 60, 80, 82, 154
   and politics discussed in church, 80
   priests ministering in prisons, 81
   punishment for attending Catholic chapel, 79
   and question of split loyalties between Britain and Rome, 85–95
Romilly, John, 88
Rosebery, Archibald P. Primrose, Earl of, 150
Ross, Robert, 146–147
Rothschild, Baron Lionel de, 8, 55–67, 78, 93, 155
   continual re-election without taking seat, 57
   proposed peerage, 64–67
Rubinstein, William, 99
Russell, Sir Charles, QC MP, 41–43, 47
Russell, Lord John, MP, 15, 56–57, 63, 86–87
R v O'Halloran, McKenna and others, 24

Salisbury, Lord, 5, 19, 23, 35, 37, 48, 92, 94–95, 134, 136–141, 153
   and Boundary Commission in Ireland, 23
   and Cleveland Street Scandal, 5, 136–141
Salomons, David, 56–57, 62–63
Scottish Reformation Society, the, 94
Self, Helen, 110
Shane, A.L., 100
Sharman Crawford, William, MP, 15
Simon, Sir John, MP, 41, 98
Smith, Goldwin, 154
Smith, Paul, 67
Smith, W.H., Conservative MP, 37, 43
Sodomy, crime of, 127–128
Somerset, Lord Arthur, 133, 135–136, 138–144, 151
Somerset, Lord Fitzroy, 80
Spooner, Richard, MP, 63
Star, The (newspaper), 136
Stead, W.T., 51–52, 101, 120–121, 129

and the 'maiden tribute of modern babylon', 120
Stedman Jones, Gareth, 7
Stephenson, Sir Augustus, Director of Public Prosecutions, 136, 142–143
Stockport riots, 30
Stringer, Keith, 4
Sturge, Joseph, 13
Sugden, Edward, Lord Chancellor of Ireland, 12
Swanson, Donald, Chief Inspector with Metropolitan Police, 106
Swift, Roger, 27–28
Swing riots, the, 18
Symonds, J.A., 130

Tait, Dr Lawson, 124–125
Temple, Sir Richard, 101
Terrorism Act 2006, 159
Test and Corporation Acts, the, 56, 60
Tillett, W.W., 17
Times, The (newspaper), 34–45, 48–50, 90–91, 101, 139
and the Parnell Special Commission, 35–50
Trelawny, Sir John, MP, 62
Truth, The (newspaper), 134, 137–138

United Protestant Societies of Brighton, 95

Vatican Decrees, the, 89–91
and the West of Scotland Protestant Association, 91

Veck, George Daniel, *see* Cleveland Street Scandal
Victoria, Queen, 28, 31, 64–67, 82, 83, 85–87, 89–93, 95, 121, 140, 154
and Rothschild's proposed peerage, *see* Rothschild,
Vigilance Association for the Defence of Personal Rights, the, 116

Walkowitz, Judith, 113, 115, 117, 121
Wallis, Frank, 83, 85, 102
Walpole, Spencer, 88
Walters, Catherine (Skittles), 110–111
Ward, Paul, 4
Warren, Sir Charles, Metropolitan Police Commissioner, 103–104, 122
Webster, Sir Richard, 42, 141–142
Wellington, Duke of, 10
Weeks, Jeffrey, 127–130, 133, 157
Whigs, 5, 19, 24, 57, 72
White, Arnold, 98, 154
White Cross League, the, 124
Whiteside, James, 18
Wilde, Oscar, 2, 5–6, 8, 78, 130, 132, 134–135, 140, 144–153
author of *De Profundis*, 146
education and background,, 145
and Lord Alfred Douglass, *see* Douglas, Lord Alfred
William, Prince, 162
Wilson, Henry, MP, 123
Wohl, Anthony, 68
Wolffe, John, 86
Wolverhampton, 28–29

Milton Keynes UK
Ingram Content Group UK Ltd.
UKHW021857080524
442410UK00040B/1027